Goals for Academic Writing

ESL students and their instructors

Edited by

Alister Cumming

Ontario Institute for Studies in Education

John Benjamins Publishing Company

Amsterdam / Philadelphia

™ The paper used in this publication meets the minimum requirements
of American National Standard for Information Sciences – Permanence
of Paper for Printed Library Materials, ANSI z39.48-1984.

Library of Congress Cataloging-in-Publication Data

Goals for academic writing : ESL students and their instructors / edited by
    Alister Cumming.
        p.   cm. (Language Learning and Language Teaching, ISSN 1569–9471
; v. 15)
    Includes bibliographical references and indexes.
        1. English language--Study and teaching--Foreign speakers--
Research. 2. English language--Rhetoric--Study and teaching--Foreign
speakers. 3. English language--Written English. 4. English language--
Rhetoric--Study and teaching--Canada. 5. Academic writing--Study and
teaching--Canada. I. Cumming, Alister H. II. Series.

    PE1128.A2.G57 2006
  808.042--dc22   2006047724
  ISBN 90 272 1969 9 (Hb; alk. paper)
  ISBN 90 272 1971 0 (Pb; alk. paper)

John Benjamins Publishing Co. · P.O. Box 36224 · 1020 ME Amsterdam · The Netherlands
John Benjamins North America · P.O. Box 27519 · Philadelphia PA 19118-0519 · USA

Goals for Academic Writing

Language Learning and Language Teaching

The *LL&LT* monograph series publishes monographs as well as edited volumes on applied and methodological issues in the field of language pedagogy. The focus of the series is on subjects such as classroom discourse and interaction; language diversity in educational settings; bilingual education; language testing and language assessment; teaching methods and teaching performance; learning trajectories in second language acquisition; and written language learning in educational settings.

Series editors

Nina Spada
Ontario Institute for Studies in Education, University of Toronto

Jan H. Hulstijn
Department of Second Language Acquisition, University of Amsterdam

Volume 15

Goals for Academic Writing: ESL students and their instructors
Edited by Alister Cumming

Contents

Foreword

William Grabe

In some ways, research on second-language (L2) writing development is rapidly superceding research on first-language (L1) writing in university settings. L2 writing research is not fettered by a need to endorse post-modernist thinking about research, and thus it is not discouraged from engaging in a full variety of empirical research approaches (cf. Haswell, 2005). L2 writing research is also carried out in contexts in which L2 students' needs for effective instruction is obvious and readily measurable; there is a greater urgency to "try to get it right." At the same time, L2 writing research is open to the full range of interpretive concepts and theoretical arguments that drive most post-modernist inquiry in L1–writing research. This book by Cumming and colleagues provides an outstanding model for how such a range of research perspectives can be integrated to examine important issues in L2 writing.

The book explores a seemingly simple question: What types of writing goals do L2 students set for themselves in university settings, how do they vary from the goals of their instructors, and how do these goals change as students move from ESL support courses to disciplinary subject courses? However, the simplicity of the question belies the complexity of the issues involved and the complexity of research efforts that need to go into the search for answers. The question also suggests a number of larger issues that can be inferred from this project: How do we understand better the nature of academic writing goals? How do contexts influence student writing goals? How can we observe and examine writing goals among students longitudinally – from pre-university to the second year in university studies? Cumming et al. sought answers to these questions through multiple research methods: questionnaires, interviews, retrospective think-aloud data, and case studies of students in differing settings. In the process they developed an important descriptive framework for the interpretation of writing goals in academic settings, and they offer a range of insights on goal setting for L2 writers as well as writing in university settings more generally.

The concept of "goals" is complex. Goals themselves imply self-regulated learning; they imply motivation (and motives for action); they imply agency (deciding to act) and a pro-active set of deliberate decisions. Goals have long been associated with writing. Bereiter and Scardamalia (1987) depicted writing as a primarily goal-oriented activity in their major volume on the psychology of composition. Goals also suggest strategic actions, and thus learning strategies as part of the act of writing and the development of writing abilities. The research project integrates many of these various perspectives through *activity theory*: an approach that sees sets of activities as driven by motives (the motivation to act) in specific contexts, carried out by individuals who vary in their personal histories. These more general motives lead to specific, concrete actions in response to particular immediate goals in specific situational contexts.

Situating writing development within activity theory emphasizes the complexity of the student writer as a focus of inquiry and the importance of goals for writing, whether the goals are driven by individual, social, situational, or institutional forces. Such a view of writing provides one window into the complexity of writing instruction in academic institutional settings, often driven by long-range, if not always well articulated or carefully examined, goals of teachers, students, curriculum planners, and institutions. In this way, the study of goals also opens up explorations of linkages among research, educational policy, and pedagogical practice.

Major features of the project

Staying with the theme of complexity, I would like to comment on eight aspects of the research project. Each is given some prominence at various points in the research described in this book, and each reflects aspects of applied linguistics and writing research that merit further exploration.

1. A contextually-grounded descriptive framework for the research

The main two-year study of students' writing goals is guided by a descriptive framework based on contextually rich information about the varying purposes and contexts of writing goals in this one setting (presented in Chapter 3). This framework, created on the bases of carefully collected data (described in Chapter 2), provides an interpretive scheme for all of the studies in the book. Although not as extensive or indepth as a full ethnography, the inquiry accounts sufficiently for the local situation and the perspectives of students and their instructors to allow the researchers to consider various contextual factors that influence writing goals – providing a way to examine continuities and differences in writing goals across an extended period of time, across types of goals, across different types of courses, and across types of actions taken. The results of the main study highlight the power of the framework. It is also interesting to note that the socioculturallyoriented, interpretive studies by Kim, Baba and Cumming (in Chapter 8) and Gentil (in Chapter 9) suggest additional categories that could be considered in this descriptive framework in the future (e.g., students' L1 literacy history, students' L2 proficiency, prior opportunities for writing particular types of assignments, levels of motivation, the scope of goal identified).

2. A multiple case study approach

One of the strengths of case study research for writing is the ability to understand the details of students' efforts to engage in writing and the consequences of these efforts. An obvious limitation of most case study research is the inability to generalize beyond the immediate setting of the study itself. Many case studies involve one, three, or perhaps five cases of students in a given learning context, and they tell a narrative of success, failure, coping, or not coping related to a major point of inquiry. The present project has a much broader scope: It involved up to 45 students, 14 instructors, at least 11 different courses, two continuous years of data collection and analysis, and a team of 10 committed researchers. Such a context for research allows for comparative analyses as well as comparisons with other case study and ethnographic literature on L2 writing. It offers the potential for exploring larger issues such as the connections among research, policy, and pedagogy; the relation between goals for writing and writing development; and patterns of variation among groups of learners.

3. Multiple theoretical frames

This project also moves beyond exploratory, ethnographically-oriented case studies in another sense. The research was explicitly guided by specific theoretical orientations that were intended both to shape the research design and to assist interpretations of the results (as described in Chapters 1, 2, and 5 to 9). While much exploratory qualitative research offer insights into a context and raises important questions for further research, this project sought both to raise questions and to provide evidence for (or against) theoretical expectations. The project is grounded by activity theory (Russell, 1997a) as a way to understand the role of goals in writing classrooms. It also draws strongly on research on learning goals, self-directed learning, and motivation from the educational psychology literature. Both orientations converge on the role of goal-directed activity in the writing instruction context. The project also makes use of social theory and rhetorical theory in interpreting motives and outcomes for several of the case study students.

Finally, the project affirms the importance of reliable, empirical data in L2 writing research. It builds comparisons from patterns of similarity and variation in the interview data collected as well as from relevant supporting data. The project forcefully rejects the notion that case study research and other primarily qualitative approaches are not empirical. Instead, the project highlights the need for controlled data collection, the categorization of observations for quantitative analyses and interpretations, and the careful use of evidence (in both prose and quantitative forms) to respond to the key research questions.

4. The importance of longitudinal research

For some time, applied linguists have recognized that language learning and language-skill learning is a process that cannot be understood fully by short-term research studies and single point-in-time sampling of students' behaviors or abilities. Tucker (2000) noted the development of longitudinal research as one of the major needs in applied linguistics for the coming decade. Leki (2000) pointed out the importance of longitudinal studies for writing research as the way to understand what students learn, or do not learn, with respect to writing development, and how social and situational settings influence that learning (see also Harklau et al., 1999; Leki, 1999; Spack, 1997; Sternglass, 1997). The current project not only adds to the research literature on longitudinal research (as described in Chapter 1); it also provides a template for others to follow. The extended time-series sampling across years, as well as the combined sampling of students, language teachers, and university faculty, create a set of data that can be examined in multiple ways for multiple sub-questions. It also permits interesting linkages to the existing research literature on L2 writing development.

5. Patterns of continuity and differences across students and over time

One of the most satisfying aspects of the project documented in this book is the ways in which a complex issue such as writing goals in university contexts is teased apart to reveal an array of patterns (summarized in Chapter 10). These patterns emerged from a careful analysis of the data and point to a range of continuities and differences. Both continuities and differences arise across ESL courses, university bridging courses, and disciplinary courses. Similarly, continuities and differences are seen when comparing the view of students and their teachers as well as patterns of student reliance on teachers versus reliance on themselves. Important additional patterns of continuity and difference appear in the actions taken by students in response to goals, in ways that students form distinct groups, and in terms of the origins of goals, responsibility for goals, and student aspirations.

6. Multiple perspectives on complex language skills

The recognition that complex issues have to be viewed from multiple perspectives is equally key for this research effort (as is argued in Chapter 1). The matter of perspective is not a choice of one perspective over another, but one of nested perspectives. The objective is not to take a cognitive approach rather than a social or situational approach. Rather, the goal is to recognize that multiple layers of evidence inform the research questions. A situated analysis also gives strength to the linkages among research, policies, and pedagogy in a given setting – a concrete example of language in education policy, seeing how pedagogy is the manifestation of policy.

The project used multiple research methods. Case study methods form a central core for the various issues explored, driven primarily by qualitative analyses of interview transcripts. The standardized interview methods and the categorization of goals into major types add a level of quantitative interpretation. They also open the way for statistical analyses of varying goal categories in relation to the kinds of actions students said they took and the differing ways that students conceptualized goals. The combination of these multiple perspectives and research methods allowed the project to go beyond emergent ethnography, to move beyond discovering good research questions, and to find evidence and possible answers to important questions.

7. Goals for writing, self-directed learning, and motivation

The specific emphasis on writing goals connects in a number of ways with motivation. The role of motivation in language skills development has been only minimally explored in either L1 or L2 writing research. Unlike discussions of motivation for general language learning situations, motivation research specifically for writing (or for reading, or for listening, or for speaking) is urgently needed. This project makes some initial moves in this direction.

Anyone who has looked at questionnaire instruments for general language learning motivation – and then considered how a questionnaire instrument would look different if only addressed to a single language skill – would recognize that motivation must be examined specifically for identifiable writing contexts. Because writing is a strongly goal-directed activity and is metacognitively demanding, the items in a motivation questionnaire for writing success need to be composed differently from those for language learning generally. Constructs associated with motivation also need to be considered and applied differently. For example, the role of goal orientation for writing is likely to be different from goal orientations for communicative language learning at lower proficiency levels. Recent research on goal orientations for advanced students at universities shows that students perform best when they hold both high levels of mastery goals and high levels of performance approach goals (e.g., for competitiveness, grades) (Harackiewicz et al., 2002a, 2002b; Pintrich, 2000a).

But we don't know yet how motivation constructs influence writing performance and development (or even which motivation constructs are most relevant) because the specific exploration of writing motivation has yet to be carried out (cf. He, 2005). One of the strengths of the current research project is that it opens the way for the exploration of motivation constructs (through goal orientations and self-regulated learning) on writing development under varying educational conditions. Among the constructs noted and worth further exploration are performance learning goals and mastery learning goals; the concepts and influence of community-of-learning orientations and intentional learning (Bereiter, 2002; Bereiter & Scardamalia, 1989; 2005); and the application of game theory to the study of students' attitudes toward writing tasks and writing instruction (Newman, 2001). It would be very helpful to writing research to see such work developed in the coming years.

8.   The locus of investigation: pre-university and university contexts

The locus of inquiry in this project focused on a set of critical transition points in academic writing development for L2 students (and generation 1.5 students as well). Prior research has pointed out the massive adjustment required of ESL students as they move from pre-university writing instruction to freshman-year writing expectations (Atkinson & Ramanathan, 1995; Harklau, 2000; Leki & Carson, 1997). There is also a second major gap between freshman writing courses and writing support courses to courses in disciplinary majors that are more writing intensive (usually in junior and senior years and in graduate programs). The current project focused on these gaps, especially the first one, in its longitudinal investigation, capturing important points in time for academic writing development: Writing in language preparation courses (or secondary schools), writing in bridging and support courses, and writing in disciplinary courses. This research project demonstrates the real gap between pre-university writing and writing in university classes and disciplines. It is for further research to determine how evidence can be best gathered that will help our understanding and that will improve educational policies and pedagogical practices in these contexts. Nonetheless, the complexity of L2 writing and the pattern of results documented in this book suggest important developmental and group trends that can serve as a basis for future instructional practices, institutional policies, and research.

CHAPTER 1

Introduction, purpose, and conceptual foundations

Alister Cumming

This book documents the processes and findings of a multi-year project that investigated the goals for writing improvement among a sample of students from diverse countries who came to Canada to study ESL (English as a Second Language) and then pursued academic studies at universities here. In addition to the goals of these students, we also analyzed instructors' goals for writing improvement, first in an intensive ESL program, and then a year later in the context of various academic programs at two universities.

The purpose of our research was threefold:

1) to describe the characteristics of these students' goals for writing improvement,
2) to relate students' perspectives about their goals to those of the instructors who taught them, and
3) to determine how these goals might differ or change between the contexts of an ESL program and first year university studies one year later.

Specifically, we contribute an analytic framework that defines the characteristics of goals for writing improvement that appeared in this context. We also demonstrate areas of fundamental similarity and notable differences among these ESL students, between the students and their instructors, and among the various instructors and the curricula of their courses. Our findings confirm that students' goals for ESL writing improvement remain relatively stable over time, but they also differ in certain respects among individuals and situations. Importantly, our focus on goals provides a way to combine, in a conceptually unified perspective, considerations of learning, teaching, writing, and second language (L2) development, rather than treating these elements separately, as has most previous research on writing in second languages (Cumming, 1998; Nassaji & Cumming, 2000; Leki, Cumming & Silva, 2006).

These findings will primarily interest educators who work with, research, or administer programs for adult students of English from culturally diverse backgrounds in universities or colleges. Our research involved people at universities in Ontario, Canada, but their situations have similarities to other parts of North America, northern Europe, Australia, and New Zealand (cf. Cumming, 2003). The international diversity of students in our research also suggests its relevance for educators in Asia, South America, Africa, and the Middle East, particularly in situations where students are learning English for future studies at universities abroad or in situations where English is a medium of communication in higher education, business, and industry. Our analyses focus on writing, so they apply directly to composition instruction. And since writing is integral to language learning, the development of literacy, and performance in programs of academic study, our analyses extend to programs of general language study, academic literacy, and diverse fields of academic and professional study.

The conceptual foundations and implications of our inquiry will interest language educators and researchers generally. Research demonstrating the value of learning goals is well established in educational psychology. Indeed, they may represent one of the most robust findings in all of psychology. But few studies have inquired systematically into the nature of goals for language learning and literacy development together. Basic descriptions are lacking in regard to goals that students, instructors, and educational programs actually strive for (Cumming, 2001a, 2001b; Cumming, Busch & Zhou, 2002), such as could guide future research, instructional practices, and curriculum policies, and evaluate the importance of goals for theories of language or literacy learning. To date only exploratory studies of goals for L2 writing development have been conducted. Some resulted from teachers' action research projects in their own composition courses (Cumming, 1986; Hoffman, 1998) while other studies emerged as explanations for individual differences in, for example, students' uses of diaries or journals in a language course (Donato & McCormick, 1994; Gillette, 1994). The suggestive value of such exploratory inquiry was an impetus for the present research and book.

Goals and language learning

Previous attempts by theorists to relate students' personal goals to their second language learning have been speculative and abstract, adopting approaches that tend toward one of three divergent directions. Some theorists have recently acknowledged the theoretical significance of individual goals in language students' motivation, but also recognized that research on motivation has mostly involved survey studies that analyze the attitudes of groups of students, not the goals of specific learners in particular circumstances of language learning. There is a need for research to identify and analyze students' particular goals for learning in ways that can explain their cognitive value and immediate impact on specific aspects of language development (Dornyei, 2003). For the present book, we undertook an extended research project that aimed to move forward theoretical and empirical knowledge precisely along these lines in reference to teaching and learning ESL writing in academic contexts.

In a second approach, theorists have classified goals for learning as part of other related constructs, such as strategies for communication, thereby blurring conceptual distinctions between them (Oxford, 1990). In our research we tried to differentiate, rather than obscure, the distinctions between (a) goals for learning and (b) acts of communication or performance in a second language. We recognize this dilemma has long plagued and undermined the educational value of communicative orientations to language teaching and of experiential approaches to writing instruction. As Widdowson (1983) argued, educators and students may easily confuse purposes of teaching and learning *for* communication (i.e., to achieve long-term aims of improving language proficiency) and *through* communication (i.e., performing classroom activities that involve communication with other students). Our analyses in the present book provide educators with detailed examples of how, when, and why goals for ESL writing improvement differ from acts of ESL writing performance while recognizing that the two necessarily interact.

A third approach has been the stipulation of general goals for learning in L2 tasks and a corresponding neglect of the centrality of individual learners' personal agency in creating and acting on their goals for learning. For example, this approach is inherent in Skehan's (1998) triad of the goals of fluency, accuracy, and complexity for the design of learning tasks in second language curricula. Skehan's research stipulates these goals as a focus for students' task performance. But who is to say, in the context of Skehan's and colleagues' experiments, that students really focus on any one of these goals with intensity, commitment, or intention? Indeed, this problem applies to most recent curricula for language education around the world that have stipulated general standards or benchmarks for students' achievements in educational programs. Such curriculum specifications tend to be done without any empirical inquiry into students' or teachers' perceptions of or investments in such goals, analyses of their uses of them for learning, nor demonstrations of students' abilities to achieve them progressively over time (Brindley, 1998; Cumming, 2001a). In the present research we have assumed, as a fundamental principle, that understanding students' and their instructors' goals for ESL writing improvement from their own perspectives is primary to understanding how students can actually improve their writing in English and how their instructors can assist them to do so (Hilgers, Hussey & Stitt-Bergh, 1999; Kuh, 1993; Lawrence & Volet, 1991).

Why goals?

Goals mediate learning, teaching, and curriculum contexts. They also influence the strategies and actions that people take to improve their abilities. In educational settings, students' goals derive from long-term personal histories, which in turn contribute to their focus on present activities, thus shaping future abilities. Teachers' goals likewise build on pedagogical knowledge and experience, the purposes and constraints of the courses they are employed to teach, and their understanding of the specific learners they encounter in their classes. The goals of educational programs are public statements of policy and purpose that students and teachers agree to cooperate and invest in over the duration of a course. Students and teachers can readily talk about, negotiate, and reflect on their goals, both individually and collectively.

These fundamental characteristics make goals a suitable focus for inquiry into the otherwise complex phenomenon of L2 literacy education. Writing, in particular, has long been recognized as a characteristically goal-oriented activity (Bereiter & Scardamalia, 1987; Graham & Harris, 1994; Hayes, 1996). Students use goals to regulate themselves through the extended mental effort required to coordinate and direct their thinking while they compose. Moreover, students incorporate relevant resources and judgments of potential readers' expected responses to plan, draft, and revise a written text that satisfies a personal sense of purpose, coherence, and expression as well as relevant social norms for literate communication. Goals stick out in this context. But goals for writing also vary. Individuals have unique personal goals for writing any one text and for developing writing abilities over time. Such goals are of greater or lesser importance to individuals and appear in different ways. In addition, goals for writing and writing improvement differ by cultural norms and expectations and in various types of texts and situations (Connor, 1996; Heath, 1983; Johns, 1997).

Indeed, acquiring a second language is highly variable and marked by differing individual and cultural orientations. People attain greater or lesser proficiency in a second language, depending on their purposes for learning, the prior knowledge and abilities they possess, the stages in their lives, their orientations toward the target language and its culture, and the conditions for learning they experience (Csizer & Dornyei, 2005; Lightbown & Spada, 1999; Mitchell & Myles, 2004; Spolsky, 1989). Increasingly, educators are required to work with students and situations that combine the complexity and variability of writing together with that of second language acquisition (see below). Analyses of learning processes and variables in these situations reveal a veritable Pandora's box of multiple, intersecting components of individual, developmental, socioloinguistic, typological, and textual diversity (Carson, 2001; Cumming, 1989, 2004; Cumming & Riazi,

2000; Grabe, 2001; Harklau, 2002; Hornberger, 1989; 2003). Amid this diversity and complexity, goals present a focal point to consider what people commonly do when they write in a second language.

But the basis for studying goals goes deeper than this. Philosophers have long claimed that goals are central to human mental states, volition, and social interaction. Since Hegel a fundamental assumption about human activity is that we are each aware of ourselves, of the objects around us, and of what we might want to do with such objects. Philosophers call this relation between self-awareness and other objects *intentionality* (Anscombe, 1957; Dennett, 1981; Searle, 1983). Intentions involve what we believe, hope, or desire. In turn, we are aware that other people have a similar consciousness. That dual awareness shapes our intentions and abilities to communicate with each other. It is an ability that develops as we mature and gain greater awareness of other people's intentions and subsequently learn to use literacy for sophisticated purposes (Astington, 1999; Davidson, 1984; Malle, Moses & Baldwin, 2001; Olson, 1994). From this perspective, goals are integral to actions. Moreover, literate and communicative abilities, such as writing and language learning and use, extend directly from our intentional states and social interactions.

To guide the present inquiry into ESL writing we have drawn on two sets of related theories that have risen to the fore in much recent research into learning in educational contexts: goal theory and activity theory. Both sets of theories attempt to explain the qualities of human learning, as well as individual differences in and development of them, by describing people's personal agency and motivation in relation to their social conditions. Both sets of theories are fundamentally "applied" in the sense of their having purposes of improving pedagogy. They offer frameworks to describe cognitive states, actions, and interactions in learning situations, aiming (a) to understand how learners themselves construct these within their social contexts and subsequently develop their abilities so as, ultimately, (b) to know how these conditions might be improved, for example, through enhanced approaches to learning, implementing specific pedagogical interventions, or changing the conditions of classroom interaction. Accordingly, both sets of theories are oriented toward phenomenological and case study data, that is, observations and learners' own accounts of their personal positions, circumstances, behaviors, and development within particular social contexts. Goal theory tends to focus more on individuals' beliefs and behaviors – adopting the conventional perspective of educational psychology, and leading to applications that can help learners better regulate their own learning. Activity theory tends to focus more on the socio-material conditions and processes that facilitate learning and long-term stages of development – adopting a culturally-oriented perspective to psychology, and leading to applications for evaluating or improving particular educational conditions. Although we (and other authors cited below) refer to each of these theories in the singular, neither is a single, explicit theory (in the sense of advocating a precise explanation for learning nor a testable set of hypotheses). Rather, goal theory and activity theory have each been applied, and reinterpreted, by various researchers who have aligned themselves with the respective theory and a common set of concepts and foci (as described below). Given their applied orientations and focus on particular educational contexts, neither goal theory nor activity theory strive to explain constituent phenomena in the way that, for example, cognitive neurolinguistics might aim to explain the biology of learning nor ethnography might aim to explain the nature of a culture.

Goal theory in psychology

Educational psychologists have established an extensive body of theory and research asserting the centrality of goals in human learning. Some educational psychologists, such as Locke and Latham (1990) in adult education and Midgely (2002) in secondary education, put goal setting at the centre of theories of learning and motivation in academic or work contexts. Midgely (2002, p. xi), for instance, described how "goal orientation theory" developed:

> within a social-cognitive framework that focuses on the purposes or goals that are pursued or perceived in an achievement setting. Rather than conceiving of individuals as possessing or lacking motivation, the focus is on how individuals think about themselves, their academic tasks, and their performance (Ames, 1987). Goals provide a framework within which individuals interpret and react to events, and result in different patterns of cognition, affect, and behavior.

Others, such as Pintrich (2000b) or Zimmerman (2001), have viewed goals as a focal component of self-regulated learning:

> A general working definition of self-regulated learning is that it is an active, constructive process whereby learners set goals for their learning and then attempt to monitor, regulate, and control their cognition, motivation, and behavior, guided and constrained by their goals and the contextual features in the environment.
> (Pintrich, 2000b, p. 453)

Reviews of the voluminous inquiry into goal setting and achievement in various domains of education and work (Austin & Vancouver, 1996; Pintrich, 2000b; Schunk & Zimmerman, 1994; Zimmerman, 2001) have provided conceptual guidance for our present research into goals for ESL writing improvement, so it is worth summarizing the main tenets of these theories and research.

First, goals appear in phases or as processes. Austin and Vancouver (1996) outlined how research has demonstrated that people first establish goals, make plans about them, strive to monitor and achieve their goals, then either persist with or revise their goals, and finally recognize that they have attained their goals or make a decision to abandon them. Pintrich (2000b) likewise describes a proto-typical sequence of phases for an individual's goal achievement that moves from forethought or activation to monitoring, control, reaction and/or reflection.

A second tenet of goal theories is that they have content. Goals have an object of some kind and these objects can be identified as the focal point of the agent's intentions. As Searle (1983, p.1) emphasized, intentions are always "about" something. The content of a goal tends to be domain-specific, that is, linked to specific contexts of human activity rather than spanning a range of different situations or types of activities. This characteristic was a principal reason for our under-taking an empirical study of goals for ESL writing improvement. We hoped to establish what may be unique about students' and their instructors' goals in this domain. Pintrich (2000b) proposed that the content of goals is defined in respect to individuals' regulation of their (a) own cognition, (b) motivations and affec-tive states, (c) behavior, and (d) contexts. Paris, Byrnes and Paris (2001) further asserted that goals are self-constructed theories of self-competence based on both internal and external sources of information, involving sequences of beliefs, desires, and actions in respect to personal estimations of possible selves, satisfac-tion about performance, standards for judging and modifying these, and feedback from others.

Third, goals have structure. Austin and Vancouver (1996) described the struc-ture of goals in terms of dimensions, properties, and organization. Some goals are more important, urgent, relevant, or encompassing than others, which is to say goals have differing values and significance. In turn, people always have multiple goals, even in extreme cases of obsession or compulsion about a single object or action. Theorists have conceptualized the relations between multiple goals, however, as various patterns of organization, including hierarchies, taxono-mies, or sets of competing factors, continua, or cycles. Locke and Latham (1990) defined learning goals in terms of two basic dimensions, their content (e.g., topic, specificity, difficulty, complexity) and intensity (including commitment, origin, and self-efficacy). But even this distinction acknowledges that goals are multidimensional, change according to situations, and differ in their salience and temporal range. Goals can be about accomplishing something as well as avoiding something; consequently goals may have opposing (positive as well as nega-tive) dimensions.

A frequently cited distinction in educational psychology is between *perfor-mance* and *mastery goals* (Ames, 1992; and for an application to ESL writing, see He, 2005). Performance goals involve doing a task or demonstrating an ability.

Mastery goals involve learning from such performance or developing an ability above and beyond doing the activity. For writing development, Bereiter and Scardamalia (1987, 1989) proposed a related distinction, between models of composing or instruction that involve students simply (a) *telling their knowledge* about a topic in order to produce content for their writing or (b) more intentionally aiming to *transform their knowledge* (and so improve their abilities or knowledge) during the process of writing. Knowledge telling is what most educational tasks require of students. Knowledge transforming is characteristic of highly skilled writers and of writing tasks done explicitly to achieve goals for learning (cf. Cumming's 1990, 1995 descriptions of ESL writers). Yet simple bipolar dichotomies cannot suffice to explain more than prevailing differences in orientations among the complexity of competing, interacting, and adaptive goals that people tend to experience in most real-life situations (Harackiewizc, Barron & Elliot, 1998; Hidi & Harackiewicz, 2000). This is particularly true for the complexity of learning to write in a second language, as Cumming, Kim and Eouanzoui (in press) have established already with data from the present research concerning the motivations of ESL students.

Activity theory

Activity theory offers a unique framework that conceptualizes goals as central to learning in social contexts. Numerous researchers have demonstrated the suitability of activity theory for long-term analyses of literacy development in classroom contexts (Russell, 1995; 1997a, 1997b; Weimelt, 2001; Wells, 1999; Winsor, 1999; Witte & Haas, 2005). Indeed, we have already undertaken such analyses in preliminary case studies from the present project (Cumming, Busch & Zhou, 2002; Yang, Baba & Cumming, 2004), as have others in related situations of adults' L2 writing development (e.g., Basturkmen & Lewis 2002; Parks & Maguire, 1999). We continue to draw upon this theory in most of the analyses in the present book.

The principles of activity theory were developed by Leont'ev (1972, 1978) in conjunction with Vygotsky's (1978) sociocultural theories of learning and more recently extended by Engeström (1987, 1999). Goals figure distinctly in this theory as the conceptual focus between people's personal beliefs, values, and actions, involvement in specific social contexts, and corresponding development of knowledge and abilities. Activity theory maintains that humans construct their knowledge through actions and interactions with others, mediated by cultural artifacts or tools, such as language and literacy practices, in historically defined circumstances (Cole, 1996; Lantolf, 2000). Learners "do not simply internalize and appropriate the consequences of activities on the social plane," but also "actively restructure their knowledge both with each other and within themselves" (John-Steiner & Meehan, 2001, p. 35). Learning occurs through successive, self-regulated social activities in historically situated settings (Engeström & Miettinen 1999; Leont'ev, 1972). Investigations of learning therefore require, not analyses of experimentally isolated tasks, but rather studies of people's long-term engagement with tasks to determine the development of behaviors in naturally occurring social contexts. According to activity theory, people act in reference to the knowledge they bring to the task and the perceived objectives needed to achieve their goal(s).

Leont'ev (1972, 1978) proposed analyzing an activity system in terms of a general *activity* that involves specific *actions* which in turn are realized through more particular *operations*. He suggested that each activity has its corresponding *motives, goals*, and *instrument conditions*. *Activities* such as learning to write in a second language are mobilized by *motives* such as intending later to study at university or pursue a career that requires writing in that language. To realize their *motives*, people take specific, relevant *actions* based on *goals* that are oriented toward transforming their intentions into real *actions* through specific *operations* in relevant *conditions*. For example, a learner taking an ESL writing course performs *actions* such as writing compositions that involve specific *operations* for learning, such as producing a clear introductory paragraph, prescribed by the course instructor. The student subsequently sets personal *goals* for achievement in each writing task within the *instrumental conditions* of classroom study and available material resources, thereby making achievements in the general *activity* of writing in English.

Engeström (1987, 1991b) expanded Leont'ev's concept of activity by elaborating on the social dimensions of learning activities. Specifically, Engeström expanded the institutional dimension of activity systems by stipulating that they involve *rules, communities*, and *division of labor* in respect to the roles of *subject, object*, and *mediating artifacts* (e.g., signs and tools). To extend the example above of a person learning to write in a second language, a student (*subject*) focuses on improving her English writing (*object*) in respect to its discourse norms (*rules*, implicitly perceived, jointly established, or explicitly taught) in the context of a classroom (*community*), performing writing tasks assigned by the teacher (*division of labor*) using a word processor, source books, and dictionaries (as *mediating artifacts*) to produce compositions in English. Learning to write in the second language involves acquiring the textual conventions of the target language while also acting to produce them according to individual goals. In doing so, learners become a functioning member of a distinct social community.

Why ESL writing?

Few other aspects of education have seen as much simultaneous growth over the past two decades in descriptive research on learning, formulations for institutional policy, and advice for pedagogical practices as has writing in second languages, particularly for English in academic settings (Grabe & Kaplan, 1996; Matsuda, 2003). The number of students from overseas attending colleges and universities in English-dominant countries (such as Australia, Canada, the U.S., the U.K., or New Zealand) and those preparing in their home countries or doing so after immigration has increased enormously in recent decades. The resulting student population has created unique concerns for educators (Eggington & Wren; 1997; Harklau, Losey & Siegel, 1999; Herriman & Burnaby, 1996). Parallel situations exist in other countries with high levels of immigration and cross-border mobility and in countries where an international language is used in higher education and/or for business, work, or travel (e.g., Chinese, French, German, Italian, Japanese, Portuguese, or Spanish) (Dickson & Cumming, 1996). In these academic contexts, attention focuses on writing because it is through written texts that students demonstrate knowledge in tests, course papers, assignments, and formal projects such as theses. Written academic literacy is central to university studies. The unique and variable characteristics of student's written texts distinguish ESL learners from their English-majority counterparts (Hinkel, 2002; Silva, 1993), leading to a perception that their writing is the ability most in need of improvement.

Despite the recent surge of publications on ESL writing in academic settings, few theoretically-informed, empirically-based perspectives have aimed to link this research, policy, and pedagogy together as a basis to evaluate or explain their relations. Indeed, a common critique of this field has been that it remains fragmented. Studies have focused on different aspects of writing (e.g., text characteristics, composing processes, and social discourse), separated studies of learning from studies of teaching and of relevant social contexts, and compartmentalized analyses for different learner groups or program types (Cumming, 1998; Grabe & Kaplan, 1996; Leki, Cumming & Silva, 2006; Silva & Brice, 2004). Where a distinctive amount of inquiry has related teaching to the learning of second-language writing, it has been in respect to just a few discrete pedagogical functions, such as instructors' responses to ESL students' writing (Ferris, 2003; Goldstein, 2004; Nassaji & Cumming, 2000).

We undertook the present inquiry to attempt to provide one unified perspective on learning, teaching, and institutional policies. Other approaches to research with the potential to unify perspectives on second-language writing, teaching, and policies include ethnographies (Losey, 1997; Ramanathan & Atkinson, 1999), narrative inquiry (Bell, 2002; Casanave, 2005), or personal histories (Belcher & Connor, 2001; Li, 1996). But we were determined to focus the present project on goals for writing improvement for several reasons. Some of these reasons are already explained above, but many of them build on the findings of recent studies of ESL writing, either from the perspective of learning, pedagogy, or policy.

Learning: case studies of ESL writing development in university settings

Important insights into writing in second languages have emerged from recent case studies describing particular individuals (or small groups of individuals) as they have developed their writing in English in particular university programs. These studies have provided vivid, holistic descriptions of the strategies, struggles, and accomplishments to improve their writing experienced by particular undergraduate (e.g., Currie, 1993; Johns, 1985, 1992; Leki, 1995, 1999, 2001a; Parks, 2000; Sasaki, 2004; Spack, 1997) and graduate students (e.g., Angelova & Riazantseva, 1999; Braine, 2002; Casanave, 1992, 2002; Connor & Kramer, 1995; Raymond & Parks, 2002; Riazi, 1997; Silva, 1992). Precedents for such inquiry have come from related studies of English mother-tongue students in university settings who similarly encounter diverse personal, intellectual, and cultural struggles in learning to write. All university students seem to find themselves struggling to meet the demands of courses, instructors, changing identities, and interpersonal relations (Berkenkotter, Huckin & Ackerman, 1988, 1991; Chiseri-Strater, 1991; Faigley & Hansen, 1985; Herrington, 1985, 1992; Ivanic, 1998; Jacobs, 1982; Jones, Turner & Street, 1999; McCarthy, 1987; Prior, 1998; Sternglass, 1997; Walvoord & McCarthy, 1990; Wolcott, 1994).

The value of these studies comes from their holistic, experiential and situated focus, longitudinal perspective (ranging from the period of a course to several years of academic studies), and complementary sources of information (interviews, observations, and text analyses) that connect individual writing processes to the social conditions that produce them (e.g., course requirements, discourse norms, background knowledge and orientations, evolving peer relations, and shifting cultural and personal identities). Braine (2002, p. 66) has even claimed that "research on the acquisition of academic literacy by graduate students *must* be in the form of case studies"[italics added] because:

> Case studies provide rich information about learners, about the strategies they use to communicate and learn, how their own personalities, attitudes, and goals interact with the learning environment, and the nature of their linguistic growth. Case studies are also descriptive, dynamic, and rely upon naturally occurring

data, and are therefore the most appropriate for studying the acquisition of academic literacy.

Case studies certainly offer insightful, holistic perspectives on these matters, distinct from text analyses, process-tracing studies, and other approaches to inquiry that have dominated studies of second-language writing. Text analyses can describe the characteristics of written texts and evaluate how these vary on certain dimensions or develop over time, but even the most thorough of text analyses cannot alone explain why students produced the relevant text features (cf. Archibald, 1994; Connor, 1996; Hinkel, 2002; Intaraprawat & Steffenson, 1995; Jarvis, Grant, Bikowski & Ferris, 2003). Process-tracing studies of ESL composing can distinguish differences in the thinking, behaviors, and uses of knowledge between differing groups of writers (e.g., more or less proficient, younger or older students) and in differing tasks or conditions (e.g., L1 vs. L2, different text types, different information sources). But even the most thorough of such process-tracing studies cannot be certain how closely people's performance in experimental-type conditions represent the writing or learning that they actually perform in natural contexts of academic studies or work (cf. Bosher, 1998; Cumming, 1989; Whalen & Menard, 1995; Sasaki, 2002; Shi, 2004; see also Smagorinsky, 1994). Ethnographies of ESL writing describe how cultural values and intergroup relations inform the production and qualities of written texts in a specific social milieu, but there are limitations in extending findings from one context to another. A second limitation is how well a researchers' involvement or interpretations may have represented the experiences of participants in that context (cf. Atkinson & Ramanathan, 1995; Casanave, 2002; Losey, 1997; Parks, 2000; see also Ramanathan & Atkinson, 1999).

Case studies also have their limitations, similar to those of other approaches to inquiry into second-language writing. One limitation is the uncertainty of knowing how well sampling of participants, tasks, texts, or contexts might actually represent other participants, behaviors, writing, or situations elsewhere. Other limitations arise from aggregating results to determine group trends and make inferences about them and from the unpredictable nature of natural events, which challenges longitudinal research aiming to compare participants' performance on the assumption that the basic conditions for comparison remain equivalent (Little, Schnabel & Baumert, 2000; Mellow, Reeder, & Forster, 1996; Miles & Huberman, 1994; Yin, 1994).

In designing the present research, we wanted to capitalize on the strengths of naturalistic case study inquiry and focus on specific, meaningful phenomena, not just events as we observed them unfold. Hence we directed our attention toward goals, using the strategies for data collection and analysis described in Chapter 2. In this respect, the present inquiry was naturalistic because we observed and did not try to alter natural educational circumstances (Guba & Lincoln, 1983). But our research was designed to focus on phenomena that we expected to be prominent in students' and their instructors' thinking and then to change over time in different contexts, so our project was developmental in design (Perret-Clermont, 1993). We approached the natural phenomena of ESL writers in an intensive, academic preparation program in order to describe, analyze, and compare particularly their goals for writing improvement. In doing so, we concur with Atkinson's (2002) argument that to move theories of language and literacy learning forward it is necessary for research to deliberately link and explain theoretically the relations between social and cognitive phenomena in natural educational settings.

Policies and pedagogies: writing and learning in ESL and university studies

Our interests in students' goals for writing improvement focused on their learning processes, which we recognized as existing with respect to specific policy and pedagogical conditions. Investigating learning processes was as much a matter of aspiring toward realism by accounting for the particular social contexts of learning as it was an effort to make the study useful for educational policy makers and practitioners. We agree with Luke (2005) who argued that educators need to "move beyond the view of literacy education as simple pedagogic machinery for the transmission of basic skills" toward a "literacy-in-education policy *in situ…* based on a rich, triangulated, and multiperspectival social science" (p. 669). We also concur with the socio-historical view of Triebel (2005) that "literacy is tied to institutional arrangements and concepts" and that "community building and identity formation are the crucial variables at the basis of literacy" (pp. 805–807).

Zamel (1995) produced a vivid yet mildly terrifying depiction of the cultural collisions confronted by ESL learners entering an American university and, conversely, experienced by the faculty and staff in their interactions. Fishman and McCarthy (2001) debate, in a detailed analysis of their own teaching practices, how goals and conditions for education differ among instructors of composition and of academic subjects. It was with such differing institutional policies and cultural practices in mind that we set out to investigate learning goals. We sought to document what changes, if any, occurred in the goals for writing improvement of a cohort of ESL students as they moved from the context of a highly supportive ESL writing program to a variety of settings in different freshman university courses. Moreover, we wanted to analyze instructors' goals for students' writing improvement and the relevant pedagogical conditions.

The transition from ESL program to mainstream university courses is a crucial one for students pursuing university degrees in a second language and in a foreign country. So we felt it was necessary to document participants' experiences. There were several reasons for doing so. First, we simply wanted to know what happened and what differences there might be. Although a few case studies (cited above) have documented cases of individuals in similar circumstances, we did not know what to expect for larger numbers or cohorts of students. We also did not know precisely what differences may exist across the types of educational programs (ESL vs. academic degree programs) and in the students' or instructors' goals for writing. Second, we wanted to see if there really was a sort of cultural disjuncture akin to the "home-school mismatch" for literacy practices that might be a reason for success or failure in university studies. Various researchers have shown that a mismatch occurs for young children from diverse cultural backgrounds when they begin schooling (Heath, 1983; King & Hornberger, 2005). Third, we wanted to gather evidence that might be useful for understanding and improving educational policies and pedagogical practices in this and other related institutions, although it should be noted that our intent was not to evaluate any particular program, course, or person's work.

The fundamental rationale for many university ESL programs in North America is that their courses prepare students for university studies. The considerable efforts that instructors and students alike put into improving English in these programs are premised on several conceptual foundations, each of which relate to understanding what the goals of students and instructors for writing improvement might be in these contexts. Programs of ESL instruction may be organized as (a) courses of English language and writing support, either on a full-time (i.e., intensive) or part-time basis, (b) sheltered academic courses for English learners, in which academic subjects are taught and studied but with attention to developing relevant ESL skills, or (c) individual services for tutoring and resources for self-directed study or diverse combinations of these structures (Brinton, Snow & Wesche, 1989; Leki, 2001b; Stoller, 2004). Within these contexts Cumming (2003a) described curriculum options structured according to particular aspects of writing (composing processes, text types, text structures, topical themes, or personal expression), organized around syllabi in particular formats (either integrating or separating writing from other language skills), and developed in respect to intended achievements in language, style, rhetoric, logic, personal expression, and academic socialization.

At a minimum, pedagogy and policies related to writing improvement have to define or at least make tacit assumptions about what writing and learning are in these contexts (Davis, Scriven, & Thomas, 1987; Reid, 2001). What conceptualizations of writing and writing improvement might we expect to encounter in a research study of ESL and academic writing? Jones, Turner and Street (1999) suggested there are three models of student writing in higher education: (a) study skills, (b) academic socialization, and (c) academic literacies.

The *study skills* model, based on psychological and linguistic theories, treats writing as atomized skills and surface features of texts and language. Numerous taxonomies of writing skills needed for university studies have been generated through needs analyses and surveys of students and faculty, many of which are widely used as a basis for the design of ESL and other programs of writing support and assessment (Bridgeman & Carlson, 1984; Cheng, Myles & Curtis, 2004; Rosenfeld, Leung, & Oltman, 2001; Zhu, 2004). For example, analyses of the texts required for university courses have often served as a benchmark for defining the skills students need to achieve writing competency (e.g., Feez, 1998; Hale, Taylor, Bridgeman, Carson, Kroll & Kantor, 1996; Hyon, 1996; Kaldor, Herriman & Rochecouste, 1998; Swales, 1990).

The *academic socialization* model assumes that students are acculturated into a new culture in the process of becoming functioning members of a particular academic discourse community and its institutional norms, genres, and practices for writing. This model has motivated most case studies of writing development cited above in studies of both English mother-tongue and ESL students in university settings. The model is perhaps most distinctly articulated in Berkenkotter and Huckin (1995) and for ESL writing curricula by Hyon (1996) and Parks and Maguire (1999). The *academic literacies* model advocated by Jones, Turner and Street (1999) similarly takes a socio-anthropological view, but adopts principles of new literacy studies, multiliteracies, and critical discourse analysis (Barton & Hamilton, 1998; Cope & Kalantzis, 2000; Lankshear, Gee, Knobel & Seale, 1997). This model portrays students as negotiating conflicting power relations and different literacy practices to develop and challenge a variety of differing repertoires for writing as well as identities appropriate to diverse modes of discourse and relations. Case studies of writing by Lam (2000), Ivanic (1998), and Lea (1999) exemplify this focus on writing that involves multiple modes of discourse, shifting personal identities, and power relations.

These differing models present a wide range of alternative prospects for the goals that students and instructors might have for ESL writing improvement. Indeed, analyses of ESL writing achievement have ranged in their units from micro-elements of English grammar and functional text structure (e.g., Bardovi-Harlig, 1997; Grant & Ginther, 2000) to holistic accounts of the negotiation of alternative identities and relations with academic knowledge and power structures (Ivanic & Camps, 2001; Spack, 1997). Another way to consider these matters is in terms of the functions that writing serves in academic studies. Sternglass (1997), in summarizing her longitudinal study of 53 college students' writing development, identified four general purposes of writing in university courses: to make knowledge conscious, to help remember facts, to analyze concepts, and to construct new knowledge. She concluded that students primarily used writing in university courses to develop critical reasoning skills over the period of their degrees. Specifically, they used writing to translate concepts into their own language, move from gathering facts to analyses of them, and adjust themselves to the task demands of specific courses and fields. This view of writing, as itself a mode of or focal context for learning and knowledge development, aligns with the pedagogical movements of Writing Across the Curriculum or Writing in the Disciplines (Bazerman, 1988; Britton, Martin, Mclead & Rosen, 1975; Langer & Appelbee, 1987; Ochsner & Fowler, 2004) and more recent extensions into the design and evaluation of Knowledge-Building Communities for technologically-mediated written communications (Bereiter, 2002; Engle & Conant, 2002).

Organization of the book

This introductory chapter has outlined the purpose and conceptual foundations of our inquiry into goals for ESL writing improvement in university contexts. The remaining chapters in this book describe the specific analyses and findings that emerged from our project. The first half of the book focuses on our main study and its findings. Chapter 2 describes the context, design, and research methods of the study, providing a necessary preface to the results presented in the following chapters. Chapter 3 analyzes the frequencies with which students reported these goals over two years of data collection, describes the basic characteristics and qualities of these goals, and evaluates whether these goals changed over time. Chapter 4 describes the goals for students' writing improvement expressed by the instructors who taught these students, both in ESL and university courses.

The second half of the book offers case studies of particular student groups and issues. Chapter 5 describes nine Chinese students and their particular goals for writing improvement in ESL and various university courses. Chapter 6 compares the perspectives of students and instructors in assessing whether students achieved their goals in particular written texts. Chapter 7 offers a detailed linguistic analysis of the expressions about ESL writing improvement that students produced during interviews about their goals. Chapter 8 extends into a third year of university studies the cases of three students, exploring issues of identity and motivation that developed over time and differed among these individuals. Chapter 9 speculates on sources of variation that, based on analyses from a parallel study in a bilingual English-French university, might extend into studies of goals for multilingual writing improvement in contexts others than the Canadian ESL and university programs in which our main research study was situated. Chapter 10 concludes the book by summarizing our findings and suggesting implications for educational policies and practices as well as future inquiry into second-language writing development.

The research team and authors in this book consisted of one professor (Alister Cumming), one post-doctoral research fellow (Guillaume Gentil), and ten doctoral students in the graduate program in Second Language Education at the Ontario Institute for Studies in Education. All of us have worked extensively as ESL writing instructors and each has had personal experiences learning English and/or other second languages. In addition to Jia Fei, other students who contributed to the project but completed their Masters' degrees before we embarked on this book were Sameena Eidoo, Cheryl Fretz (who produced a unique analysis of some of the present data in Fretz, 2003), and Su Zhang. Our project was a highly collaborative activity, so it is worth our acknowledging that all contributors of chapters to this book contributed integrally to most aspects of the project as a whole.

Acknowledgements

Funding for this research came primarily from the Social Sciences and Humanities Research Council of Canada, standard grant 410–2001–0791, supplemented by part-time research assistantships from the Ontario Institute for Studies in Education of the University of Toronto to Kyoko Baba, Khaled Barkaoui, Michael Busch, Jia Fei, Tae-Young Kim, Usman Erdosy, Luxin Yang, and Ally Zhou. Guillaume Gentil was supported by a postdoctoral fellowship from the Fonds québécois de la recherche sur la société et la culture over the year 2003–2004 while he was in Toronto. We are especially grateful to the students and their instructors who participated in the study. We have concealed the names of all students, instructors, and courses in this book with pseudonyms in order to protect their confidentiality. We thank Michelle Pon for many and various forms of administrative assistance. We also thank William Grabe for his Foreword and for his comments on the draft manuscript, which helped to improve its coherence and to suggest certain implications arising from it. The editors of this book series – Kees Vaes, Jan Hulstijn, and Nina Spada – likewise deserve our thanks for their useful comments and corrections on the final versions of the manuscript as well as their patience in awaiting these.

Section I. The Main Study

CHAPTER 2

Context and design
of the research

Alister Cumming

This chapter documents the context and participants of our research, the data we gathered, and our methods of analyses. As described in Chapter 1, our purposes were primarily to describe the goals for writing improvement that a sample of ESL learners and their instructors had as well as to determine whether these goals changed as the students moved from a pre-university ESL program into various academic programs at university the following year.

Context and participants

Our starting point was an established ESL program that had the advertised policy of preparing students from overseas to enter academic programs at universities in Canada the following year. The ESL program was an intensive, full-time set of courses held 5 days per week over one three-month academic term. As described in its syllabus, the curriculum integrated "four skill areas (speaking, listening, reading and writing) to improve overall English comprehension and production." Some courses focused on particular language skills (e.g., writing, grammar) and others on topical themes involving various language modalities (reading, listening, speaking, and writing) culminating in students' production of academic-type tasks. (See Chapter 4 for further descriptions of syllabi and teaching approaches). We first conducted a preliminary set of case studies in this context (published as Cumming, Busch & Zhou, 2002) to establish the approaches to data collection and analyses suitable for our purposes. The ESL program proved to have students from around the world who were aiming to improve their English in order to continue their studies at universities in Canada. The program's staff consisted of certified and experienced ESL instructors.

We sent solicitation letters first to instructors in the ESL program and then (for the instructors who agreed to participate in the research) distributed notices to their students, asking for volunteers to participate in the study. Five ESL instructors volunteered, giving themselves the pseudonyms Faith, Leeanne, Linda,

Lulu, and Maria. Forty-five of their students likewise volunteered, about half of the students in their classes. The students also provided pseudonyms that maintained their ethnicity and gender but preserved their confidentiality. Profiles of the students and their instructors appear in Appendix A. We called this initial part of our project Phase 1, which took place from September to April of the first school year.

As shown in Appendix A, students participating in Phase 1 were mostly in their early or mid 20s (but 3 were in their 30s) and had come to Canada from various countries in Asia (14 from China, 7 from Korea, 3 from Japan, 3 from Thailand, and 2 from Vietnam), the Middle East or North Africa (4 from Iran, 3 from Israel, 2 from Morocco, and 1 from Saudi Arabia), Latin America (3 from Mexico, 1 from Chile, and 1 from Ecuador), and Europe (1 from the Ukraine). There were about twice as many females as males among them. Eighteen of the students had prior university or college degrees from their home countries and a few had some limited work experience. But for most, the completion of high school was their highest previous level of education. All had studied English part-time in their home countries, mostly for periods of six to eight years, as part of their previous degrees. Their average score on the institutional version of the TOEFL (Test of English as a Foreign Language) was 550, which is the score level required for admission to undergraduate programs at many universities in North America. So these students were relatively proficient in English but had not fully mastered the language. Before we contacted them, the students had resided in Canada for periods ranging from 1 to 36 months.

Phase 2 of our project occurred from September to April of the following school year. We contacted the students who had participated in Phase 1 to ask if they were willing to do a second, parallel set of interviews about their goals for writing improvement in the context of their university courses. Unfortunately, most students from Phase 1 had entered universities in other parts of the world, either in their home countries or elsewhere, so they were not available for interviews. Nonetheless, 15 (or a third) of the students from Phase 1 agreed to participate in Phase 2. They were in academic programs at one of two universities in southern Ontario – with the exception of one student, Lee, who opted to complete a final year of high school in Toronto to obtain grades that would get her into university the following year. We asked these students to nominate, for interviews with us, one of their instructors who taught them in a course that involved the most writing. Nine instructors agreed, one of whom taught two of the students. They came from a range of academic disciplines, including architecture, Asian studies, commerce, computer science, economics, engineering, literature, and political science. A nearly equal number, 9 instructors, declined our invitations. Some acknowledged that they were part-time instructors holding full-time jobs outside the university, whereas others said they did not have the available time. Profiles of the students in Phase 2 and the pseudonyms of their academic courses and instructors who agreed to be interviewed appear in Appendix B.

The 15 students who continued into Phase 2 were a less heterogeneous group than those in Phase 1. Most were Asian (10 Chinese, 2 Japanese, and 1 Korean), the exceptions being one Iranian and one Russian student. Most were female. Seven were in programs of commerce or economics, two were in programs of architecture, two in engineering, two in computer science, one in political science, and one was completing the final year of Canadian secondary school.

The five ESL instructors who participated in Phase 1 were appropriately qualified (with Masters' degrees either in Education, English, or Applied Linguistics) and experienced (i.e., had taught English for 7 to 12 years). Five of the instructors who participated in Phase 2 had regular university appointments in the professorial stream, whereas three were contracted or continuing instructors (who taught courses for basic or professional writing), and one was a high school teacher (who taught Lee).

Data and instruments

We collected four types of data from students at the beginning and end of Phases 1 and 2: (a) initial profile questionnaires (for basic demographic information), (b) semi-structured interviews about goals for writing improvement, (c) samples of their writing in courses, and (d) stimulated recalls concerning goals for the writing samples. We collected parallel interviews and stimulated recall data from their instructors in addition to interviewing them about the content and aims of their courses, requesting course outlines or syllabi, and observing some of their classes to document the general patterns of interaction and atmosphere in the classrooms (rather than for explicit analyses).

The interviews and stimulated recalls with students were conducted near the beginning and end of their courses in both Phases 1 and 2. Students who participated in Phase 1 did two interviews, which we later refer to as Interview 1 and Interview 2. Students who also participated in Phase 2 did two additional interviews in total. We refer to those in Phase 2 as Interviews 3 and 4. The interviews with instructors and observations of their classes (in both Phases 1 and 2) were conducted mid-way through the courses. The instructors produced stimulated recalls about their students' writing after the courses were completed and grades submitted, so the instructors would not know which of their students participated in our study.

Various members of our research team conducted the interviews and stimulated recall protocols, so we made efforts to standardize our protocols for these, and also for transcribing audio tapes of them. In addition to rehearsing the interviews and stimulated recalls, we developed a manual for data collection and coding (Busch, 2002) to ensure the interviews and stimulated recalls were equivalent in their administration and content. The design of our research assumed that each of the interviews, stimulated recalls, and writing samples were equivalent, to the extent this is possible in a natural context, and parallel in content and sequence across students and instructors – so as to facilitate comparisons over time, i.e., between beginnings and ends of courses, across Phases 1 and 2, and between groups of participants, i.e., students vs. instructors, or among groups of students.

Interviews. We developed a semi-structured interview protocol, displayed in Appendix C, based on pilot studies (reported in Cumming, Busch & Zhou, 2002) and several months of field tests with ESL students (in programs other than the one where we collected data for the project). We also conducted mock interviews among ourselves on the research team, followed by subsequent revisions and refinements of the instruments for feasibility, phrasing, and quality of data produced. The interview protocol first asked a student in general terms about his or her goals for writing improvement in English, and then prompted the student (through a sequence of 20 questions) to describe and give examples of goals that s/he had for specific aspects of writing (e.g., grammar, composing processes, rhetoric, etc.). For instructors, the content and sequence of interview questions were parallel (to questions addressed to students), but the questions focused on their goals for students' writing improvement in the instructor's course. We conducted the interviews individually with students or professors in a quiet meeting room or office, audio taping and then later transcribing them in full. The interviews lasted about one hour, ranging in duration from 45 to 90 minutes.

To ensure consistency in the interviews, we developed a 16–point list of guidelines for conducting and sequencing the interviews as well as an 11–point checklist of steps to take for data collection (Busch, 2002). Members of the research team also read and discussed principles for interviewing from such sources as Fontana and Frey (2000), Rubin and Rubin (1995), and Spradley (1979). Each participant received a nominal fee per interview. Most interviews were conducted fully in English since the students' high proficiency enabled them to do so. But given the large numbers of participating students from China, Japan, and Korea, we included in our research team native speakers of these languages (Kyoko Baba, Tae-Young Kim, Luxin Yang, and Ally Zhou), who conducted their interviews with students by allowing them the option of using either English or their native languages. In these instances, the interviews tended to switch between English and either Mandarin, Japanese, or Korean, respectively. While transcribing the interviews, however, utterances originally spoken in Mandarin, Japanese, or Korean were translated into English and then verified by a second native speaker of that language prior to analysis.

Stimulated Recall Protocols and Writing Samples. We asked each student to bring to their interviews a writing sample from one of their courses, preferably one of their best pieces of writing. After completing the interview as described above, we asked each student to explain his or her goals generally for the piece of writing. They were asked whether these goals derived from the student or their instructor and whether the respective goals had been fulfilled. Next, they went through the piece of writing, sentence by sentence or section by section, depending on the length of the sample text, and explained verbally the goals they had for each sentence or section of the written text. In this latter procedure we followed principles for stimulated recall protocols described by Gass and Mackey (2000), Smagorinsky (1994), and Woods (1996). We aimed to obtain a detailed account of individual students' goals in reference to the specific text they had produced and found personally significant. The samples of students' writing ranged greatly in genre, length, and quality, however, as described in later chapters of this book. We were satisfied that students' self-selection of their writing yielded texts of personal interest or importance for the students and so were relevant to their goals for writing improvement and represented writing that they actually did in courses. But the variability in text types compromised our abilities to compare the full set of writing samples we received across the two phases of the research or at the beginning and end of each phase. The stimulated recalls lasted about 15 to 25 minutes.

For instructors, we conducted parallel sets of stimulated recalls concerning the same pieces of their students' writing for which the students had earlier produced stimulated recalls. As with the students, we asked the instructors (a) to state their goals generally for the writing task; (b) to tell us whether these goals derived from the student or the instructor; and (c) to tell us whether the respective goals had been fulfilled. Next, the teacher went through the piece of writing, sentence by sentence or section by section depending on the length of the sample text, explaining verbally the goals the student appeared to have for each sentence or section of the written text and to evaluate whether these text segments fulfilled the instructors' course goals. ESL instructors had a number of students from their courses participating in the research. Each of these students produced two samples of writing at the beginning and end of their courses and later provided stimulated recalls about them. The ESL instructors subsequently selected a sample of the most legible pieces of writing to produce their own stimulated recalls. University instructors had only one (or in one case, two) student from their courses participating in our research, each of whom had previously produced one or two writing samples and stimulated recalls about them.

Transcriptions. We transcribed the interviews in full, using standard punctuation and spelling for spoken dialogue and following a limited set of conventions adopted from ten Have (1999), specifically, to signal pauses (.. for 1 to 2 seconds, ... 3 seconds or more), overlapping speech (round parentheses), transcribers' comments (square parentheses), incomplete words (two hyphens), repetition (commas), indications of questions (?) or excitement (!), uncertainty about words (??), and inaudible words (xxx). We laid out the transcriptions in a standard fashion, numbering sections for later coding in reference to the numbered items in our interview schedule (see Appendix C) and also for the sequence of turns in the interviews and then stimulated recall protocols. Extracts in subsequent chapters of this book that quote speech from these interviews use: plain text for utterances originally spoken in English, italics for discourse originally spoken in another language then translated into English by the transcriber, and underlining for discourse originally written in one of the students' writing samples or instructors' course materials.

Analyses

Our analyses focused on developing a scheme to describe the statements about goals for writing improvement that students and instructors produced, applying this scheme to code transcripts of the interviews and stimulated recalls, then tallying the frequency of each category of goal statement and comparing the distribution across phases of the research and types of participants. We did this to establish whether the frequencies differed and in what way. We present the scheme itself in Chapter 3 because we consider it a major outcome of this research as well as a comprehensive means for describing goals for writing improvement among adult ESL learners. Results of other case studies and their respective methods of analysis appear in subsequent chapters of the book.

Developing the coding scheme. Our process of developing a coding scheme to describe goals for ESL writing improvement was at once grounded empirically in iterative reviews of the data we obtained from interviews and stimulated recalls – in the manner of grounded theory (Strauss, 1987) and the constant comparative method (Miles & Huberman, 1994). But the process was also informed conceptually by our reading and discussions of theories and research about goals, intentionality, self-regulated learning, and composition pedagogy as described in Chapter 1. This interactive combination of bottom-up and top-down processes extended over a period of two years through meetings we held once or twice a month and in individual tasks of description and coding between these meetings. We endeavored first to develop an interview schedule that elicited adequate information about students' goals for writing improvement, then to refine it through piloting with ESL learners and ourselves, seeking to make sure that we prompted students to talk about key aspects of their writing and theoretically important features of their goals within a reasonable period of time. We next adapted the contents of the interview schedule so that it would be parallel for instructors and suitable to their unique perspectives and roles in teaching ESL writing. Once we collected and transcribed our first sets of data in Phase 1, we constructed a set of terms and operational definitions to identify, describe, and systematically code goals. While reviewing the data, we revised our initial constructs extensively then proceeded to code the data as described in Chapter 3. As explained in Chapter 1, people and writing tend to have multiple goals, none of which map simply or directly from linguistic expressions to conceptual interpretations. So we opted to code each goal statement for multiple features, i.e., polytonic rather than monotonic coding (Smagorinsky, 1994).

Applying the coding scheme. Four members of our research team (Busch, Cummings, Yang, and Zhou) coded the interview data after reaching levels of inter-coder agreement of between 75% and 85% on multiple segments of the data. This level of agreement means that our interpretations of goals and their characteristics were relatively consistent. All coding of verbal data was done with NVivo (Bazeley & Richards, 2000; Richards & Richards, 2002), a "code and retrieve" software program.

We observed some problematic issues that defied systematic coding and resolved them by making decisions based on our theoretical understanding of goals. We mention them here for the benefit of others who may undertake similar research. Some statements about goals were incomplete in the sense that participants did not provide all the information we would have liked. In these instances, incomplete passages were coded provided that they contained a statement regarding one of the following: an antecedent desire, belief, object of the goal, plan, or action in progress. If none of these five components were present, then the passage was not coded as a goal. Common instances of such fragmentation were describing the object or topic of a goal but not any actions associated with it. Likewise, people sometimes expressed their desires, expectations, or preferences (e.g., through verbal phrases such as "I like to...", "I hope to...", "I think I should...") rather than goals they actually intend to act on. Other times people expressed statements about general improvement (e.g., "I want to improve my writing") or hypothetical situations (e.g., "If I did this, then I could...") which were not sufficiently precise to be considered goals. Statements about some goals proved to be nested within others, and we coded these only once. Some students spoke about goals they had prior to starting their ESL or university programs, and likewise we did not code these.

Statistical analyses. Most of our quantitative results (described in Chapters 3 and 4) are presented as simple tallies of the frequencies of goals or characteristics associated them or as percentages of these for groups of students or instructors. To determine whether these frequencies changed over time or differed among groups, we employed (as reported in Chapter 3) an innovative method for analyzing symmetrical relations among categorical data called dual scaling (Nishisato, 1994; Nishisato & Nishisato, 1994). Dual scaling is akin to principal components analysis but does not require the assumptions of inferential statistics. As demonstrated in an earlier analysis of our data from Phase 1 of this study, this technique helped to show how clusters of goal attributes grouped together by students and by interviews, indicating trends in the data that account for the complexity of our coding scheme of goals in respect to students' characteristics and changes over time (Cumming, Eouanzoui, Gentil, & Yang, 2004). We also attempted to analyze these data through time-series analyses. That is, we tried to model the co-movements over time among the variables in our coding scheme of goals, assuming that each of the students' four interviews was an equivalent data point in a time-series design, for which we could identify a vector model that minimized the variance in the frequency of the expression of types of goals. We found, however, that this method was of restricted value for the multi-faceted, categorical nature of our data and coding schemes as well as the relatively small number of students (i.e., 15) who participated in both phases of our research and the small number of data points we had for them (i.e., 4 interviews). Such analyses might, we realized, be more fruitful with a larger data set, more data points over longer time intervals, and purposes of inquiry that involve predicting future performance from past trends.

CHAPTER 3

Students' goals for ESL and university courses

Ally Zhou, Michael Busch, Guillaume Gentil,
Keanre Eouanzoui, and Alister Cumming

This chapter presents the main results of our research. We first explain our framework to describe students' goals for writing improvement then exemplify them in the case of one ESL student's goals. Next, we present the frequencies with which students reported each feature of their goals, comparing the frequencies reported during the ESL program then, a year later, during programs of university studies. These frequencies indicate how often students, as a whole, expressed certain types of goals or features of them. Accordingly, we have displayed them in the form of bar charts. To examine further the ways in which the students may have changed their goals between the ESL and university programs we present and interpret the results of dual scaling analyses across the four sets of parallel interviews.

What is a goal for ESL writing improvement?

Figure 3.1 displays our framework, consisting of 36 coding categories, for describing goals for ESL writing improvement, the development of which we described in Chapter 2. A fundamental principle is that a goal must be stated fully as a proposition (a point we quickly realized in trying to identify what was, and was not, a statement about a goal in our interview data). Our operational definition of a goal includes students': (1) explicit statements of desire or need in regard to the learning of L2 composition or related abilities; (2) direct acknowledgments of a desire, need, or problem in response to a question about a goal; or (3) descriptions of a dilemma, problem, conflict, or disjunction about learning. (A detailed linguistic analysis of the students' expression of their goals for writing improvement in English appears in Chapter 7.)

Force of a goal

A goal may appear in several possible states of realization or cycles of development, as suggested by genetic approaches to activity theory. We have called these states the *force* of a goal. A student may first formulate a goal as a *dilemma*, recognizing a problem, conflict, or uncertainty about actions to take when writing. Second, a goal may be in a fully realized state as an *intention*, expressing something that students want or desire along with actions for regulating their behavior to do so. Third, a student may already have accomplished a goal and be referring back to it as an *outcome*, which is satisfactorily accomplished or resolved.

Objects of goals

Students' goals are about something. That is, goals have semiotic content or object-oriented actions associated with them. The following objects (and our operational definitions of them in parentheses) were most frequently mentioned by students in their goals for writing improvement:

- *language* (the vocabulary and grammar of English, ranging from clauses to morphemes or punctuation),
- *rhetoric or genres* (including conventional discourse or text structures and elements of them),
- *composing processes* (planning, drafting, editing, and revising a text),
- *ideas and knowledge* (concepts and information for written texts),
- *affective states* (learners' emotional dispositions concerning writing),
- *learning and transfer* (processes of transforming knowledge and skills), and
- *identity and self-awareness* (awareness of self, self-image, or self-concept related to social functions of writing).

Actions taken

Students' goals involve doing something. A basic principle of psychological functioning is that people use goals to mediate semiotic or material objects in the world around them. The actions that students most frequently associated with their goals for writing improvement involved:

- *seeking assistance from instructors* (e.g., by asking questions, for explanations, or for individual guidance),
- *seeking assistance from others* (such as friends, classmates, or native speakers of English),

GOAL (stated as a proposition)

FORCE OF GOAL
  Dilemma
  Intention
  Outcome

OBJECTS
  Language
  Rhetoric or genres
  Composing processes
  Ideas and knowledge
  Affective states
  Learning and transfer
  Identity and self-awareness

ACTIONS TAKEN
  Assistance from instructors
  Assistance from other people
  Self-regulation or heuristics
  Tools or resources
  Studying
  Alter conditions or stimulation
  Reading

CONTEXT OF ACTIONS
  ESL classes
  Academic classes
  Tests
  Work
  Family
  Home

ASPIRATIONS
  University studies
  Tests
  Career

ORIGINS OF GOALS
  Student
  Instructors
  Peers
  Family
  Work

RESPONSIBILITY FOR GOALS
  Student
  Instructors
  Peers
  Others

Figure 3.1. A framework to describe goals to improve ESL writing

- *self-regulation or use of heuristics* (e.g., through phases of planning, monitoring, self-control, or reaction or reflection, or through explicit strategies such as translation, mind-mapping, or memorizing),
- *using tools or resources* (such as the Internet, dictionaries, radio, TV, and grammar books),
- *studying* (e.g., through completing course assignments or prescribed activities, such as journal writing),
- *altering conditions for writing or stimulation* (e.g., finding a peaceful location to write, going to an Internet chat room, drinking coffee), or
- *reading* (i.e., texts in English, such as novels, newspapers, or magazines).

Context of actions

Actions take place in a context. The students we interviewed mostly described acting on their goals for writing improvement within the environments of classrooms or courses, as might be expected of full-time students. To demarcate the study of language and of academic subject matter, we distinguished these classroom contexts in terms of *ESL classes* and *academic classes*. Students also described their goals for writing improvement in respect to other contexts, including *tests* they were preparing for (e.g., for university admissions or professional qualifications), *work* situations (e.g., tasks or expectations for writing associated with jobs previously held or to be sought in the future), *family* members (e.g., parents, spouses, or siblings who helped or provided guidance with writing), or others in their *home* environments (e.g., roommates, neighbors, or friends).

Aspirations

In addition to students' immediate contexts, their goals for writing improvement were sometimes phrased in reference to long-term academic or career plans or aspirations, including future *university studies*, *tests* they would have to take, or expectations for writing in their intended *career* or employment.

Origins of goals

A sixth characteristic of goals is that they come from somewhere. Students cited numerous sources for the creation or origin of their goals for writing improvement: *themselves*, their *instructors*, their *peers* (including classmates and peers), their *family* members (including spouses, parents, and siblings), and *work* situations.

Responsibility for goals

In turn, someone is responsible for carrying out or determining that a goal is achieved. In this regard, students mentioned four categories of people: *themselves*, their *instructors*, their *peers*, or *others* (including family, friends, and employers).

Darina's goals

To exemplify these characteristics of goals for writing improvement, we present some extracts from interviews with Darina during her ESL studies. Darina had been a physician in the Ukraine for four years before coming to Canada to study English. She was the most professionally experienced of the students who participated in both phases of our research, and so quite able to talk about her goals explicitly in reference to her work and career plans. Her long-term *aspiration* was to study computer science at university – as she did, in fact, do the following year – to combine her knowledge of medicine with computer applications, or as she put it, "Maybe with some programming in medicine, in medical field. It would be easier for me to do programming in this field, in medicine, because I am familiar with this activity." In her future academic studies and career Darina was expecting to write extensively: "I think that I will be writing a lot maybe reports, reports, papers, research papers also."

In the following three extracts from her interviews, Darina expressed different goals, all originating from her ESL instructor, in the form of (a) a dilemma about the object of language (articles), (b) an intention about the object of rhetoric (specifically, coherence), and (c) an outcome about the object of language (vocabulary):

(a)   I think it's articles is my weakest point. My teacher said that in general my writing is not bad and that articles are my weakest point. (Darina, Interview 1)

(b)   *Interviewer*: Are there specific types of writing that you're trying to improve in your writing in English?
       Essays.. essays. To improve coherence and unity in essays. To make my essay more logical…introduction and main ideas and supporting ideas. Right now, we're working on essays. (Darina, Interview 1)

(c)   *Interviewer*: Anything you want to change about your writing process as a result of your teacher's feedback?
       Probably I would put some phrases, replace. I would replace some phrases for more advanced, more sophisticated phrases. Some things more appropriate than my phrases in this piece of writing. (Darina, Stimulated Recall, Interview 2)

The actions that Darina subsequently described taking about these goals involved her assuming her own responsibility for studying, using heuristics to remember new vocabulary, seeking help from her instructor (in her ESL class) and from a friend (in her home context), reading, and self-regulation through writing and conversational practice:

> Uh.. I'm studying rules about articles. And I try to remember some group of words which use particular articles.. like expressions.   (Darina, Interview 1)

> Writing in English: spelling and articles. I am doing, I'm trying to do some exercises for articles. Our teacher give us a lot of practice with articles. I try, I usually do this exercises very accurately. I try to do it in time and after that I have conversations with the teacher, and I listen to her suggestions.   (Darina, Interview 2)

> Yes. I try, I'm trying to improve my vocabulary by learning more advanced, more sophisticated language. I usually write it down and try to remember it and trying to repeat it. Um I try to get this word, to memorize this word, and I'm trying to use this word as much as possible to memorize it for the future.

> *Interviewer*: Where do you usually notice new vocabulary?

> Darina: Where? Right now it's in class. Sometimes we have new topics, which are unfamiliar to me, for example from articles. Usually I try to highlight new words and write them down. I have special exercise book for my new vocabulary, and I am trying to get through these new words and memorize them. Sometimes I try to use these words in conversation. For example, I have Canadian friend, I usually use new word, "Listen, I learned today this word."   (Darina, Interview 2)

Frequencies of goals in ESL and university courses

The 15 students who participated over the two phases of our study expressed a total of 490 goals during their two interviews in the ESL program (Phase 1) and 376 goals during their two interviews in university courses (Phase 2). (As a point of comparison, the 45 students in Phase 1 of our research expressed 1,409 goals during their two interviews, or a ratio of about 31 goals per person or 15 goals per interview, which is equivalent to the ratio of those expressed by the 15 students in their Phase 1 interviews.) The interviews in Phase 2 tended to be briefer, seemingly because students became familiar with our interview questions and interviewers, and the students appeared to be, after four parallel interviews, more efficient in responding to our questions or describing their goals.

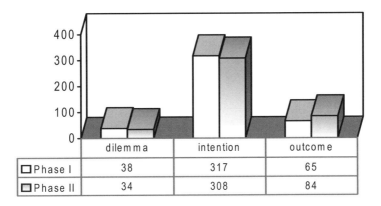

Figure 3.2. Force of goals.

Force of goals

As shown in Figure 3.2, students tended to express most of their goals as intentions during their ESL (Phase 1) and university (Phase 2) courses. The smaller proportion of goals expressed as dilemmas likewise remained relatively consistent across both Phases of our research. But the equally small frequency of goals expressed as outcomes increased between Phases 1 and 2. As the students entered their first year of university programs, some seem to have gained confidence in their abilities and accomplished some of the goals they had previously set for their ESL learning (e.g., for composing processes, as described in Chapters 5 and 8).

Objects of goals

Figure 3.3 shows that, over their ESL and university courses, students' goals mostly tended to involve, in the following order, improving their (1) language, (2) rhetoric, and (3) ideas and knowledge. The frequency of these objects of goals declined slightly from Phase 1 to 2, seemingly because of the decrease in the number of goals expressed overall in the two sets of interviews, though perhaps also because some university professors put less emphasis on writing or English proficiency than had the ESL instructors in Phase 1 (see Chapter 5). Smaller, but distinct, proportions of the students' goals also focused on their composing processes, affective states, and identity and self-awareness, in approximately equal portions in the ESL and the university courses. The one slight increase evident in overall frequency was in the category of learning and transfer, as several students expressed goals that involved their applying skills or knowledge from their ESL

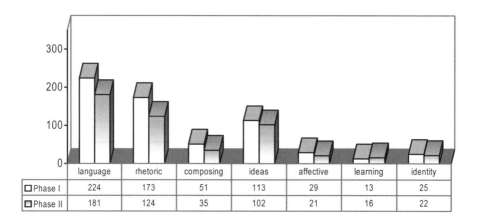

	language	rhetoric	composing	ideas	affective	learning	identity
☐ Phase I	224	173	51	113	29	13	25
☐ Phase II	181	124	35	102	21	16	22

Figure 3.3. Objects of goals.

courses (e.g., about composing processes or text structures) to write assignments in their university courses (again described in Chapter 5).

Actions taken

The actions that students described taking to achieve their goals are tallied in Figure 3.4. Students said they relied mainly on studying course materials to achieve their goals in their ESL as well as their university courses. Seeking assistance from instructors was distinctly more prevalent in the ESL than the university context, and numerous students even found some of their university instructors inaccessible or relatively unconcerned about their writing (as described in Chapter 5). In turn, students said they acted on their goals more frequently, during university studies than ESL studies, in respect to readings for courses, notably to learn technical or discipline-specific vocabulary and genres (e.g., "What I can do now is only read textbooks repeatedly…I don't think I can acquire all the knowledge in the textbooks. So I just read and increase my knowledge to prepare for my next writing"), but they also did other types of reading (e.g., "I try to improve my vocabulary in my writing by reading a lot of short articles on the CBC Web site"). Indeed, the students portrayed their goals and processes of studying as becoming more self-directed during their university courses than their ESL courses, even though the frequency of such statements did not increase. The uses of resources that the students established during their ESL courses appear to have extended into their university courses, for example, in regards to uses of the Internet, dictionaries, and grammar or style guides; obtaining help from friends, classmates, or native English speakers; and regulating themselves while writing.

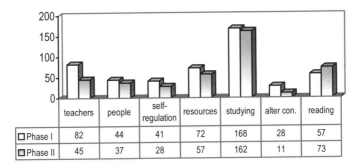

	teachers	people	self-regulation	resources	studying	alter con.	reading
☐ Phase I	82	44	41	72	168	28	57
☐ Phase II	45	37	28	57	162	11	73

Figure 3.4. Actions taken.

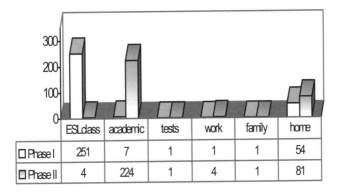

	ESLclass	academic	tests	work	family	home
☐ Phase I	251	7	1	1	1	54
☐ Phase II	4	224	1	4	1	81

Figure 3.5. Contexts of actions.

Contexts of actions

As would be expected and as illustrated in Figure 3.5, the contexts that students described for acting on their goals were mainly in ESL classes in Phase 1 and, conversely, mainly in academic classes in Phase 2. A few students did, however, take ESL or writing courses during their first year of university studies, which explains the appearance of this category during the Phase 2 interviews. Interestingly, the students' goals for writing improvement in respect to their home contexts increased during their university studies, as they made more friends, socialized with more Canadian classmates, or lived in accommodations with Canadians who could assist them with their writing (see Chapters 5 and 8).

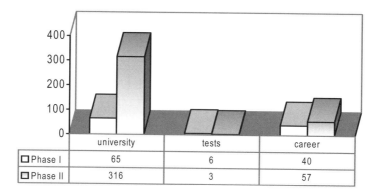

	university	tests	career
☐ Phase I	65	6	40
☐ Phase II	316	3	57

Figure 3.6. Aspirations.

Aspirations

Likewise, the significance and immediate realities of university studies came to shape the students' goals for writing improvement in the university context to an extent that had scarcely existed during their ESL program. This trend is shown dramatically in Figure 3.6, where there is an increase of 386% in goal statements related to university studies from Phases 1 to 2. As Figure 3.6 also shows, students increased their goals for writing related to their long-term careers, seemingly as they became more aware of the particularities of these during their university studies. Writing improvement to pass tests concerned the students less after they had already gained admission to university programs, and so did not have to worry about tests for this purpose.

Origins of and responsibilities for goals

Figures 3.7 and 3.8 suggest that these students continued to see themselves as the main originators of their goals for writing improvement in their ESL and in their university courses as well as to bear the primary responsibilities for achieving them. In university courses, the students saw their professors as having limited responsibilities for their writing goals or even as a source of origin for them, compared to their previous ESL instructors. As described in Chapter 5, many students perceived their university professors as having responsibilities for teaching academic subject matter, not English or writing (and these were roles that, in fact, many of these instructors themselves tended to profess, as described in Chapter 4). Likewise, the students' family members, friends, student peers, or employers were seldom mentioned as having responsibilities for originating or carrying out the students' goals.

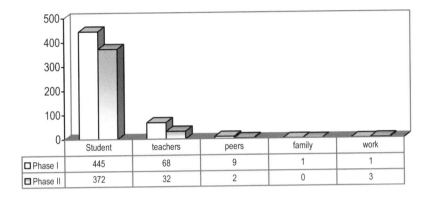

	Student	teachers	peers	family	work
☐ Phase I	445	68	9	1	1
☐ Phase II	372	32	2	0	3

Figure 3.7. Origins of goals.

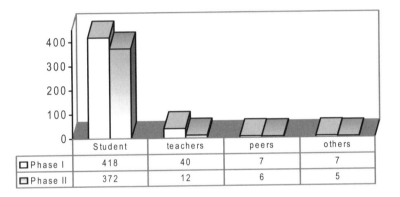

	Student	teachers	peers	others
☐ Phase I	418	40	7	7
☐ Phase II	372	12	6	5

Figure 3.8. Responsibilities for goals.

How did the students' goals vary and change?

Dual scaling analyses

In an earlier analysis of data from Phase 1 of our study we used dual scaling to compare the goals that 45 students expressed at the beginning of their ESL studies (i.e., Interview 1) with those they expressed almost three months later, near the end of the ESL program (i.e., Interview 2) (Cumming, Eouanzoui, Gentil & Yang, 2004). We did not observe noticeable changes in students' goals for ESL writing improvement over the period of the ESL program. But we were able to identify patterns in clusters of students' conceptualizations of their goals. For example, in terms of objects of goals, one group of students appeared predominantly concerned about improving their grammar and vocabulary whereas another group tended to focus more on the clarity and organization of ideas in their writing. Similarly, we could distinguish groups of students based on the kinds of actions they said they took to accomplish their goals: One group appeared more reliant on teacher's and others' assistance, a second group relied more on studying and reading, while a third group tended especially to use resources such as dictionaries and grammar books. Despite these differences among clusters of students in respect to the features of their goals, few patterns appeared along the time dimension. That is, student variables tended to map in relation to the characteristics of goals they expressed rather than variables related to their interviews (i.e., Interview 1 vs. Interview 2). We interpreted these results as indications of consistency in the students' formulations of goals and of their strategies for goal achievement, related to their remaining in the same context of ESL writing instruction with objectives of preparing themselves for academic studies in English-medium universities.

In the present section we apply dual scaling again to examine whether patterns appeared in the 15 students' goals for writing improvement between their ESL program (Interviews 1 and 2) and their university courses (Interviews 3 and 4). We analyzed the frequency of occurrence, as presented above, for the five main characteristics of goals (objects, actions, aspirations, origins, and responsibilities) through Dual 3 statistical software (Nishisato & Nishisato, 1983), considering the distribution of the frequencies of the students' goals per category, per student, and per interview. We present below, however, only the results for the analyses of objects of goals, actions taken, and responsibilities for goals because these represent the most salient and meaningful characteristics of the students' goals for writing improvement and for ease of interpretation in view of the complexity of information that dual scaling analyses produce.

The solutions in dual scaling are, for categorical data, akin to the components in principal components analysis for numerical data (see for more details, Nishisato, 1994; Nishisato & Nishisato, 1994). The number of solutions depends upon the type of categorical data. In the case of frequency tables, the total number of solutions is the smaller number out of the number of rows (say, n) and columns (say, m) minus one (i.e., minimum {n, m} – 1), giving rise to the number of solutions taken in combinations of two at a time to produce a graphical display, as in Figures 3.9, 3.10, and 3.11 below. That is, for a 45–by–6 contingency table, the total number of solutions is 5 and the corresponding total combinations of two solutions is 10 (or $\frac{number\_solutions \times (number\_solutions - 1)}{2}$). Although dual scaling produces multiple solutions to any data analysis, for reasons of parsimony we present below only plots of Solution 1 versus Solution 2, considering this to approximate an optimal representation of our data matrices. In the dual-scaling plots displayed below, the two axes are the first two solutions (Solution 1 juxtaposed against Solution 2) of the equation. The dual scaling analyses optimize the between-row (students) and between-column (goal category variables) discrimination as well as the correlation between responses weighted by row weights and those by column weights. The frequency data on which these dual-scaling analyses are based appear above, in the Figures with bar charts, for the relevant category of goals. In the Figures that follow, the relevant categories of goals are identified by triangles and the students by diamonds.

The dual-scaled data provide a kind of map showing the relative distance between each student and each goal category for each interview, this distance being a function of the number of times each student expressed each goal category during each interview. That is, the closer a student is to a goal category, the greater the number of times he or she had expressed this particular goal category during the interview. Furthermore, the analyses represent the distance between a student and a particular goal category for each of the four interviews. That is, if a student expressed one goal category many times in all four interviews, he or she mapped on the graph close to this category for all interviews. Alternatively, if this student expressed the goal category frequently in the first and second interviews then seldom in the third and fourth interviews, then that person mapped close to this category for the Phase 1 interviews but far from the category in the Phase 2 interviews. In this way, the plotted graphs from the dual scaling analyses help to identify consistencies or changes in the students' responses in terms of the relative distance between the categorical responses in the Phase 1 interviews and those in Phase 2 interviews. These analyses are essentially exploratory, however, in the sense that we have had to interpret the patterns we perceive in the plotted graphs in order to make sense of the data they display. There are no tests of statistical significance or effect sizes appropriate to dual scaling analyses such as might guide these interpretations.

Objects of goals

The dual-scaled graph in Figure 3.9 provides a two-dimensional representation of the distribution of the frequencies of goal statements per student, object type, and interview number. Together, the first two solutions represent 35% of the variability for students' expressions about the objects of their goals. Most students cluster near the origin around the three most frequently cited objects of goals: language, rhetoric, and ideas. Interestingly, the Southern hemisphere includes both Phase 1 (i.e., Interviews 1 and 2) and Phase 2 (i.e., Interviews 3 and 4) variables, whereas the Northern hemisphere includes almost exclusively Phase 2 variables (except for goals with the object of language in Interview 2, which is near the origin). Furthermore, the East end of the Southeast quadrant includes only composing and affective variables from Phase 1, which are diametrically opposed

Objects: interview 1, 2, 3, and 4

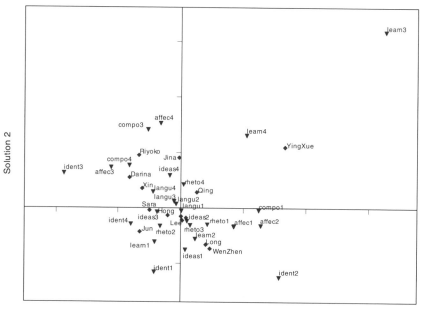

Figure 3.9. Dual scaling of objects of goals in interviews 1, 2, 3, and 4.

Note: Triangles represent objects of goals (i.e., language, composing processes, rhetoric, ideas, affect, learning, and identity); numbers 1, 2, 3, and 4 refer to their mention in the sequence of the 4 interviews; diamonds represent pseudonyms of students.

to the composing and affective variables in Phase 2 in the Northwest quadrant. A final observation is that goals related to learning and transfer in Interviews 3 and 4 map into the Northeast quadrant around one particular student, Yingxue (who produced 38% of the goal statements for the learning and transfer category in Phase 2), and not far from Jina (who produced 19% of these goals) and Qing (who produced 13% of them).

The clustering of students either around variables (i.e., language, rhetoric, and idea) or around the phases (e.g., composing and affective states in Interviews 3 and 4 vs. composing and affective states in Interviews 1 and 2) suggests that some students shifted their focus from one kind of object to another between their ESL and their university courses. For instance, Rihoko, who maps in the Northwest Phase 2 quadrant, focused her objects of goals almost exclusively on language and rhetoric in Phase 1. In Phase 2, while she remained concerned over language and rhetoric, she broadened her goals to include statements about composing, affect, and identity as well as ideas. Similarly, and mapping not far from Rihoko, Darina and Xin focused their goals mostly on three objects (language, rhetoric, and ideas) in Phase 1. In Phase 2, while still concerned about language, ideas, and to a lesser extent rhetoric, they expressed new or more goals related to composing and affective states. Conversely, Long, who maps in the Phase 1 Southeast quadrant, expressed fewer goals related to composing (0 vs. 7) and ideas (3 vs. 13) in Phase 2 than in Phase 1, while his goal statements focused on language (16 vs. 20) and rhetoric (13 vs. 12) remained high and stable across phases. Yingxue focused on learning in both Interviews 3 and 4, while this object of goals was absent from her Phase 1 interviews.

Remarkably, despite these noticeable changes of focus in some students' objects of goals from Phase 1 to Phase 2, the students tended to focus on similar objects of goals across the two interviews within each phase. Moreover, while the students' goal statements show some between-phase variability for some object categories (composing, affective states, and learning), they show less between-phase variability for other object categories (language, rhetoric, ideas). Language, rhetoric, and ideas were the most frequent categories in all interviews: These objects of goals were consistently emphasized by all students in both phases. Statements about identity accounted for less than 4% of the goals expressed in both phases and showed the greatest variability. Students expressed between 1 and 4 identity-related goals either in both interviews of one phase only (i.e., Darina, Lee, Jina) or in three interviews only (Hong, Jun, Long, Whenzen, Xin) or in one interview only (e.g., Qing, Sara, Yingzue). This variability is shown on Figure 3.9 by the mapping of the identity variables in distant locations in three quadrants.

The interview transcripts confirm these patterns of consistency and change from Phase 1 to Phase 2. For instance, not only were language-related issues the most frequent objects of goals in the four interviews with Darina, the objects she emphasized – articles, spelling, vocabulary, tenses – and often the very phrasing she used were remarkably similar in both phases. Thus, her concern over developing "more advanced, more sophisticated language" voiced in Interview 1 is eerily echoed in Interview 4, over one year later, when she says that she "would like to use more advanced, more sophisticated words." Similarly, Darina's awareness of article usage being a special area in need of improvement – "because we don't have it in Russian" – is a recurring theme across all four of her interviews. On the other hand, composing processes – e.g., improving her planning strategies and learning how to obtain peer feedback – were new objects of goals, reflecting, perhaps, the influence of the ESL writing instruction she received.

Likewise, Rihoko's overarching concern over making her writing "more complex" as well as the sophisticated metalanguage she used to describe how she aimed to achieve this (studying "adjective clauses and adverb clauses" avoiding "agreement errors" when using "relative pronouns") appear across all of her interviews. (See also discussion of Rihoko's case in Chapter 8.) At the same time, in addition to expressing new kinds of objects of goals in Phase 2 (e.g., composing processes and affective states), Rihoko changed the formulation of the specific objects she focused on for other object categories. For instance, in all interviews, Rihoko made a couple of goal statements about the object category, "rhetoric structures and genres." But the genres she wanted to improve varied from generic academic text types (e.g., research essays) and self-expressive narrative genres in Interviews 1 and 2 to the descriptive genres specific to her discipline, architecture, in Interviews 3 and 4.

Expressions of identity-oriented goals also tended to vary from one interview to the next for each participant. For instance, in Interview 1, Whenzen formulated her identity in terms of adjusting her "Chinese" ways of thinking and writing to "Canadian" ways. In Interview 2, she shared her belief that while in Canada, she was learning how to affirm herself in life and her writing – to think and choose for herself and to express her stance in her writing – rather than doing what her parents and teachers told her to do. In Interview 3, Whenzen did not mention any identity goals. In Interview 4, she formulated the goal to learn how to "write like a manager." In sum, there were consistencies and changes in the objects of students' goal statements, suggesting both the continuity of their predispositions, perceptions, and intentions as well as their adaptive responses to changing academic and cultural environments and exigencies (a point we explore further in Chapter 8).

Actions taken

Figure 3.10 shows the first two solutions of dual scaling for the actions that the students said they took to try to achieve their goals. Although the graph is complex, several zones can be distinguished. First, instructors' assistance clusters for all four interviews around a few students (e.g., Long) in the Southwest quadrant. Second, the action of studying clusters around a number of students (e.g., Xin, Jina, Yi, Kazuko, and Jun) not far from the origin and mostly in the Southeast quadrant (with the exception of studying in Interview 3, which is near the origin but in the Northeast quadrant). A third cluster overlapping the Northeast and Southeast quadrant includes a number of students (Rihoko, Jina, Sara, Yi, and Kazuko) around three types of action (use of resources, seeking assistance from others, and reading) for Phase 2 only. Not far from this cluster, Darina maps near statements about self-regulation in Interviews 3 and 4, which are diametrically opposed to statements about self-regulation in Interviews 1 and 2 (in the Western hemisphere). Fourth, uses of resources mentioned during Interviews 1 and 2 cluster together in the Southern hemisphere and away from the resources mentioned for Interviews 3 and 4 further North. While the other variables are relatively scattered, all but one of the variables about altering conditions for writing appear in the Northwest quadrant. Interestingly, the Northeast quadrant includes only Phase 2 variables, whereas the Southwest quadrant, diametrically opposed, includes actions taken to obtain assistance from instructors, mentioned during Interviews 1 to 4, but only Phase 1 variables. This distinction reflects the finding, discussed above in regards to Figure 3.8 and described further in Chapters 4 and 5, that the students found their ESL instructors more accessible and helpful than their mainstream university instructors in regards their individual writing improvement.

Thus, as with their statements about the objects of their goals, the students' statements about the actions that they took to achieve their goals for writing improvement show some between-phase variability for some actions (self-regulation, use of resources, seeking others' assistance, and reading), but less so for other actions (seeking help from teachers, studying, and altering conditions for writing). In other words, some students appear to have changed some, but not all, of the actions they reported using for accomplishing their writing goals as they progressed from pre-university ESL courses to first-year academic courses. For instance, almost all students reported using studying as their most frequent actions in all four interviews. On the other hand, some reported using resources more frequently in the Phase 1 interviews than in the Phase 2 interviews (and others reported the converse). While all students reported using reading to act on their goals in the Phase 2 interviews, five students (Darina, Jun, Rihoko, Sara, and Kazuko) hardly or never reported taking that action in the Phase 1 interviews. Conversely, most students reported relying on teachers' assistance in the Phase 1 interviews, but some (Jina, Mark, and Rihoko) no longer did in the Phase 2 interviews. However, some students (notably Long, Lee, and Qing) reported consistent uses of teachers' assistance in all four interviews. In contrast, other students (Darina, Rihoko) did not report taking this action at all. The consistency of these statements helps explain why overall the teachers' assistance variables cluster together for all four interviews.

In sum, whereas the simple frequency of statements about actions taken (i.e., Figure 3.4) suggests an equivalence from Phase 1 to Phase 2 in the total number of students' statements about the actions they took to achieve their goals, with the exception of teachers' assistance and reading, the dual-scaled graph here (Figure 3.10) provides a more nuanced picture of the students' reported actions taken for goal achievement, highlighting various areas of both consistency and change.

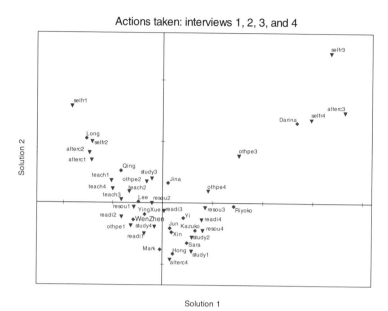

Figure 3.10. Dual scaling of actions taken in interviews 1, 2, 3, and 4.

Note: Triangles represent actions taken (i.e., assistance from teachers, assistance from *others*, self-regulation, use of resources, studying, altering conditions, reading); numbers 1, 2, 3, and 4 refer to their mention in the sequence of the 4 interviews; diamonds represent pseudonyms of students.

Responsibilities for goals

Figure 3.11 shows the first two solutions of dual scaling for statements about responsibilities for goals, representing over 55% of the variability in these data. (These patterns resemble those for the statements about origins of goals, as well, which showed scarcely any change between Phases 1 and 2, so we have not displayed them here.) Almost all students cluster around the variables for students, near the origin of the graph, indicating that students saw themselves as primarily responsible for carrying out their goals for writing improvement. Interestingly, however, three groups of students are discernible: a majority group who located the origins of their goals only or mostly in themselves (the "students" group near the origin), and two minority groups who also mentioned teachers (in the Northwest quadrant) and peers (in respect, either to the ESL student peers in Phase 1, e.g., Whenzen, or to university students in their classes in Phase 2, e.g., Yingxue). For instance, Yingxue and Whenzen cluster in Figure 3.11 near statements about

Responsibility for goals: interviews 1, 2, 3, and 4

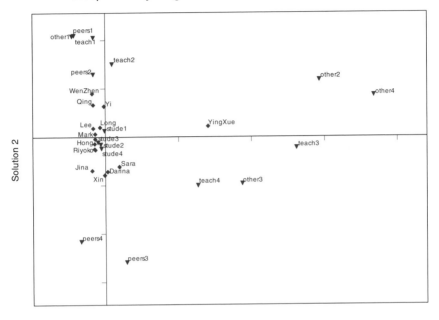

Figure 3.11. Dual scaling of responsibilities for goals in interviews 1, 2, 3, and 4.

Note: Triangles represent who was said to have responsibilities for goals (i.e., students, teachers, peers, or others); numbers 1, 2, 3, and 4 refer to their mention in the sequence of the 4 interviews; diamonds represent pseudonyms of students.

responsibilities for goals residing in peers and with instructors because they were among the few students who, in addition to identifying themselves as the originators and responsible for their goals for writing improvement, also sometimes mentioned their instructors and peers.

Summary

In sum, these analyses produce images of consistency, individual variability, and socio-contextual influences on goals for writing improvement. We have been able to describe categorically and systematically the goals that these students expressed for improving their writing in English. These goals have complex dimensions and realizations, as suggested by goal theory and studies of goals in other domains

(Austin & Vancouver, 1996; Pintrich, 2000b) as well as by previous research demonstrating the multi-faceted characteristics of writing in second-languages (Cumming, 1998; 2001b; Leki, Cumming, & Silva, 2006).

The objects of goals that students most frequently expressed were to improve their language, rhetoric, and ideas and knowledge in their writing. But other aspects of writing were also distinctly considered as the objects of goals, including composing processes, ideas and knowledge, affective states, learning and transfer, and identity and self-awareness. Writing in English at university was not a single entity or skill but rather for these students represented a complex array of interrelated abilities, processes, and relationships, as suggested by academic socialization and academic literacies models of writing (Jones, Turner & Street, 1999). The frequency with which these objects were mentioned remained relatively consistent, though declined slightly, between the ESL and university courses. The consistency attests to the stability of learning goals (cf. Leont'ev, 1972; Pintrich, 2000b) as well as the complexity of writing in a second language (cf. Cumming, 1998; Silva & Brice, 2004). The slight decrease over time may have resulted from the students' increasing familiarity with the interview format. Nonetheless, the dual scaling analyses show that most students tended to retain their focus on the same objects of goals over the period of our research, although a minority shifted their focus between the ESL and university courses, notably broadening out their range of goals during their university studies to include objects such as composing processes, affective states, and learning, in addition to the core objects of language, rhetoric, and ideas.

The students indicated that most of their goals were related directly to the contexts of instruction in which they were currently engaged. In Phase 1, students expressed their goals mostly in relation to their ESL courses. In Phase 2, students expressed their goals mostly in relation to their university courses. At both times, however, influences from home situations and family members also formed some of the contexts for certain students' goals. These trends confirm a principal tenet of activity theory and other socio-culturally oriented theories of learning: People learn language and literacy from and in relation to the resources, people, interactions, models, and rules available in their immediate social contexts (Engström, 1999; Lantolf, 2000; Wells, 1999; Winsor, 1999). Educational experiences appear to have shaped these students' conceptualizations of their learning though influences from family, acquaintances, and peers played a role too.

This principle is evident, as well, in considering the long-term aspirations that motivated these students' goals for improving their writing in English. As the students moved into university courses, and came to appreciate the specific demands for writing in particular academic courses, they increased dramatically their aspirations to improve their writing for these purposes. In turn, their concerns about improving their writing in order to pass university admissions tests diminished almost completely (once they actually were in universities), an indication of the impact that such tests may have on ESL students' approaches to their learning (Bailey, 1999). Likewise, some students seem to have gained, while studying academic courses in their disciplines, greater awareness of the demands for writing for their future careers. These trends support arguments (presented in Chapters 1 and 4) for the value of writing and language instruction in the context of academic courses at universities, viewed either from the perspective of curriculum policy (Brinton, Snow and Wesche, 2003) or of activity theory (Bazerman & Russell, 2003). In turn, the value of intensive support from ESL instructors prior to university studies is evident in these students' recognition that, although they themselves have primary responsibilities for stipulating and carrying out their goals for writing improvement, instructors in ESL courses played a greater or more distinctive role in these processes than did instructors of academic courses – a point that emerges more distinctly from data presented in Chapters 4 and 5.

CHAPTER 4

A study of contrasts:
ESL and university instructors'
goals for writing improvement

Jill Cummings, Usman Erdősy, and Alister Cumming

In this chapter we describe and contrast the goals for writing improvement of the ESL and university instructors who taught the ESL students who participated in our study. This analysis and comparison of the instructors' goals is important because the goals that students talked about – as documented and analyzed in other chapters in this book – centered on their learning of academic writing in the classes that they attended. For instance, 83% of students' goals reported during interviews in Phase I of our research related directly to the contexts of their ESL courses (see Chapter 3). For this reason it is vital to understand the goals, activities, and perceptions of the instructors who taught, and indeed, who created these contexts. Other research has shown how various ESL learners strive to match and appropriate the aims for writing improvement modeled, suggested, or advocated by their instructors (Cumming, 1986; Cumming, Busch & Zhou, 2002; Fishman & McCarthy, 2001; Hoffman, 1998; Nassaji & Cumming, 2000). In this regard, differences or similarities in students' goals for their writing improvement may arise from the ESL or university instruction that they receive.

As activity theory suggests, classroom instruction creates the activity systems in which students develop their writing abilities in English (Bazerman & Russell, 2003; Russell, 1997a). With this conceptualization in mind, we designed our interviews, stimulated recalls, and observations with the instructors to elicit information to describe key qualities of these activity systems, though we cannot claim to have the extent or rigor of ethnographic data that would be needed to account for these activity systems in detail. That is, we conceived of the classroom contexts as environments managed primarily by the instructors, who (like the ESL students for their goals for writing improvement) would have, as stipulated by Leont'ev (1978) and Engeström (1991b), distinct but interconnecting levels of realization.

First, and most generally, we assumed that the *activities* established in class-rooms and written assignments would be fundamental units of human behavior, embedded in the social and institutional contexts of rules, communities, and divisions of labor among instructors and students. Second, these activities would exist to satisfy *motives*, such as aspirations to write effectively in English or a specific field of academic study, providing an energizing function to actors. Third, we expected instructors to have *goals*, both for students' writing improvement and for their learning of course content, that would serve as focal or operational principles to direct themselves and their students, bridging the gap between abstract activities and concrete actions. Fourth, we expected to see instructors undertake specific, tangible a*ctions,* for instance in their teaching and in their responding to students' writing, that would realize abstract activities in relation to goals. In turn, we expected students to engage in *intermediate actions*, such as composing or performing tasks, to fulfill their instructors' goals. These actions, we assumed, would jointly correspond to the kinds of routines that Cumming (1992) described in his observational study of ESL instructors teaching. Further, these actions would consist in smaller clusters of *operations* (and even automatized behaviors) that determine how things are done (compared to actions, which determine what was done).

We considered goal theory as well in our trying to prompt instructors to articulate the goals they had for their courses, for their students' development of English writing, and for specific writing tasks. We attempted to observe, for instance, whether instructors might express goals for students' *mastery* of English writing or for their simply *performing* writing tasks – a distinction that Midgely (2002) argued is crucial in pedagogy that promotes meaningful, enduring learning. Such pedagogical orientations may, or may not, have been overtly stated in the open-ended interviews that we conducted, though we did ask instructors explicitly in their stimulated recalls whether they thought students had, or had not, achieved the particular goals set for each written assignment they commented on (see Chapter 6 for the results of these analyses). Information about such orientations also emerged implicitly, for example, in instructors describing whether they prompted students to produce multiple, rewritten drafts of their written assignments (which, in principle, should promote *mastery-oriented* learning) or simply single passes at writing tasks (which may tend to promote goals of just *performing* writing).

The ESL instructors' goals and pedagogy for writing were intended to prepare students for and to complement the goals, pedagogy, and writing tasks that the students might encounter in university courses the following year. At the same time, the ESL instructors could not predict exactly what situations the students would encounter in their academic studies, or precisely what expectations for literacy in English the university courses might entail. There are many unknowns here, making an understanding of instructors' goals and activities for writing improvement as important as an understanding of the students' goals. As Polio (2003, p. 58) observed, "Surprisingly little has been written [about} what actually transpires in L2 writing classrooms." Moreover, how closely should we expect the contexts of ESL and university courses to correspond? As Tait (1999, p. 10) observed, "Writing teachers, content area instructors, and L2 students do not necessarily agree on the desired outcomes of courses targeted to improve L2 writing."

For these reasons, we have documented and contrasted the goals that instructors articulated for improving students' writing from their pre-university ESL program to mainstream, content-based university courses. We focus in the present chapter on these two research questions:

1. What similarities and differences appeared in the goals and instruction of the pre-university ESL teachers and the university instructors and professors?
2. What are the implications for writing instruction and curricula in pre-university ESL and university contexts?

Policy Issues in Writing Instruction in Pre-University and University Contexts

Brinton, Snow and Wesche (2003, p. 242) identified four primary features of academic literacy in post-secondary education in North America: (i) linguistic characteristics; (ii) background knowledge; (iii) cognitive knowledge (e.g. strategic and critical thinking); and, (iv) knowledge of the discourse community. We adopted this conceptual framework for the present analysis because of its comprehensiveness and proximity to the situations and goals described by the instructors in this study, equally for the ESL and university instructors. At the same time, our analyses are also informed by issues arising from previous research on learning, teaching, and curriculum policy for ESL students in pre-university and university studies.

Genres of academic writing across the curriculum

A central policy issue in discussions of curriculum for writing instruction at universities is the extent to which (a) courses should be designed as preparatory to university studies, as the present ESL program was, or whether (b) responsibilities for writing instruction should be distributed across the curriculum, and shared by all university instructors in respect to their areas of academic specialization, rather than situated in separate writing courses. Spack (1997) and Zamel (1995), for example, have recommended that "writing across the curriculum" be a feature of all university courses, particularly for students from culturally diverse backgrounds. They have advocated pre-university ESL instructors and university professors work jointly to facilitate ESL students' participation and learning of writing in their discipline-specific studies.

In regards to preparatory courses of writing instruction for universities, a key issue is how pedagogy incorporates the writing demands of specific text genres in academic disciplines. Russell (1997a) and Bazerman and Russell's (2003) studies of general academic preparation writing courses for native speakers of English in American universities have suggested that such courses tend to be overly general in their content, so academic preparation writing courses need to align more specifically in genre-types to the disciplines that students will pursue. Russell (1997a) recommended that courses in general academic preparation writing be provided as ongoing mainstream university courses that promote student participation and interaction with their intended disciplines of study, rather than as the unrealistic "one time pre or early entry" remedial courses intended as a "stop gap measure" to "fix" writing and writers before they enter their disciplines. Appealing to activity theory, Russell (1997a) and Bazerman and Russell (2003) advocated that the goals and content of writing programs be made discipline-specific, and thereby consistent with the actual goals and genuine academic interests of students. They claimed this approach would make students' writing experiences meaningful and facilitate the transfer of writing skills to content-specific courses. They argued that teaching general writing skills to students without linking them to their discipline-specific studies is like teaching someone to play basketball in hopes that they will be able to transfer "general ball-playing skills" to other "ball sports" such as softball and football.

Horowitz (1986), Leki and Carson (1997), Leki (2001b), and Johns (2003) have likewise called for a discipline-specific orientation in ESL courses for academic preparation, particularly attention to the genres of academic writing required in university studies. Leki and Carson's (1997) analysis of ESL students' impressions of their pre-university courses concluded that pre-university ESL (or EAP) courses should: (a) focus directly on the academic tasks that students will eventually pursue; (b) be appropriately complex in their intellectual demands; and, (c) be "text responsible" in the sense of requiring students to write to real academic demands rather than for personal expression or linguistic development. Leki (2001a) extended this theme, providing multiple models of exemplary courses for academic preparation writing courses around the world while stressing the importance of teaching critical thinking in relation to genre-specific tasks.

Social contexts and learning transfer

Crucial to these debates, as it is to our present analysis, is the issue of how and why pedagogy in ESL and university courses should correspond. Fishman and McCarthy (2001) adopted the perspective that the goals, orientations, and situations of instructors of writing and of academic subjects inevitably differ. They analyzed one ESL student's progress in a writing-intensive, introductory philosophy course. They found that, even though the student and professor's goals initially did not match, the student eventually did strive to meet the professor's expectations and made progress in her writing. What seemed to overcome or compensate for the "mismatch" of goals between professor and student was the opportunity for the student to interact purposefully with her peers, giving her a social motive and support for accomplishing the class assignments. Fishman and McCarthy suggested that this was a process of socialization and goal realization that the student might never have been able to experience in a non-collaborative course setting; nor in the context of an ESL program which did not have discipline-specific course content.

Equally important to issues of academic socialization are those of learning transfer. How do students transfer the writing abilities that they learn in ESL courses to perform in academic courses? James (2003), for instance, documented how students made use of or transferred such skills as organizing their compositions, peer editing, reading for specific details, and group work management that they had acquired in preparatory ESL courses to approach assignments such as reports for their engineering courses. (See chapter 5 for similar findings about the transfer of skills and strategies from ESL to university courses.) Widdowson (1983) argued for the benefits of a general approach to English language education to develop capacities in students which they could later apply to future academic studies or employment, rather than a narrowly focused training approach to specific-purposes language pedagogy. Widdowson argued that such specific-purposes pedagogy limits instruction to helping students acquire specific skills that might be limited or unpredictable for future use. This distinction between general purposes and specific purposes (related to writing for a particular academic or professional discipline) appears to be a fundamental basis for variation in the curricula for ESL writing instruction around the world, though the outcomes of either curriculum orientation are not well-established (Cumming, 2003a).

Method

As indicated in Appendices A and B, five ESL instructors and nine university instructors participated in our study. As explained in Chapter 2, the ESL instructors volunteered to participate in our research in response to a solicitation letter, whereas the university instructors were nominated by students (already participating in our study). The ESL instructors provided two interviews, one near the beginning and one near the conclusion of their course, and stimulated recalls about their students' writing samples, following the protocols described in Chapter 2 and displayed in Appendix C. We observed fourteen of the ESL instructors' classes and took field notes about the routines, tasks, interactions and materials in the classes. The university instructors provided parallel data, but only one interview, stimulated recall, and classroom observation was carried out with each university instructor. The ESL classes met 4 times a week (for 16 hours per week) over 12 to 14 weeks, whereas the university classes met once or twice a week (for 3 hours per week) over 12 to 14 weeks;

Context and participants

The ESL instructors – Faith, Leeanne, Linda, Lulu, and Maria – taught the integrated-skills courses in the advanced, pre-university EAP program during Phase 1 of the project. Two of these instructors (Faith and Maria) were observed and interviewed twice for courses they taught – first during the September–December semester; then later in the January–April term, so the data on goals we report below has been tallied in regards to seven ESL classes (i.e., counting Faith and Maria's courses twice – for each course for which we observed and interviewed them).

We have divided (for reasons explained below) the nine instructors of university courses into two groups based on the types of courses they taught. One type of course was bridging and foundation courses intended to introduce ESL students (and in some cases native-English first year students) to discourse and writing conventions and theoretical foundations of academic disciplines. The Canadian universities where we conducted the research do not typically require a first-year composition course for all students (as is the policy at many American universities); rather, bridging and foundation courses like the ones described in this study are usually available to native and non-native speakers of English as they enter university, although they are not compulsory. The second type of courses involved mainstream university courses in which the instructor focused exclusively on discipline-specific content (e.g. Landscape Design) and classes were comprised of both non-native English speakers (NNES) and native English speakers (NES).

All university courses were credit-bearing courses, except Mary's, as explained in Chapter 2, which was a credit (Ontario Academic Credit) course specific to international business and for completion of grade 13 of secondary school.

The bridging or foundation courses and their instructors we have called (as indicated in Appendix B): Professional Writing for Engineering, taught by Bruce to mostly NNES students in Engineering; Arts of Discourse: Ancient and Modern, taught by Gloria as a foundation course in the Humanities to a combination of NNES and NES students; Introduction to Canadian Language and Culture, taught by Julianne as a bridging course mainly for NNES students; Oriental Arts, taught by Richard as a foundation course in the Humanities to NNES and NES students; Writing for Engineering, taught by Sally as a bridging course for NNES students in Engineering; and International Business, taught by Mary exclusively to NNES students completing the final year of high school.

The mainstream university courses and their instructors we have called: Landscape Design, which was taught by Aliz to NES and NNES students in a graduate program in Landscape Design; Behavior in Institutions and Businesses, taught by Hatton to NES and NNES students in an undergraduate Commerce Program; and Foundations of Economic Theory, taught by Willy to NES and NNES students in an undergraduate program in Economics (See Appendix B).

Analyses

We began our analyses with impressionistic interpretations about the curricula of the courses based on our observations of classroom teaching, inspection of course outlines and assignments, and the instructors' descriptions of the purposes and scope of the courses. We then analyzed the instructors' statements about their goals for their students' writing improvement, identifying and coding the goals they expressed in each interview in the same manner as for the students' goals (as described in Chapters 2 and 3). We focused on three of the categories from our coding scheme – objects of goals, actions taken, and responsibilities for goals – that we considered relevant to the perspectives of instructors and based on the interview data we obtained. We calculated and compared the frequency of these goals and their characteristics for the ESL courses (Phase 1) and university courses (Phase 2) after converting the frequencies to percentages (because of the differences in numbers of instructors, courses, and interviews). To evaluate whether there were differences in the frequencies of goals for writing improvement across the course types, we made post-hoc comparisons by analysis of variance across the goals expressed for the three course types (ESL, Bridging and Foundation, and Mainstream university courses, i.e., see Figure 4.1 below).

Findings and discussion

We have already alluded to a basic finding from our analyses: There was not a simple dichotomy between ESL and university courses as we had expected when designing our research. Rather, four relatively distinct types of courses could be distinguished, following the framework of Brinton, Snow and Wesche (2003). Obvious curricular distinctions appeared among the university courses selected by the ESL students in our research to discuss in the interviews as writing intensive courses.

Four types of courses

The first type was, as we expected, *non-credit, intensive ESL courses*, which describes all of the courses in Phase 1 of our research. As Brinton, Snow and Wesche (2003) suggest, such courses focus on developing language skills and knowledge in respect to cognitive knowledge and learning or task-oriented strategies. In these classes, perhaps best called EAP (English for Academic Purposes), instructors presented general academic themes, genres, and reading and listening texts as a means for developing general academic English proficiency and writing skills. None of the content in these courses was specific to any particular academic discipline or discourse. All of the EAP instructors themselves said they strived to provide a variety of general academic writing themes and materials in an effort to meet the variety of discipline interests and goals of their pre-university students. The EAP instructors knew their individual students well because of the intensity of (daily) instruction and their relatively small class sizes (15 to 22 students per class).

The second type, *bridging courses*, applied to the two courses on writing for Engineering students taught by Bruce and Sally, the academic skills course about Canadian society taught by Julianne, and the course in International Business for high school credit taught by Mary. These courses were distinct in their overt attention to English language, critical thinking and writing, but they had a limited focus on background or subject matter knowledge (Brinton, Snow & Wesche, 2003). These courses differed from the previous category of pre-university ESL courses by providing students with academic credit toward degree programs and their slightly lesser attention to language knowledge and skills. Conversely, the bridging courses differed from the next two categories of courses in their being taught by instructors whose qualifications were primarily in ESL and/or rhetoric and composition rather than in a particular academic discipline. Their "bridging" element consisted of organizing curricula from the starting point of general writing and language skills, then developing students' academically oriented writing competencies through the discourse and subject matter of the course topic. For example, the engineering writing courses foregrounded processes for composing and general text types (as was also the case in the ESL courses in Phase 1), and content related to engineering served as a vehicle to prompt students to write on relevant tasks rather than as an intended outcome from their participation in the courses. The size of bridging classes was 20 to 25 students per course, similar to the pre-university EAP course.

The third type of course can be called *foundation courses*. Their stated purpose was to introduce students – both NES and NNES – to the knowledge and writing conventions of academic discourse communities. One such course was a comparative study of communication in ancient and modern societies; the other focused on East Asian Art. Both were taken as options in the Humanities by students (in our research) from programs in Commerce or Economics, so these foundation courses were not their major areas of academic study. Language and cognitive skills were not overtly emphasized in the course content and delivery, although they figured in the assessment of students' performance and were addressed by instructors through feedback on written assignments. NNES students were not "sheltered" (or segregated) in these classes, but took the courses alongside native speakers of English. Academic subject matter was treated on a general, introductory level, but nonetheless was the focus of teaching about discipline-specific conventions for constructing written arguments. There were between 25 and 45 students in the foundation (and also the mainstream) courses, which made for an atmosphere where instructors were less personally involved with individual students than in the ESL or bridging courses.

The fourth type of courses, *mainstream university courses*, focused entirely on academic content, representing the NNES students' target environment for study. One was a graduate course in Landscape Design, and two were introductory undergraduate courses on the topics of economics and of organizational behavior, respectively. The content of these courses focused overtly on discipline-specific knowledge. Students were assumed to know relevant cognitive, language, and rhetorical skills and conventions, so instructors only treated these features of academic literacy development implicitly. These elements were often embedded in discussions of substantive content issues; they surfaced explicitly mostly in the ways that the instructors responded to and assessed written assignments.

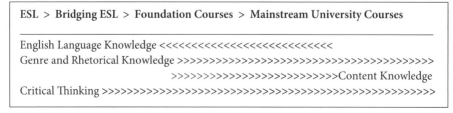

Figure 4.1. Continuum of course types from pre-University ESL to University

This range of course types form a continuum, as shown in Figure 4.1, for students to develop academic literacy and improve their writing progressively through a transition from pre-university, to freshman, then to mainstream university studies. We need to interpret goals for writing improvement – students and instructors' alike – within these contexts and expectations. Language abilities (grammar and vocabulary) were a primary focus in ESL courses but featured only implicitly in the other courses. Genre and rhetorical knowledge gained increasing importance along the continuum; they were treated explicitly in the ESL, bridging, and foundation courses but implicitly in the mainstream university courses. Content knowledge was the explicit focus of mainstream university courses as well as the primary emphasis of the foundation courses. However, a consistent point of instruction across all the courses was the development of students' critical thinking. ESL instructors encouraged students to express personal opinions and to respond critically to ideas in their compositions, and the instructors of mainstream university courses expressed similar expectations in respect to the academic content of their disciplines.

Two points of comparison across the four types of courses are worth making, based on our observations of the classes and inspection of writing assignments and materials in them. First, the writing assignments were remarkably similar in genres across all types of courses, all requiring students to: take notes, write summaries and paraphrase, produce critical analysis and response writing, compose reports and descriptions, and write essays of argument and persuasion. It seemed that the ESL and bridging instructors had successfully modeled the genres of university writing in their courses, even though the content of the tasks they assigned were based on general academic themes rather than discipline-specific subject matter.

A second observation is that – in the transition toward university mainstream courses – the courses showed a decrease in teacher scaffolding or personal assistance for students. Fewer practice-focused activities and more direct writing activities were required in the bridging and university courses. ESL instructors scaffolded their students' transition to academic writing in English through individual conferencing with students about their writing, attention to composing processes, facilitating peer editing, asking for multiple drafts and submissions of papers, and using writing portfolios to document students' long-term development of their writing or subsequent drafts of their compositions. University professors generally relied on written feedback on students' assignments and "one time submission" of written work. Thus there was an overall decrease in interaction regarding writing between instructors and their students in the transition from ESL to university courses. We might assume, as well, that the ESL instructors' scaffolding of their students' writing promoted a mastery orientation to their goals for writing improvement (cf. Midgely, 2002), whereas the university instructors' single assignments promoted a performance orientation to students' goals for writing improvement (though the university instructors may well have exercised a mastery orientation to course content, particularly in the mainstream university courses).

Objects of goals

Distinctions between these four types of courses make simple contrasts between the goals for writing improvement of ESL and university instructors tenuous. Nonetheless, Figure 4.2 shows the frequency (in percentages) of the two groups of instructors' expressions (during their interviews) of objects of goals for students' writing improvement in their courses, contrasting the two phases of our study (ESL=Phase I; University=Phase 2). Both groups of instructors emphasized goals related to language most frequently, followed by rhetoric and genres, then knowledge and ideas. Contrasts between the two groups of instructors appear in their relative focus on composing processes, primarily because of the bridging courses, most of which focused explicitly on teaching composing processes. Goals related to affect, learning and transfer, and students' identity were seldom mentioned by either group of instructors, but the ESL instructors did refer to their students' identities with some frequency, a point we discuss further below.

The ESL instructors said that they focused their teaching explicitly on students' development of the English language, particularly their grammar and vocabulary. For example,

> We would like the students to improve grammar in as much as it impacts ability to convey what they have to say.   (Leeanne, Interview 1)

> [We want students] to improve language proficiency in all skills; to improve their English.   (Maria, Interview 1)

> [We want students] to overcome vocabulary weaknesses with examples and definitions; to develop strategies for dealing with them. … to learn alternate ways of expressing things using complex structures.   (Faith, Interview 1)

In contrast and not surprisingly, most of the university professors' statements about language were either related to students' learning the terminology of their fields, or they were acknowledgements that they did not view language as a focus of their pedagogy. For example,

> I don't think that [writing] is my responsibility… I teach Chinese Art. (Richard)

> I don't mark the papers for writing. Inevitably, the students' writing skills affect how well they can communicate… I don't correct spelling…grammar. I don't do any of that kind of evaluation.   (Hatton)

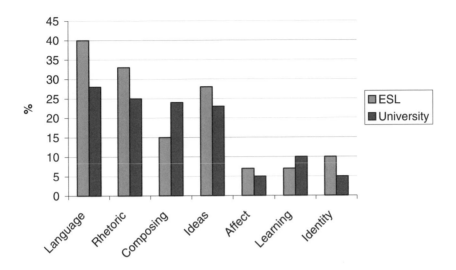

Figure 4.2. Objects of goals for writing improvement expressed by the ESL and university instructors.

> I think if they get control over the writing process a lot of the grammar issues take
> care of themselves.   (Bruce)

Actions taken

The ESL and university instructors had a similar distribution of references in their interviews to types of actions that they expected students to take to improve their writing in English, as shown in Figure 4.3. The actions that both groups of instructors most frequently discussed were: (i) seeking assistance from the teacher; (ii) studying and completing course assignments; and (iii) reading. The ESL instructors referred to actions in respect to their own instructional assistance given to students in 85 % of their statements about actions; in contrast to 55 % of the statements about actions which referred to the instructors' own assistance to students by the university instructors. For instance, the ESL instructors frequently discussed conferencing individually with students about their writing:

> Well, of course, it's very individual depending on their first language…There's
> seldom one grammar point that everybody has trouble with, so I really work with
> them individually.   (Faith, Interview 1)

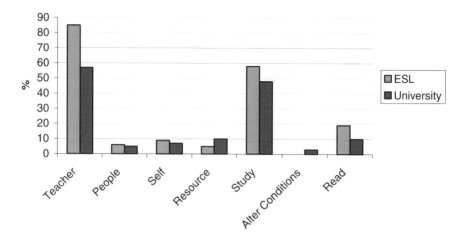

Figure 4.3. Actions taken for the goals for writing improvement expressed by the ESL and university instructors.

> I make it very clear that they are free to come and talk to me about their writing at any time...and they have to take advantage of it.   (Linda, Interview 1)

The university instructors, in contrast to the ESL instructors, did not discuss individual assistance to students often. The mainstream university instructors expected the students to handle the writing of assignments independently without much instructional assistance or feedback. For example, Willy, who taught an introductory Economics course, stated that:

> Once again, I wouldn't say we do anything that reflects the English competency of the answer but rather the economics of the answer. So we're not assessing any writing in this course. I think it's the bottom line. Will I welcome that? Um... a part of me says: "Yes, I [would] welcome it" because I do believe that students should leave university quite competently able to write in English as this is an English-based university. ...Um in practical terms, I have enough challenge in marking the economics of it...But you know it could be mandated. If we all have to do it, I would do it.   (Willy)

The bridging and foundation university instructors such as Bruce (who taught English for Engineering) and Gloria (who taught Arts of Speech: Ancient and Modern) were more attuned to ESL students' writing needs for assistance. For example:

> I draw attention to a particular grammar issue and I'll give them some individual feedback on that, but all my experience has led me to believe that the

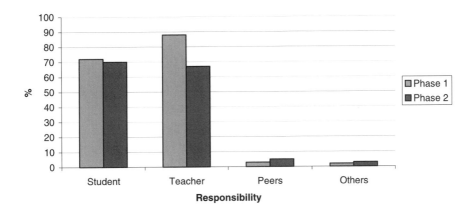

Figure 4.4. Responsibilities for goals for writing improvement expressed by the ESL (1) and university instructors (2).

best approach to improving student grammar is to get them to improve their writing in the broad bases of rhetorical strategy and writing process. That's what ultimately makes the difference, when they know what they are talking about and what they want to say, their grammar is generally better than when they are groping blindly for the next sentence, so that's how I approach that.   (Bruce)

Because the class is small, and especially because this year and last year this is the only class I'm teaching since I'm retired…I try to approach it on a very individual basis. And so I meet, I invite the students, if they have any questions, to come in and meet with me.   (Gloria)

This image of the ESL instructors being more involved and responsible for students' actions for writing improvements was also reflected in the instructors' goals statements regarding responsibility for students' writing improvement as shown in Figure 4.4. We noted that the ESL instructors expressed more goals referring to their own teacher responsibility as significant for students' writing improvement in their goal statements as compared to the university instructors; that is, 88 % of the ESL instructors' goals referred to teacher responsibility for writing improvement as compared to 67 % for the university instructors' goals.

Among the actions that the instructors said they expected students to take to achieve their writing goals, reading was a noteworthy point of comparison. ESL instructors related students' reading to their writing improvement in 20 % of their goal statements (Figure 4.3). The ESL instructors linked reading explicitly to students' writing tasks, typically by stipulating writing assignments that required some prior reading about topics to be written about. Due to the range in their students' goals and interests, however, the ESL instructors tended to assign reading texts that were "general interest materials" taken primarily from current affairs articles of recent newspapers and magazines. The ESL instructors saw their job as helping students to make sense of reading material before writing, and they taught reading as a vehicle for writing, thinking and language development. They provided numerous pre-writing discussions and group tasks related to the reading that students would respond to in their writing assignments.

In contrast, the university instructors viewed their roles as primarily dispensing content information, not scaffolding writing from background readings. This finding corresponds to distinctions observed in many previous studies contrasting the approaches and policies of ESL composition and mainstream university instructors (e.g., Brinton, Wesche & Snow, 2003; Zamel, 1995).The university instructors in our study observed their NNES students struggling due to their lack of reading and language abilities as well as inexperience in reading and writing from complex academic texts. The university instructors mentioned reading in only 9 % of their statements about goals for students' writing improvement. These remarks were typically laments about their students' problems related to reading, or writing in ways that involved "copying" that was "close to plagiarism." For example,

> They're not readers for the most part. They don't read a lot. Depending on the degree of their second language, they read even less than they might otherwise. They tend to read what they have to read. For the way they use reading in writing…um… too often there is a degree of plagiarism, a very close modeling of reading that they've done.   (Bruce)

> Some students are very capable…of assimilating information and reproducing it, and others didn't seem to. So I wondered about the level of their reading comprehension, or their strategies, which we did talk about… But some of them were much more competent than others. There's a real range.   (Sally)

The instructors of mainstream university courses further observed how students' limited reading abilities impinged on their academic writing performance. For example, Hatton expressed concern that "reading is a bit of an issue" because students found it difficult to do case analyses of previously unread texts under time pressure on the final exam. Aliz, who expected each student to complete a graduate seminar based on specific readings, expressed dissatisfaction that:

> I don't think that one of my students from ESL did the reading that was required. [She] did a design exercise, so she avoided a lot of that writing. The other, kind of [did]. I don't think she really got it, but there was a seminar aspect which correlated the reading to the writing.   (Aliz)

Some of the instructors of bridging or foundation courses, however, did perceive reading as a means of learning to develop writing abilities, as many of their students did (see Chapter 3), although the instructors had relatively few pedagogical strategies for scaffolding relations between reading and writing (as Grabe, 2003, has observed for university instructors generally):

> [Reading] quite directly influences the students' writing in some ways where you can see them working, using similar sentence structures and particularly paragraph structures… For things like introductions for different components of reports. So that they are using the readings as models. And I encourage that, although we combine that with discussions of plagiarism…   (Sally)

> A lot of times we're asking them to, in writing essays or in writing anything, to reproduce a form that they've almost never read. I mean how many essays do you read, you know ?... So I do a lot of um… reading with them…ah… And I do make explicit connections between reading and writing. Again, we spend a lot of time sort of looking at the signposts, of signals of order that the writers use.
> (Julianne)

Both the ESL and university instructors talked a great deal about their expectations for studying as a means for students to achieve writing improvement, particularly through completing course assignments. The ESL instructors referred to studying in 58% of their statements about goals for students' writing improvement, and the university instructors mentioned studying in 48% of their statements about students' goals.

The ESL instructors talked about studying in reference to the assignments that students were required to complete in their EAP courses: various types of summary and response writings, note-taking practice, and timed writings tasks, journal writing, and a final mini-research paper. Most of these instructors focused students' attention on the processes of composing as actions for completing these writing assignments. They involved students in pre-writing activities, peer and self editing, and completing a number of drafts of their compositions. Faith explained these expectations for writing practice and studying in this way:

> What I usually do is give them an editing handout that they can use to check specific aspects of their writing. Like one would be subject-verb agreement or consistency of verb tenses. So they would look for each aspect of the handout in their own writing…And we do peer editing – get students to use that checklist and read their fellow students' writing. And uh… when we have a timed writing I insist that they spend at least 5–10 minutes out of 50 editing their work, knowing what their own mistakes are, what do they usually have problems with, what is their weakness and to focus on that. (Faith, Interview 1)

The university instructors, in contrast, mentioned fewer actions for studying than the ESL instructors did, and focused in their interviews mainly on the completion of course assignments which included midterm tests, final exams, reports in business-oriented courses, engineering reports in the English for Engineering courses, essays in the Canadian Studies, Oriental Arts, and Arts of Speech courses, and project designs and reports in the Landscape Architecture course.

The actions for acting on goals that involved students' uses of resources (such as writing clinics, textbooks, and dictionaries) differed slightly among the university and ESL instructors (mentioned in12% and 4% of their statements about goals, respectively). The ESL instructors talked about themselves directly providing assistance to students, for example, through individual conferencing and feedback. The ESL instructors encouraged students to refer to their course textbook for grammar assistance and thesauruses and dictionaries for vocabulary development, as Lulu described in the following:

> I want them to use a broader range of vocabulary. I want them to be aware of the power of words. As I said at the beginning of the interview…we'll read a text for the vocabulary…I'll point out "This is okay, but there are better choices." I insist that they get a thesaurus. … I say: " Use a dictionary. Use a thesaurus."
> (Lulu, Interview 1)

Some of the university instructors talked about referring students to writing clinics as a resource for their writing improvement; others were not sure what resources their students used to help them improve their writing. For example, Willy (who taught Introduction to Economics) responded to our interview questions about the tools and resources that students might use to help them write (Question 20) by stating: "I don't know. Don't know." Gloria (who taught Arts of Speech), on the other hand, was detailed about her explanation of resources for writing improvement:

> Well, I know that one student who showed me a kind of summary of grammar on sheets they had. They do use computers; they do use spell checks and grammar checks on computers. I showed them it's very important that if there are words that have more than one spelling that they get the right one. It's not good enough to have the word. I do encourage them to use dictionaries, and I hope they use them, but I don't know…But whether they did or not, I don't know.   (Gloria)

In contrast, Richard (who taught Oriental Arts) noted that writing clinics and centers were the primary resource that he thought that students might use:

> I don't know what tools…Probably writing centers operate. Uh, I do know that.. uh…they [the writing clinics] won't write papers for you that you bring in. I think students who have problems bring essays and papers either in draft form or

papers that have been marked down because of bad English; then get individual help…uh… how to improve writings. Well, this is the way to do it. You know, you have to sit down with somebody who knows how to write properly, and it's a skill… I suppose that's what they do, but I'm just guessing.   (Richard)

Differences in frequency of goals

To establish whether there were differences in the frequencies of the instructors' goals, we grouped the instructors into three groups: ESL instructors (group 1), university instructors teaching bridging and foundation courses (group 2), and university professors teaching mainstream academic courses (group 3). Analyses of variance with post-hoc comparisons produced only the following contrasts that were statistically significant, as shown in Table 4.1. All but one of these differences in goals were between the ESL instructors and the professors teaching mainstream university courses:

1. The ESL instructors articulated more goal statements concerning the writing of their students than did the professors teaching mainstream university courses.
2. The ESL instructors referred to rhetoric as the object of their goals for writing improvement more frequently than did the university professors.
3. Instructors in all three groups – ESL, bridging and foundation, and mainstream university instructors – differed significantly in their frequency of expressing students' identity and affect as the object of their goals. The ESL instructors did so most frequently, and the mainstream university professors least frequently.
4. ESL instructors identified themselves ("the teacher") as the origin of actions that students took to achieve their goals more frequently than did the instructors of mainstream university courses. However, the ESL instructors also identified the students as the agents responsible for achieving writing goals more frequently than did the mainstream university professors.

Overall, the paucity of contrasts between these three groups of instructors reflects the progressive continuum of differences in their instructional emphases (on language, writing, and academic content) already described above in discussing Figure 4.1, rather than there being sharp distinctions between these pedagogical approaches (i.e., between ESL, bridging or foundation, and mainstream courses). Only in respect to goals related to students' "identity and affect" did significant contrasts appear at each step in the continuum (shown in Figure 4.1) – from ESL, to bridging and foundation, to mainstream academic courses – and this concern may be a reflection of the intensity of instruction and small class sizes as much as

Table 4.1. Statistically significant post-hoc pair wise comparisons between frequencies of goal characteristics expressed by ESL, bridging and foundation, and mainstream university instructors.

	Type of Comparison	Group	Group	Mean Difference	SE	95% C.I. Lower Bound	Upper Bound
Number of goals	Scheffé	1	3	15.21	3.53	5.55	24.86
Object / Rhetoric	Scheffé	1	3	4.75	1.67	.19	9.30
Object / Identity & Affect	Dunnett	1	3	2.50	1.01	.34	4.65
	Dunnett	2	3	1.33	1.06	.64	2.01
Actions taken / teachers	Scheffé	1	3	15.75	4.10	4.55	26.94
Goal origins / teachers	Scheffé	1	3	13.54	3.97	2.69	24.38
Responsibility / Student	Scheffé	1	3	14.08	4.26	2.44	25.72

Note: For comparisons, Scheffé assumes equal variances across groups but Dunnett's C does not. Groups were 1 (ESL instructors), 2 (bridging and foundation instructors), and 3 (mainstream university instructors).

a concern for students' personal development in their goals for writing improvement. Likewise, that professors teaching mainstream academic were less likely to see students as agents responsible for achieving their own goals, in contrast to the ESL instructors, may reflect their more traditional and less participatory modes of teaching through lectures rather than small group or personalized writing activities.

Summary

Distinguishing between ESL and university instructors' goals and orientations towards writing improvement for students is important, not only to inform curriculum policies in ESL and university programs, but also as a means of understanding the qualities of experience that ESL students encounter as they develop their writing abilities while they move from pre-university ESL courses to their mainstream university courses. The primary image emerging from our analyses here is of a continuum of gradual progressions. Instructors' goals for ESL students' writing improvement did differ between the pre-university ESL program and the mainstream university courses, when these course types were contrasted distinctly against each other. But the reality of the activity systems that the students in our research encountered was more of a progression from courses that intensively supported their individual development of academic writing in English (in the pre-university ESL program) to courses that increasingly expected students to be able to express their knowledge about academic subject matter in modes of English writing appropriate to the academic discipline and tasks assigned (in the mainstream university courses). In between these extremes were bridging and foundation courses that mediated these differing conditions for writing while providing varying extents of direct, individualized instruction about English language and writing and critical thinking and reading skills. The implications that these contrasts suggest for university policies, pedagogical development among university instructors, theories of learning for ESL students, and further research are discussed in Chapter 10.

Section II. Case Studies

CHAPTER 5

Nine Chinese students writing in Canadian university courses

Luxin Yang

This chapter describes the goals and activities for writing improvement expressed by nine Chinese ESL students who participated in the two phases of our project, starting from their studies at an ESL academic preparation program (Phase 1) through to their first-year of university studies (Phase 2). I describe the writing goals and practices of the individual students and then summarize five themes central to their accounts of their writing in their first year of university courses. Following the tenets of activity theory (Engeström, 1991b, 1999; Leont'ev, 1972, 1978) outlined in Chapter 1, I have composed these descriptions as accounts of the activity of learning to write in English as experienced uniquely by these nine students, emphasizing how their learning to write in English is not simply learning the textual conventions of the target language, but also learning to do the conventional acts of a particular community and thus becoming a functioning member of that community. Accordingly, for each student I present, in terms of Engeström's (1999) multifaced categories, descriptions of *activity systems* that involve each person as a *subject* persevering to improve the *object* of academic English writing through uses of *mediating artefacts* in particular *communities* that have *rules* and *divisions of labour* and resulting in specific *outcomes*. As in other chapters in this book, I have placed the goals for English writing improvement, along with the actions that students took to realize these goals, as the central, focal element in these activity systems.

Methods

The present analysis is of data that I and another Chinese-speaking member (Ally Zhou) of our research team collected bilingually (using both Chinese and English) from the nine Chinese students in Phase 2 of our project (i.e., during their first year of university studies), following the schedule for data collection described in Chapter 2. Quotations presented below in italics were originally spoken in Chinese, whereas those in regular typeface were originally spoken in English (and the latter are presented verbatim without correction of grammatical infelicities).

Following qualitative research methods of analytic induction (Goetz & LeCompte 1984) and constant comparison (Miles & Huberman 1994), I read the interview transcripts iteratively, searching for recurring themes or patterns related to the principles of activity theory, in addition to inspecting the students' written drafts to corroborate the participants' reflections and my interpretations of them.

The nine students were all Mandarin-speakers from Mainland China. Five were female (who we have called Hong, Wenzhen, Xin, Yi, and Yingxue), and four were male (who we have called Jun, Long, Mark, and Qing). Hong was in her early 30s, whereas the other students were all in their early 20s. At the time of data collection, Hong was in her first year of a masters' program in Landscape Design. The others were in their first years of undergraduate programs in Commerce (Jun, Wenzhen & Yingxue), Economics (Mark & Yi), Engineering (Long & Qing), or Computer Science (Xin) at one of two Canadian universities in Southern Ontario. Yingxue started her university studies in January 2002, whereas the others all began their university programs in September 2002. The pseudonyms we gave to the courses they selected for interviews were: Landscape Design (Hong), Oriental Arts (Jun & Xin), Writing for Engineering (Long), Professional Writing for Engineering (Long & Qing), Foundations of Economic Theory (Mark), Arts of Discourse: Ancient and Modern (Wenzhen), Cultural History of Asia (Yi), and Behavior in Institutions and Businesses (Yingxue). As observed in Chapter 2, and itemized in Appendix B, Chinese-background students were the largest sub-population of students participating in Phases 1 and 2 of our study.

Writing practices in English: individual goals and actions

Jun, Xin, Long, Qing, Wenzhen, Yi and Yingxue took only one course each semester that had many writing requirements. These included writing a proposal, research paper, case analysis, lab report, reading response, or in-class essay. Hong, as a graduate student, needed to write at least one term paper for every course she took. Mark did not take any courses that required him to do any extended writing other than short answers in the exams for one introductory course in economics. Basically, the students attended primarily to their immediate goals for writing to fulfill course assignments and obtain satisfactory course grades. On the one hand, the nine students varied in their individual goals for English writing improvement and the actions that they took. On the other hand, they shared common learning goals and types of activity systems. They all wanted to enlarge their English vocabulary. They had particular views about the value of writing support from university instructors. They sensed the impact of their previous ESL studies on their abilities to self-regulate their composing process. They perceived specific strengths and weaknesses in their English grammar. They had certain perceptions of their bilingual identities in writing.

Hong

Hong, a graduate student in Landscape Design, aimed to improve her writing of site analyses (a pre-stage task for an architectural design), responses to course readings (to deepen her understanding), and research papers. She focused on rhetorical organization and proper expression in her writing while trying to learn more about North American culture related to her field:

> I think the most important thing for me is organization. ... Next problem is vocabulary..... sometimes I feel I can't explain, express my mind very clearly.
> (Hong, Interview 3)

> I think for this semester I will focus on the writing style... I need to learn more culture in North America. This is the main purpose for me because in North America and China, they have totally different cultures. So if I still keep the style in China, I don't think they will accept it easily.   (Hong, Interview 4)

To achieve her learning goals, Hong often borrowed her classmates' well-written assignments to learn their methods of organizing and presenting ideas. She also asked her more capable classmates to check her written drafts of assignments:

> I think my classmates help me, but everybody is busy. They won't say, tell me how to write or something. They just lend me their writing. If I have any questions, I can ask about it and they'll answer me.   (Hong, Interview 3)

> I think my classmates and friends give me a lot of help, such as now in my class, of course there are a lot of native speaker and some of them got higher degree like Ph.D. from other field like social study or something. They can help me to improve the logical thing in the writing and the organization. This is my weakness, especially organization.   (Hong, Interview 4)

In addition, Hong read extensively to improve her English proficiency overall and particularly in terms of grammar, vocabulary, and the organization of ideas:

> [Does reading influence how you write?] Yes, very much, because I can learn the method used, and grammar, because just as I mentioned, grammar is my big problem. After I read article and materials, I can learn something from it, I cannot copy it, but I can learn from it. I can use the same grammar, the same structure in my writing, and also the style.   (Hong, Interview 3)

> Because from the reading materials and other information, I can get first of all, vocabulary, and they use a lot of beautiful vocabulary. Another thing is logical.. how to say that, it's context or something like *coherence...* and the discussion,

because in my field, our writing must include the discussion and argument
because different people have different opinions for one project and I can learn a
lot from the reading materials.   (Hong, Interview 4)

Over the academic year, Hong came to feel comfortable when writing in English.
In the middle of the second semester, she remarked, "Now, I feel okay, because
every time when the professor gives us a topic, I can write it in a short time
(Interview 4)."

Jun

Jun's long-term writing goal was to write as effectively and clearly as do native-
speaking writers of English. Jun wanted his writing to be understood and accepted
by Canadian readers.

[I want my writing to have] a good content, good style, style is just the way
that I write, the language that I use, just make it more local, attractive [to the
readers], concise.   (Jun, Interview 4)

Unlike when he was in the ESL program the previous year, Jun did not aim to
improve any specific aspect of his English writing other than completing course
readings and assignments and reading textbooks and other material extensively:

I'm not, you know, doing something to improve my writing on purpose. I just,
you know, read some articles, some English articles, from Internet every day. I
think that's, that's what I'm doing now.   (Jun, Interview 4)

In the first semester, Jun wrote in-class essays and a bibliography assignment for
the course Oriental Arts, a compulsory Humanities courses for undergraduate
students. He remarked,

I chose this course in my first year, also because I hoped that I could improve my
writing, so that when I get to second or third year, it'll be better. I hoped it wouldn't
be too difficult, since I'm Chinese and I have some background in Chinese Arts.
At class, although sometimes I might not understand the English, I do understand
the contents.   (Jun, Interview 3)

In this first semester, the only help Jun received on his writing were general
instructions and feedback from his professor. In the second semester, Jun made a
friend with a Canadian classmate who checked his writing occasionally, correcting
certain awkward words that Jun used. Jun did well on his in-class essays and the
final research paper. He got a mark of A+ (90%) for his final research paper on a
Chinese traditional painting, for which he had read ten books. Jun was satisfied
with his ideas in the research paper, but he thought that he could still improve his

language in terms of word choices. At this point, Jun stated that language was not a huge barrier in his English writing, and he felt he could write faster and with enhanced knowledge than before. In his words, "if I got the idea, if I know how the way I interpret it, it's better, you know, it's faster that I write than before, if I got the idea (Jun, Interview 4)."

Long

Long aimed, like his father, to do business in the field of engineering. Following his father's advice that the important element in business writing was clarity rather than creativity, Long tried to make his writing clear, well-organized and easily understood:

> As I mentioned last time, I just want to be clear and well organized, like to use some correct words and to make the professor understand me is very important. I don't want to write a boring, long paragraph to be very academic and nobody can understand. Maybe just short, but clear organized, this is what I think, since my professor said like you don't have to write that long stuff, but you just dis-cuss one question, if you can define this question, discuss it very clearly, then that's enough.   (Long, Interview 4)

In the first semester, Long took the course Writing for Engineering, where he learned to write lab reports, which he thought important and essential for engi-neering students but which he had not previously encountered in ESL courses. After two months of study, Long appeared to understand the format of the genre of lab reports as well as how expectations varied with the nature of an experiment or field of inquiry:

> We have first an introduction, and then background, and then method, to write down your process for method, and… write down your result and discussion, analyze your result and recommend something in the conclusion.
>   (Long, Interview 3)

> When you do chemical experiment, you do a book research, it's totally different, so how you organize it is also important, and how you express your result or your, like, your process in detail is also a different way.   (Long, Interview 3)

Long found it somewhat difficult to write in English in the first semester, because he had not done any English writing for four months since he left the ESL program. Moreover, he did not feel knowledgeable about the academic topics he was assigned. Long identified the two major weaknesses in his English writing as his limited vocabulary and poor organization of ideas: "I know the idea about how to solve this problem [in the assignment], but I don't know how to express it" (Interview 4).

The heavy readings that Long had for the engineering program prompted him to learn engineering-related vocabulary and knowledge, unlike the general academic vocabulary and issues he had studied in the ESL program the previous year. He tried to remember some words on a daily basis while reading course materials and fiction. Long also tried to use these words precisely, especially English-Chinese cognates that had slightly different senses in either language:

> You know, originally I learn English from Chinese. There must be some differences between two languages. So basically some different word, when they translate it into Chinese, it's the same meaning, so I have to make sure they have difference when I do academic writing.
> (Long, Interview 4)

By his second semester of university studies, Long felt relatively confident about his English writing:

> I can think how to write my sentence now. At first it's kind of strange, you know. For some time I even write on Chinese sentence, and translate. Now I think I'm OK, like I can, as long as I consider idea, I can write something down. You know what I mean? I can think and write. I don't have to think the whole idea and write the whole thing.
> (Long, Interview 4)

Mark

In general, Mark aimed to write fluently, using vocabulary in academic registers and varied sentence structures. At the beginning of the first semester, Mark expressed confidence in his writing, for example, observing that he could express some of his ideas directly in English:

> Instead of translating some word, I just use the word I know, check the dictionary, what dictionary say. I use English-English dictionary, not English-Chinese dictionary. If I still don't understand, I will check the Chinese one.
> (Mark, Interview 3)

Mark did not do any essay-type assignments in the first year except for some short answers and surveys. Perhaps because of this lack of writing practice, toward the end of his first year Mark felt his English writing competence was declining:

> When I write this assignment, I feel like my writing is kind of getting worse than before because since last September, I didn't write anything in English, like essay or something. When I write, I feel uncomfortable to write and the word... choose to write the word... I can't find the right one. I just use the same one every time.
> (Mark, Interview 4)

To improve his English writing, particularly his vocabulary and syntax, Mark started to review books on academic writing and to read newspapers and books of fiction daily. But Mark did not practice any writing of his own volition, as he was burdened with a heavy workload for his courses, though he paid attention to the terminology in his course readings, particularly so he could use it when writing short answers in exams.

Qing

Qing aimed to make his writing easily understood. In his first-year studies, Qing mainly wrote for an academic writing course designed for engineering students (Professional Writing for Engineering), but he did not need to write for his other courses such as math. English writing was a challenge for Qing, so he felt he needed more practice:

> I think it's quite hard to write in English because I don't speak English,…but I have to do it because later on I need to use it, so I feel it's hard…. I think if I write more, I practice more, and then I will feel better and that will be easier later on.
> (Qing, Interview 3)

In the first semester, Qing worked on writing research proposals and lab reports, which his instructors taught explicitly, and which he learned about but did not master (getting a C- grade):

> Now I know how to write a proposal, but still I couldn't write a very good proposal. … I couldn't get high mark, so which means my paper is not good enough. But now I know how to write a proposal and the format.   (Qing, Interview 3)

In the second semester, Qing continued to practice writing lab reports, which he aimed to write clearly, concisely, and accurately. Qing discussed and exchanged his writing with his classmates, asked his professors for clarification on assignments, and sought help on course websites (where professors had posted model writing samples from previous courses):

> I just read some examples from the past year by the other students on the website, and read the other people's work, and then think that by myself, then try to do well, follow their instruction, there is some certain rules for this type of writing.
> (Qing, Interview 4)

Wenzhen

Wenzhen retained (from her ESL program) her long-term goal of writing in English fluently and easily, but added (during her university studies) the goal of making her arguments as specific as possible in course assignments. In her first year, Wenzhen wrote extensively for a two-semester humanities course (Arts of

Discourse: Ancient and Modern), whereas her other courses only required short answers in exams. Wenzhen struggled to complete satisfactorily eight analytic essays for the humanities course. The professor did not give the class any deadlines for the essay assignments so that the students could pace themselves to complete the eight essays over two semesters. The professor also encouraged students to talk to her in person when they had difficulties with the assignments. Although she had several appointments with the professor, Wenzhen still felt that English writing was not easy for her:

> I still don't think it's easy for me, because I don't write often these days. Since I finished academic preparation course, I don't write any more before the class begins. So I think writing isn't easy for me.   (Wenzhen, Interview 3)

Wenzhen made efforts to develop specific arguments for the essay assignments. But she had ambivalent feelings towards English writing:

> *If I write about something I'm interested in and I spend a lot of time reading, then I will have a sense of accomplishment when I hand it in. But it's often like this: at the beginning I feel very bored and unmotivated, but as I keep working on it, it gets better and I feel happy when I hand it in.*   (Wenzhen, Interview 4)

Xin

Xin wanted to write as well as her Canadian classmates, going beyond the use of common words and basic structures in her English writing. But she did not have clear goals to do this. In her first-year university courses, Xin wrote only for one humanities course (Oriental Arts), for which she wrote three in-class essays, one bibliography, and one research paper. Xin felt that her English writing ability was declining due to lack of practice in her courses:

> I'm not like those engineering students who have the general writing goals. I mean, I'm working on computer science, actually we just work on those codes, don't have to do that kind of academic writing, related to computer science.
>   (Xin, Interview 4)

For the in-class essays, Xin did not have a chance to make changes if she was not satisfied with the grades. However, Xin asked her professor via e-mail for details of the requirements on the bibliography assignment and, for the research paper, she incorporated her professor's comments on her oral presentation into her written submission:

> For those short essays, of course, they were treated as term tests, right? So I don't think we can rewrite or you know, how can I say, do some changes. But for the research paper, because we did the oral presentation first, and I did the presenta-

tion, using PowerPoint, so I always wrote down everything that was supposed to be my research paper. You know, not just in those pieces of information, but you know in those whole sentences. He [the professor] gave me some suggestions, like to change some vocabulary, so I did those changes in my research paper when I was writing my research paper, actually. (Xin, Interview 4)

Yi

Yi did not do any English writing for seven months after leaving the ESL program, until the middle of her first semester, when she started a research essay for the humanities course (Cultural History of Asia). She felt incompetent writing in English:

I always feel my writing in English, my English writing is so simple, because, sometimes, like first when I write in English, I usually think ideas in Chinese and translate to English, sometimes it doesn't work in English, so, I think I have to change this. (Yi, Interview 3)

In general, Yi wanted to have rich content in her writing and proper use of English grammar (e.g., complex sentences, tenses, and conjunctions). She also aimed to enlarge her academic vocabulary, which she thought she could achieve by reading course materials, attending lectures, and doing assignments.

I want more content in my essay, and, I want to improve my grammar skill, and, format... I think for the grammar, I mean, when I write, I have to be careful, pay more attention to grammar. And for the content, then I can read more and more, then I have something, I have knowledge that I can write down. (Yi, Interview 3)

For vocabulary... I think... sometimes I know words, it's like a simple word. And I want something with the same meaning but more complicated, like more academic and more formal that I can write in an essay, I can use in an essay. [To learn more academic vocabulary,] I'm reading newspaper, or maybe reading from textbooks, academic books. (Yi, Interview 4)

In her second university semester, Yi said that she tried to strengthen her written arguments by accommodating different points of view or ideas.

Interviewer: Are there any special types of writing that you want to do?
Yi: Maybe like argumentation.
Interviewer: So how are you trying to improve your argumentative writing?
Yi: Maybe trying to say the same thing from two different points of view. That would help me...Maybe talk to peoples, [laughs] people, because they have different ideas. That would help if I write an argumentation. And yeah, get my information from newspaper and books. (Yi, Interview 4)

Yingxue

As during the ESL program, Yingxue aimed to write as well as native writers of English. But she recognized a gap between what she wanted to say and what she could say in English: "If I'm in a rush, in a hurry, *I still feel I can't express myself fully. Like I said, during the exam I didn't have enough time, I wasn't familiar with the case, so I couldn't write well. That was my problem* (Interview 4)." During her first term, Yingxue took a humanities course about cross cultural differences, which was oriented toward language studies, with the intention of further improving her English writing ability. After that Yingxue perceived that she did not make much progress in her English writing. The main reason was that she was busy with a heavy workload for her courses; she focused on completing her course assignments and learning field-related vocabulary rather than English writing per se.

> *I want to learn writing, following the courses. I'll learn the vocabulary specific to that field when I take that kind of courses. I don't have my own goals. I'll just follow the courses.*   (Yingxue, Interview 3)

Also Yingxue figured out that she did not need to write well to get high marks for most of her major courses:

> *For short-answer questions, you just memorize what the teacher said and write them down. We don't write much.*   (Yingxue, Interview 3)

At the time of the third Interview, Yingxue was taking the course Behavior in Institutions and Businesses, for which she had to do case analyses in the exams and a final research paper. However, Yingxue was aware that she could not get high marks on the case analyses because of her limited ability to analyze the cases, rather than her writing ability:

> *Maybe, we [ESL students] can't express the ideas so clearly, so well. Or even though we write our analysis in Chinese, we may not analyze it well, thoroughly. Maybe it has to do with experience. Some people have job experience, so they can do a good analysis of some case.*   (Yingxue, Interview 3)

> *As far as writing is concerned, the professors are satisfied. But in terms of content or whether I can meet his requirements, that's a different story. It also depends on whether I understand the topic or whether I am interested in the topic. Like when we had English course before, we read four different books. If you don't understand this book, maybe you can't write these essays well. But if you read other books and understand them, then your essays will be very good, maybe.*
>   (Yingxue, Interview 4)

Yingxue's self-reflections were confirmed by her course instructor's comments during our interview with him. The instructor observed that Yingxue wrote well but she did not have strong arguments or rich content in her case analysis, perhaps because she did not comprehend the cases or his requirements well. Other than her writing of case analyses, Yingxue did not have any specific aspects that she tried to improve in her English writing. Yingxue got a grade of A+ for the humanities course but just C+ for the course on Behavior in Institutions and Businesses (which was her major). These results confused her: "I don't know what's the difference between them, or what the teacher thinks about the paper, and their rules or regulations about the paper" (Interview 3).

Common themes

The following themes were prevalent across all of the interviews with these nine students: vocabulary, support from instructors, self-regulation of composing processes and uses of resources, grammar, and bilingual identities.

Vocabulary

All nine students indicated that they needed to enlarge their English vocabulary to fill the gap between what they wanted to say and what they could express in writing. They considered that reading, attending lectures, and interacting with Canadians were important ways to learn vocabulary and writing conventions, gain information, and understand English culture:

> One is reading, one is um.. listen to a lecture from other school's professor and the famous designer because in our field a lot of vocabulary is totally different from other field. And ... I can feel the... they coin a lot of new words that I can't find in dictionary. So I think listening to a lecture is a good way.   (Hong, Interview 3)

> I need to know more vocabulary because later on I need to write in business or something, so I need to know more and more to communicate with others; otherwise, I ..even I write down something, it's too simple. And something I don't know how to express it, so I need to enlarge my vocabulary to write, to do the writing. ... For vocabulary, I think just read more books and... find some word you [I] don't know, check in the dictionary and try to remember it.   (Qing, Interview 3)

> Nowadays, you know, I'm taking economics classes, so there's a bunch of new words for me in the textbooks, or in my study. So I find it's much easier for me to catch these words, ... when I read the economics books, those words are repeated. You know what I mean?   (Xin, Interview 3)

> Actually in my writing, you know, if I want to use some new vocabulary in my writing, of course I have to get it first, right? So these days, like I watch TV every

> day, read those textbooks, and chat with those CBC [Canadian-born Chinese]
> friends on line, using English.   (Xin, Interview 4)

However, Wenzhen and Yingxue observed that course-related vocabulary was of
limited value to improve their English writing abilities generally:

> I don't think [I learn] lots of new vocabulary [from course readings]. They all just
> concentrate on one area, like accounting course, they concentrate on some, all the
> vocabulary about accounting. It's limited, not related to all areas; like newspaper,
> they have different topics. But like economics, or accounting course, they all about
> economics, maybe this kind of, maybe hundreds of words all about economics.
> It's not quite useful for me to improve my writing, I think.
>   (Wenzhen, Interview 4)

Support from university instructors

Some instructors, especially those of writing courses for engineering students,
taught the students explicitly how to write reports and provided detailed instructions for assignments and comments on the students' writing. The students found
this support beneficial:

> Every time she [the instructor] gave me some comments, like my organization,
> like my sentence structure, my vocabulary. She even told me how can I improve
> it, how to say it clearly.   (Long, Interview 3)

Many professors, however, did not provide much guidance or assistance, expecting
the students to already know how to write:

> They [my professors] don't help us, they just let us write and give us a score. They
> said writing is not our business. They just give us [assignments], because we have
> some task design, they concentrate on design.... writing is second, is not required
> so much. You come here, you study with other students, you must have the same
> language level. They don't think about your language problem, they just want to
> see the good writing and good design.   (Hong, Interview 3)

> *The biggest difference, I think, is that the university course instructors assume that
> you don't have serious writing problems. Even if they see a serious problem, they
> won't tell you about it. So I won't be able to get help in terms of language from these
> course instructors. I feel this is the difference.*   (Jun, Interview 3)

> *His job is to teach you theories, not to write. Only ESL courses teach you how
> to write.*   (Yingxue, Interview 3).

Mark and Qing observed that university professors focused on course content but
ESL instructors paid attention to both language and content in students' writing.
Qing remarked that grammar errors were not serious problems in his writing for
engineering courses as long as he had a clear explanation.

> When I was in ESL, teachers not only [focus] about the meaning, but they focus sometimes on the structure or the grammar or the spelling. But sometimes, the professors in other program, they just focus on the meaning, yeah, if you are right or wrong, not the grammar. ... I hope they can correct some of the grammar. I know they are busy. They cannot correct all of them. At least they can mark there is something wrong here, and I can double check.   (Mark, Interview 4)

> For me, international student, grammar is important. For engineering, I think they don't care much about grammar as long as you can explain what you want to say, they can understand, that's enough.... They care more about the number you have, so it's not a big deal if you make a grammar mistake. You will not lose a lot mark on that.   (Qing, interview 4)

In short, the participants appeared to accept that university professors were not obliged to help them write well in English because they were not language teachers. However, the students wished that the professors could point out both content and writing problems in their written assignments, as they had experienced and found helpful in their previous ESL courses.

Self-regulation of composing and use of resources

The students tended to use the approaches for composing (e.g., outlining, modeling on exemplars, editing) that they had developed in their ESL program to produce their assignments in academic courses. They adopted the focus on language or rhetoric from the ESL courses to a focus on content and ideas in the academic courses, according to their professors' expectations and using resources such as other students, family members, computers, or dictionaries:

> [When I've got a topic,] I will read some materials related to this topic, find the materials. I get some information from the Internet, get some images for the projects. I need to know. And then I start to write the outline...reread some materials and information, and then write down what I am thinking...after writing, I will check. I think the most I will check 3 times on my own and then maybe I will ask my classmates to check it for me.   (Hong, Interview 4)

> I think to write, first you have to have information, what to quote, you have to have the content, so you have to read a lot to know what you are going to write... then you have to know how to write it, like the format of the writing, so we got textbook, there are some examples like the proposal writing, so I just read it and to see the format of writing and how they start, because they are the good writings. Then once I know the format, how to do it, then you just start to do it and write it on computer because they'll correct your grammar or spelling mistake. Some word if I don't know, just check in the dictionary and find it out. I make outline first because I have to make sure I'm on the right track.   (Qing, Interview 3)

First, ... try to understand what I'm supposed to write, and second try to get an outline in my mind, and third, trying to get some related equivalent materials, if that's necessary or possible. Fourth, write...write down the general idea of what I've got, and then, actually that's the original version of my essay. Next, I'll do some, like ... if I do have time, I will check like word spellings, structure and idea or the basic idea of the whole essay, if I do have time.   (Xin, Interview 4)

[First] *Brainstorming: just read the requirements, and think about what to write generally. Then* [I] *write an outline: what to write for the introduction, body, conclusion parts. Then I'll just start writing. This way, it saves time and keeps me focused.*   (Yingxue, Interview 4)

For example, Long started his writing of a lab report with an outline, but the outline was a compulsory step, called a "planning sheet", for his lab report assignments. Long pointed out differences in outline writing for assignments in the ESL and the engineering courses:

For engineering, you have to provide almost details, like, what I usually say is half of the report to the professor. It's in very details. You know what I mean? Like every subsection you have to do. But for ESL, it's more general, you don't have to pay much attention, you just get the idea about how probably I'm going to write it, not like engineer stuff, you already got the ideas, then you just write it.
                                                                                (Long, Interview 4)

The students also attended to procedures for editing and revising that they had developed in the ESL program. They tended to reread their texts several times, checking grammar and content on their own. If possible, they would ask their friends or capable peers to give comments.

Actually I have to read it again, this is for the first time, I try to understand myself whether I'm in the right track or not. If not, I will like change some idea, like some topic sentence or some conclusion sentence. I will change it to make my article to be understandable, you know, to be more understandable. And second time I'm going to check the vocabulary mistake. If I know, like how to correct it, I'm going to correct it. If I don't know, I'm going to try to explain in another way. And third, I'm going to check the grammar.   (Long, Interview 3)

First I use computer [Word program] to help me to correct my grammar. And then I'll read my essay over and over again and to see is that the one that I want to describe, I want to say. Is that the same meaning I want to say: like, if it is, that's okay; if not, I'll change a little bit.   (Yi, Interview 4)

Actually I'll read the essay first, and then think about like, ok, do I, have I got the right idea of the, you know, of the topic? And, ok, so I will check those main ideas, follow the thesis statements and the main ideas, you know the supporting ideas.

And, well, if *I've got the thesis statement and it's in the right direction,* then I begin to check the sentence structure or word spellings.   (Xin, Interview 4)

I ask my relative to revise it for me. He's in applied science... He often writes. I asked him to check if there's anything that he doesn't understand. Maybe I won't realize it when I read it, but he can see it.   (Yingxue, Interview 3)

Grammar

The nine students thought that they had sound knowledge about English grammar from their previous EFL studies in China, but they recognized they had grammatical problems in their writing such as the use of verb tenses and articles. Several of the students focused on improving their grammar:

Generally, we learn a lot of grammar rules during our study of English, but I don't think we touched the high level, ...like a comma, sometimes I don't know how to use it very well. That's why I can't remember, I can't understand the article very well, because they use a lot of grammar. I'm confused: there's very long sentence and they use a lot of commas, and then I'm confused.   (Hong, Interview 3)

I think I'm good at what I learned, but something I haven't learned yet, I don't know. I'm sure I'm not good at it. What I mean is like, I should try to learn some more grammars ... Maybe sentence structure, phrases, some special phrases you have to use in special case, and some special vocabulary that you have to use in that way, something like that. I have to learn more.   (Long, Interview 3)

I don't have any problems about grammar, like multiple-choice in grammar, I ... when I use, when I write, I will make some mistake, but I don't notice it. But as long as somebody like, point out the problem, I will certainly realize how I can correct it.   (Wenzhen, Interview 3)

Several students indicated that they felt they were getting better at the application of grammar rules in their writing after a period of studying in the ESL program and university in Canada. For example, they thought less about grammar while writing and could spot and correct their grammar errors by themselves most of the time.

When I first came to Canada, I can recite, there are many grammar rules in my mind, but now, I'm just saying in English and write in English without thinking grammar. I cannot give those concrete examples that I wrongly use grammar rules.   (Jun, Interview 3)

Because every time after I write an essay, the grammar mistake will happen. But after I check it, I can correct it by myself.   (Hong, Interview 4)

Not quite a lot [of grammar problems]. *Not as many as before, at least I can realize when I make mistakes. Like before, in the ESL course, I don't know what I wrote wrong, but now I feel writing is not complicated. Before, I might think in Chinese and then translate it into English, so there might be problems with expressions and grammar, or tense. Now I don't think it's a big problem for me any more.*

(Yingxue, Interview 3)

Bilingual identities

The students recognized differences between the rhetoric of Chinese and English, and their capacities to compose in either language. For example, Jun commented:

English writing is very different from Chinese writing. Chinese writing may be less direct. The contents might be different, too. You might want to reserve something when you write in Chinese. But when you write in English, you may want to write more.   (Jun, Interview 3)

Long indicated that cultural differences might have impact on his English writing:

Actually as I practice this writing, I found that you know, it's not only the English grammar is the problem, it's also the culture between the East and the West countries problems. Like to express a kind of idea, the Eastern countries people, they mainly is not a straight way, they are going away and then come back, but the Western way, it's like the straight. ... because a lot of times I find my professor told me that my writing is not that straight to understand. He can understand, but it's at very last. It should appear at the beginning. That's the Eastern country people, how they write the stuff.   (Long, Interview 4)

Some considered their expression of themselves to be similar in either language, whereas others thought they differed. As the following quotations show, the students felt that their current English proficiency was still a barrier for them to express their ideas completely:

Yeah, it's difficult [to write in English]. I feel different when I write in English and when I write in Chinese. I can write Chinese more, like the content will be more natural, but in English, I always feel a little childish. Actually I did some writings in third person, but I don't think I've did any writing in Chinese in third person position.   (Yi, Interview 3)

If I wrote the articles in Chinese, it's easier for me to find concrete words in Chinese, to find words in Arts area. That's the difference, I think. *When I write, the ideas are the same, whether I write in Chinese or in English.* (Jun, Interview 4)

I think it's the same. When I write in English, for example, I answer the questions in English, if I answer the questions in Chinese, I still get the same answer.

(Mark, Interview 4)

I think it's the same thing, just expressing myself, just a different language, but myself is the same, no matter it's English or Chinese.   (Wenzhen, Interview 4)

I can only say that I can't express myself well in English.   (Yingxue, Interview 3)

Summary

A notable outcome from this analysis is that students did much less writing in their first-year university courses than they had done in the ESL program the previous year. Some indicated that their English writing competence was declining as a consequence. Most wrote in English only for assignments (e.g., research papers, lab reports) or exams. In terms of activity theory, we might observe that where an activity system for writing improvement had been established during ESL courses, that activity system languished for many students over their summer break, and then was only activated to a certain degree and for particular functions during the first year of university studies. The students' initial and broad-based goals of learning to write clearly and fluently in English were subsumed by their immediate goals to pass examinations, complete assignments on time, and get good grades in courses. Viewed in the terms of activity theory, the prevailing rules of the community dictated that the students shift their objects of activity to achieve in university courses outcomes that differed from those expected in the ESL program. To do so successfully in the university courses, all the students realized the importance of enlarging their academic vocabulary (cf. Engber, 1995), which became a primary goal and operational tool in this context. In general, the students tried to learn vocabulary through the mediating artefacts of reading course-related materials and attending lectures. They observed that their university professors helped them gain content-related knowledge rather than teaching them to write well, paying attention primarily to their understanding of course content in grading assignments and exams. As a result, some students abandoned their goals of writing improvement in English. They felt they did not need to write well to get high marks because they were evaluated mainly through exams in short-answer or multiple-choice formats. Finally, these nine students perceived that they maintained similar identities while writing in either Chinese or English, except for experiencing limitations in their vocabulary and cultural awareness to express their ideas fully and clearly in English.

CHAPTER 6

Students' and instructors' assessments of the attainment of writing goals

Khaled Barkaoui and Jia Fei

How successful were the ESL students in achieving their goals for writing improvement? What might have influenced their relative success? In this chapter we attempt to answer these questions by comparing the perceptions and criteria that a sub-sample of ESL learners and their course instructors expressed when reviewing and producing stimulated recalls about compositions that the students had written as assignments for their courses. Basing this analysis primarily on goal theory, we draw on Pintrich's (2000b) view of self-assessment as a central element in self-regulated, goal-oriented learning. Specifically, we focus on processes of reaction and reflection about learning goals, which Pintrich proposed are a fourth phase in a cycle of self-regulated learning, preceded by phases of (1) forethought, planning, and activation, (2) monitoring, and (3) control. The phase of reaction and reflection involves self-reactions, self-evaluations, and attributions. From this perspective, goals have the dual function of serving as targets to strive for and as "standards for evaluating one's performance" (Locke & Latham, 1994, p. 18; cf. Bandura, 1986; Hoffmann, 1998). A goal identifies the object or outcome one aims for and is also the standard by which one measures one's performance.

These ideas are crucial to understanding, as well, the activity systems in which the ESL students functioned in their ESL and their university courses, as articulated in Chapter 4 of the present book. Of particular interest from the perspective of activity theory is determining the extent to which students and instructors alike were aware of and explicit about their goals for writing improvement, both in particular tasks and in courses overall, as well as in relation to each other as functioning members of particular communities of learning activity. In the terms of activity theory advocated by Engeström (1999) and Leont'ev (1972), the present analysis focuses at the micro-levels of actions and operations through which goals and literate texts are realized, impressions of them jointly constructed and evaluated by students and instructors, and learning facilitated by students' appropriation of relevant instructional goals. As also highlighted in Chapters 1 and 4, there are also important curricular implications, particularly for students who study in foreign cultural contexts, associated with knowing the extent to which students and instructors are aware of, and appreciate or cater to, each others' goals and expectations for literate performance. Studies such as Block (1994) and Barkhuizen (1998) have depicted the perspectives of ESL students and their instructors to often be in conflict and so to result in misunderstandings.

With these notions in mind we posed the following research questions for a subsample of our data:

1. What are students' and instructors' goals for writing assignments for ESL and content courses?
2. How do students and instructors evaluate students' goal attainment and L2 texts?
3. What criteria do students and instructors employ when assessing students' goal attainment and L2 texts?
4. What factors seem to affect students' assessment of their L2 texts and goal attainment?

Method

Data and participants

We selected for this analysis a subsample of students who had participated in both phases of the research and for whom we had sufficient data on comparable writing tasks as well as stimulated recall protocols about these written texts, both from the students as well as instructors. In addition to attrition in Phase 2 of the research, the available data were limited because we had asked students to bring to interviews self-selected samples of their writing, some of which proved to be in unusual genres (e.g., poems, journal entries). Moreover, some university instructors declined to be interviewed, and those who did participate produced stimulated recalls on only a portion of their students' pieces of writing. We set the criterion for inclusion in this analysis as data from only those students whose writing samples matched at least one of three dimensions in Hale et. al's (1996) scheme for classifying university writing tasks: genre, cognitive demand, and rhetorical task (see Table 7.1).

The students whose data fit these criteria were eight females and three males (as described in Table 7.2 and Appendix A). Eight came from the People's Republic of China, two from Japan, and one from Iran. With the exception of one who had a B.A., the students were recent high school graduates. Like the larger sample of students in our study, they aimed to study in a variety of academic fields (e.g., commerce, science, psychology), had scores on the Institutional TOEFL of between 493 and 570 ($M = 541.5$, $SD = 25.06$), and had studied English for at least

Table 7.1. Description of 22 writing samples

Dimension	Category	ESL Courses	University Courses
Genre	Essay	10	5
	Report on observation with interpretation	0	4
	Book/Movie review	1	1
	Library research report	0	1
Cognitive Demand	Apply/analyze/synthesize/evaluate	8	11
	Retrieve/organize	3	0
Rhetorical Task	Argument	6	4
	Exposition	5	6
	Description	0	1

one year before coming to Canada. Six had been in Canada for less than one year at the start of the study, and the other five had been in Canada between 1 and 2 years. Their experiences in L1 writing varied. Three reported no extensive experience in writing in their native language, four said they had some writing experience in high school, and another two reported some professional experience, such as writing for newspapers.

Data, as described in Chapter 2, consisted of writing samples students had brought to interviews and stimulated recalls about them, produced by the eleven students and also, separately, by four of their ESL instructors and, a year later, by five of their instructors in academic courses. The stimulated recalls asked students to describe their goals for the written papers as well as the goals that their instructors had for the pieces of writing, their assessment of the achievement of these goals, a general evaluation of the papers overall, and students' interpretations of and reactions to instructors' feedback. The same interview schedule was used in both phases of the research, and instructors were asked to produce parallel versions of the stimulated recalls, responding to the same questions as the students had. We were able to analyze 22 stimulated protocols from the students but only seven from four ESL instructors and six from five university instructors. Table 7.2 lists the pseudonyms of the participating students and their instructors in each phase of the research.

Table 7.2. Participating students and instructors

Student	Nationality	ESL course instructor	University course instructor
Kazuko	Japanese	Lulu	Did not participate
Rihoko	Japanese	Leeanne	Did not participate
Sarah	Iranian	Linda	Julianne
Hong	Chinese	Did not participate	Aliz
Lee	Chinese	Did not participate	Mary
Long	Chinese	Maria	Did not participate
Yi	Chinese	Did not participate	Did not participate
Qing	Chinese	Did not participate	Did not participate
Jun	Chinese	Lulu	Richard
Wen Zhen	Chinese	Linda	Gloria
Xin	Chinese	Lulu	Richard

Analyses

We analyzed the stimulated recall protocols to identify and compare: (a) students' and instructors' respective goals for the written papers across the two types of courses, (b) students' and instructors' assessments of students' goal attainment and quality of the written texts, (c) criteria that the students and instructors employed when assessing students' texts and goal attainment, and (d) factors that appear to have affected students' assessments of their L2 texts and goal attainment. Our analyses were interpretive, based on our careful reading of the transcripts of the stimulated recall protocols and of students' corresponding writing samples, aiming to identify themes and patterns related to the research questions posed.

To answer our first research question we classified the goals for the writing samples as reported by participating students and instructors in two ways. First, we classified the *level* of the goal based on the Ng and Bereiter's (1991) distinction between (a) task-completion goals, that is, to accomplish a given task, (b) instructional goals, related to the main points of teaching, presented either implicitly or explicitly to learners, and (c) knowledge-building goals, based on individuals' efforts to construct their personal sense of phenomena or the world. Second, we classified the *object* of the goals expressed for each writing task in terms of the relevant categories used for the project as a whole (see Chapters 2 and 4), specifically (a) language (grammar and vocabulary), (b) ideas and knowledge, and (c) rhetoric or genres. We coded each goal as being at one level and as having one or more objects. We relied on these categories of levels and objects in answering the other three research questions, as well, but we pursued more interpretative and comparative analyses of the prompted recall data in these parts of the study.

Findings

Students' goals

As shown in Table 7.3, most of the students' goals – nine in Phase 1 (ESL program) and seven in Phase 2 (university programs) – were task-completion, although more students (four) reported instructional goals in Phase 2 than had in Phase 1 (two students). None of the students reported knowledge-building goals, as described by Ng and Bereiter (1991), though some of the goals that we classified as instructional goals verged on this category in view of the students' developing their English language or rhetorical abilities (e.g., see extract from Kazuko below). Task-completion goals entailed the student aiming to complete a written assignment simply to fulfill a requirement or obtain a grade. For example, Sarah said she had the goal of writing to meet the requirements of an assigned task, and Qing's goal for writing his proposal was "to get a high mark":

> Um.., my own goals is … my own goals is just writing these and then solve those problems that I think I did it.   (Sarah, Interview 2)

> I'm trying to write a good proposal, the purpose, to get a good mark from the professor, to get a high mark.   (Qing, Interview 4)

In contrast, instructional goals involved the student making efforts to learn something beyond the requirements of the specific task. For example, Kazuko expressed goals of improving her sentence structures and bibliographic referencing abilities while she wrote, which transcended the goals set by the course instructor for her assignment:

> Ah, in this composition I was trying to organize sentences well. And I wanted to cite references properly. Actually, the comment here says "unclear," but I intended to write it so that each paragraph has its internal consistency.
>
> (Kazuko, Interview 4)

For the objects of their goals, as shown in Table 7.3, most students said that developing or demonstrating their knowledge and ideas were their goals for their writing in both phases of our research, and a few reported goals related to improving their rhetorical or language abilities:

> The purpose of this writing, it was um… I have to write essay about the differences in rules between my own language and English and some of the misunderstandings that may result from it. […] And that's all I had to do, I guess. It was not really specific purpose. I didn't write it for myself. I did it for my prof.
>
> (Sarah, Interview 4)

Table 7.3. Levels and objects of students' goals for their writing samples

	Phase 1	Phase 2
Level of goal		
Task completion	9	7
Instructional	2	4
Object of goal		
Ideas and knowledge	9	10
Rhetoric or genre	3	2
Language	1	1

> I try to.. not to have mistake, especially grammar mistake. Spelling mistake is OK for me, but grammar mistake I cannot. (laughs) […] And I try to um.. sometimes I don't know how to express my, express exact meaning. And I try not to translate what I think to what I write.   (Lee, Interview 2)

Instructors' goals

Among the four ESL and five university instructors, most reported that their goals for the writing assignments were instructional, as shown in Table 7.4. In contrast, most students identified the instructors' goals as related to task completion. Instructors and students alike tended to identify more than one object for goals for each writing assignment in both the ESL and university courses. All the participating instructors and students expressed similar objects for the goals of their writing assignments (i.e., knowledge and ideas) in Phase 2, but in Phase 1 students and instructors agreed more on the rhetorical goals (4 cases out of 6) but fewer agreed on goals related to knowledge (2 cases) or to language (1 case). As also shown in Table 7.4, students in Phase 1 identified more knowledge-related goals (6), but the instructors reported that the goals of the same assignments were primarily related to rhetoric (6 cases) and language (5 cases).

Comparing instructors' and students' goals

The majority of students (seven in each phase) did not distinguish between their own and their instructor's goals in terms of level or of object. A few did, however. Yi, for instance, was aware of the difference between her own goal and the instructor's goal for the assignment; she reported that she achieved her goals but not the instructor's:

Table 7. 4. Levels and objects of instructors' goals for writing samples as reported by students and by instructors

	Phase 1		Phase 2	
	Instructor (n = 7 cases)	Student (n = 9)	Instructor (n = 6 cases)	Student (n = 11)
Level of goal				
Task completion	1	6	2	8
Instructional	6	3	4	3
Object of goal				
Ideas and knowledge	3	6	6	10
Rhetoric or genre	6	4	1	1
Language	5	1	0	1

> I think I only achieved my own goals. I write everything I understand here, but I don't think I achieved the instructor's goals.   (Yi, Interview 4)

The students' own goals (as reported by the students) and the instructors' goals (as reported by the instructors) for the assignments tended to differ, particularly in Phase 1. There were more divergences (4 cases in each phase) than convergences (2 in Phase 1 and 3 in Phase 2) between the two sets of goals. The students seemed more able to identify or express their instructors' goals that were related to knowledge and ideas in both phases, but they were less successful in identifying goals related to language and rhetoric, particularly for assignments in Phase 1. In the seven cases in Phase 1, students either failed to identify the instructors' goals for the assignments (3 cases) or were only vaguely aware of them (3 cases). For instance, Sarah identified the teacher's goal for an assignment in Phase 1 as being related to knowledge and ideas. She explained that they read about and discussed a topic in class and then the instructor asked them to write their opinion about the topic. Linda, Sarah's ESL teacher, in contrast, identified the assignment's goal as primarily related to rhetoric and language (report writing and "language of inferencing") (see quotation from Linda below). One explanation Linda offered for this discrepancy in interpreting the assignment's goal was the newness and difficulty of the task:

> So, the point was to get them to work with data, to understand it, to make cross-comparisons, to summarize. And, then I wanted them to, uh, to make inferences, based on the data, and the idea was not to go way off the wall with their inferences, but to keep them actually centered on what the data said. So, I wasn't interested in their opinions, OK? Uh, I didn't realize when I assigned it that that was actually going to be one of the hardest aspects of this thing, for most students, was to keep close to the data.   (Linda, Sarah's ESL instructor, Interview 2)

In Phase 2, students were more successful than in Phase 1 in identifying their instructors' objects of goals for writing assignments, particularly goals related to knowledge and ideas. For example, Lee identified the goal of his assignment in Phase 2 as collecting and organizing information about a specific topic for both an oral and a written presentation:

> The purpose.. I have to.. the instruction because I have to talk about all the things in the list one by one.. then organize them and give some my personal opinions, but very little bit. […] I think she [the instructor] tried to .. she tried to ask us how to find information and understand how it affects the market. I think this is her purpose. (Lee, Interview 4)

Similarly, Mary, Lee's university instructor, identified the goal of the assignment as related primarily to knowledge and ideas:

> Well, they had to do a presentation. They had to marry a resource to a business and talk about the two together. […] Yeah. That was it. Marry a resource to a business and tell us all about it. Educate us. That was their task. And then a 1000 word essay attached to it. (Mary, Lee's university instructor, Interview 4)

Note also the contrast in Mary's goals for her assignment (in a university course) compared to the goals for the assignment described by Linda (in the ESL program) above. There was a characteristic shift in focus from language and rhetoric for Linda in Phase 1 to knowledge and ideas for Mary in Phase 2.

Evaluation of goal attainment

Five students out of ten reported that they achieved their goals for the assignments in both phases of the research. As Table 7.5 shows, however, eight students reported that they attained their goals in Phase 2 compared to six in Phase 1. Only two students reported that they did not achieve their own goals for their writing in both phases. Three students reported that they achieved their goals in relation to one assignment only.

Table 7.5 also indicates that eight students out of eleven reported that they achieved what they perceived to be their instructors' goals in Phase 2, whereas only six (out of 9) reported that they did in Phase 1. Five students stated that they achieved their instructors' goals for the assignments in either phase. These were mostly the same students who reported achieving their own goals in both phases. Three students reported reaching their goals in relation to one assignment only. An exception, Rihoko, explained that she did not achieve the instructor's (nor her own) goals in either phase. The instructors' and students' assessments of their attaining the instructors' goals tended to converge in Phase 2 (6 cases out of 6) but not in Phase 1 (2 cases out of 6).

Table 7.5. Students' assessments of attainment of goals set by students and by instructors

	Students' own goals		Instructors' goals	
	Phase 1	Phase 2	Phase 1	Phase 2
Goal attained	6	8	6	8
Goal not attained	4	3	3	3
Missing data	1	0	2	0

In sum, most learners did not distinguish between their own and their instructors' goals for the writing assignments. The students generally reinterpreted or appropriated their instructors' goals for writing. As some of the instructors' responses imply (e.g., see quotations from Linda above), the students' assumptions that the two goals were identical were not always warranted, particularly in Phase 1 and when the nature of the instructors' goals were complex or difficult to grasp (e.g., language, rhetoric).

Assessment of written texts

When assessing their written texts, the majority of the students considered their expression of ideas and knowledge (10 cases), rhetoric (9 cases) and, to a lesser extent, language (7 in Phase 1 and 6 in Phase 2) in both phases of our research. Most students positively evaluated their expression of knowledge and ideas in their texts (8 students) and, to a lesser extent, their rhetoric (4 students) in both phases. Only one student was satisfied with her language use in Phase 1. In most cases the students were able to assess their writing in terms of knowledge and ideas and to identify problems and solutions at this level, indicating more confidence in evaluating and attaining knowledge-related goals than rhetoric and language-related ones. For example, Hong focused mainly on knowledge and ideas when assessing her text in Phase 1. Her major concern was the need to add more details to the text to support her argument. But when asked about language, Hong was not able to assess her essay overall, simply saying that she did her best:

> I think I need to uh I still need to show more detail in it, and find more information to explain my opinion, because this is the purpose of this writing, is to argue, but I need to find something to support my ideas. I need more detail for it. [...] Language? um, anyway I tried my best to use the correct grammar and uh the right word.   (Hong, Interview 2)

When evaluating the students' texts during the stimulated recalls, instructors focused on rhetoric and language more than knowledge and ideas in Phase 1 (6 out of 7) and on knowledge and ideas and language in Phase 2 (5 out of 6). Most instructors in Phase 1 commented that the writing samples were less effective in terms of language (6 cases) and rhetoric (5) than in terms of knowledge (2). In Phase 2 the six instructors reacted negatively to the content (4 cases) and language (6) of the papers.

Comparison of the instructors' and students' comments indicates that both groups tended to remark on similar aspects of the texts in Phase 1 (average 4 cases out of 6) but not in Phase 2 (average 1 out of 5). Notably, in Phase 2, the university instructors commented on language, rhetoric, and use of references, in addition to knowledge and ideas, whereas the students focused mainly on knowledge and ideas. Possible explanations for this discrepancy are that (a) the students identified the main goals of the assignments in Phase 2 as related to knowledge and ideas and (b) they might have expected university instructors to be concerned mainly with content but not language or textual form (cf. Fishman & McCarthy, 2001).

Students' assessment criteria

Students used a variety of criteria to assess their goal attainment and texts. Most frequently students in Phase 1 referred to their:

- overall impression of the essay (3 cases), a vague criterion that may indicate inability to articulate specific criteria,
  [Interviewer: Do you think you achieve the goals?] Um, yes, I can say so. But it's not very um it's not perfect.   (Hong, Interview 2)
- knowledge and ideas (3 cases),
  Yes. I just give some examples, the first example is about European Union, their very successful example about free trade in the world …
                                                                      (WenZhen, Interview 2)
- rhetoric (4 cases), including organization, effects on audience, and clarity of expression,
  [I think I achieved the goal] because in my opinion this essay is kind of easy to understand that what is my opinion, so, and also it's clear that, uh, maybe, uh, any, a lot, any kind of people can understand what I wrote. I, I guess, or, I think.   (Kazuko, Interview 2)
- and language (2 cases),
  [I achieved the goal] 80%. […] because I wrote some examples and uh I think the introduction and conclusion are OK. So are the body paragraphs. Sometimes I have grammar mistakes and uh sometimes I can't express something very clearly. So maybe my teacher is confused by something in this essay. Uh, just like that.   (Xin, Interview 2)

The criterion most frequently mentioned in Phase 2 concerned knowledge and ideas, particularly the quantity of ideas/information included in the written text (7 cases). Jun, for example, believed that he attained the assignment's goal because he knew a lot about the topic: [Do you think you achieve the goals?] "Well, I think so, because I have lots of Chinese arts background, I think." Another student, Lee, evaluated her text in terms of the amount of information included and text length, reporting that she did not attain this standard:

> [I did not achieve the goal] because I can.. because I think there are so many things I have to improve, I should give more details, and I should have more information because I didn't finish.. I didn't have all the information my teacher list. And… I… and the examples, she asked us to give more detailed examples and to have .. to explain it affects the market. I don't think I explain you know good in this essay.
>
> (Lee, Interview 4)

Kazuko referred to two other criteria when assessing her text and goal attainment in Phase 2: complexity or strength of expression and proper use of bibliographic references:

> Um, I think my expressions are superficial. I think my power of expression is weak. I would like to have written more smoothly. This is comprehensible, because I wrote simple things. Although my writing is easy to understand, it's too comprehensible. It lacks expressiveness, but I wrote simply and clearly. I wanted to use references properly, but I'm not sure if I could do so.
>
> (Kazuko, Interview 4)

As these extracts indicate, several students were able to consider and weigh multiple criteria when assessing their texts and goal attainment, doing so more extensively in Phase 2 than they had in Phase 1. For instance, Wenzhen reported that although her text in Phase 1 had some language problems, these problems were "basic", compared to those related to rhetoric and style. In Phase 2, Jun and Long were able to distinguish the grammatical and rhetorical aspects of their writing, identify language problems (e.g., grammar mistakes), and assess their seriousness with reference to their effects on the message they intended to convey (Jun: "but I think I state my idea clearly"). Similarly, Sarah felt that her writing suffered from language problems (mechanics and grammar), but she evaluated the rhetorical aspects of her paper positively and considered the language problem as "minor" compared to its rhetoric.

Three students identified influences from their mother tongues as problems for their writing in English. Jun, for instance, reported that his first language influenced the content and organization of his essay. His assessment of the organization of his essay was based on a belief that he still thinks in Chinese and on a vague notion of good English writing. Likewise, Kazuko attributed her failure to achieve her writing goals in Phase 2 to cross-lingual transfer ("I tend to write in a Japanese way").

Instructors' assessment criteria

The four ESL instructors in Phase 1 made reference to various aspects of writing (ideas, rhetoric, and language) when assessing students' writing samples, but their comments focused primarily on language and rhetoric. In contrast, the university instructors in Phase 2 were concerned primarily with ideas and knowledge (content). Although the university instructors considered their students' language and rhetoric they did so in terms of their effects on the content of the papers. For example, Richard's assessment of Jun's text in Phase 2 focused on knowledge and ideas, rhetoric, and language, but his main concern was knowledge and ideas. Richard's comments on language ("wordy") and rhetoric (details and organization) related closely to the knowledge and ideas that Jun was attempting to express:

> Well, I see, If you… I think it's too wordy in places uhm. That instead of, of… Say how to put this… In some cases, there's too much detail for two-hour essay covering a very broad subject. And I think that this student could've improved things, this is even a bigger problem, the inability to distinguish between the degrees of importance. […] The student wasted time on non-essential sets at the expense of using the time better to get at the things that are more important. […] Yeah. I would've like to see less description.
> (Richard, Jun's university instructor, Interview 2)

One aspect of writing not considered by the ESL instructors in Phase 1 but mentioned by three university instructors in Phase 2 was the use of source texts and plagiarism. Mary, for instance, evaluated Lee's text in terms of its use of external resources to address the task requirements. Mary reported that Lee failed in this respect, perhaps because of her limited L2 proficiency and/or time constraints (a timed essay). Similarly, Aliz pointed to instances of plagiarism in Hong's paper but indicated that this did not affect his reaction to the essay because he was concerned with the student getting the message across given her limited English proficiency.

Comparing instructors' and students' assessment criteria

As pointed out above, there were more discrepancies (5 cases out of 7) between the instructors' and students' assessments of texts and of the attainment of instructors' goals in Phase 1 than in Phase 2. The main reason for these discrepancies seems to be differing perceptions of instructors' goals for the written assignments, which in turn led to students and instructors applying different assessment criteria to evaluate students' texts and their goals. For example, in the extracts cited above, Sarah identified the primary goal of her ESL instructor's assignment in Phase 1 as related to knowledge and ideas, and so Sarah reported that she attained this goal. But her ESL instructor thought that the assignment's goal concerned the "language of inferencing" and so evaluated Sarah's paper negatively in terms of language ("her accuracy needs work"), rhetoric (support of opinion), and task fulfillment ("less opinion and more inferences based on data"). Kazuko and her ESL instructor also employed different criteria and reached different decisions about the student's attainment of the instructor's goal:

> Because in my opinion this essay is kind of easy to understand that what is my opinion, so, and also it's clear that, uh, maybe, uh, any, a lot, any kind of people can understand what I wrote. I, I guess, or, I think   (Kazuko, Interview 2)

Kazuko reported that she attained the assignment goal because the goal (expressing her opinion) was easy to achieve and because she felt she expressed her opinion clearly. Lulu, Kazuko's ESL instructor, however, based her assessment of goal attainment on different criteria, that of the student's ability to express herself and make her voice heard. The instructor valued self-expression and voice more than text structure and content and, as a result, did not think that this piece of writing was successful or one of Kazuko's best:

> It wasn't so much that she didn't express her opinions. The way she expressed them was no longer heartfelt. It was all: I'm going to say body a, body b, body c. And it was like a template. It didn't sound like [Kazuko] anymore.
>   (Lulu, Kazuko's ESL instructor, Interview 2)

By comparison, in Phase 2, there were six cases of instructor-student agreement about attainment of instructors' goals for written assignments. The principal criterion used by both parties related to knowledge and ideas, suggesting, not surprisingly, that content goals may be more evident, explicit, or expected in university courses than in ESL courses. As discussed above, where perceptions and criteria for goals conflicted in university courses, it was often that instructors perceived that limitations in students' language or rhetorical abilities interfered with their expression of knowledge or ideas. For example, Xin discussed the content, organization, and language of her paper, expressing satisfaction with the first two aspects but not with her language, but her instructor expressed dissatisfaction with the content of the paper, particularly in terms of the student's inability to distinguish between important and minor details.

Factors affecting students' assessments of text quality and goal attainment

Three factors seem to have particularly affected the students' assessments of their texts and goal attainment, as indicated in the prompted recall data: feedback from instructors, attributions of failure and success, and personal standards and involvement.

Instructors' Feedback. To assess the effectiveness of their written texts and attainment of instructors' goals, the students relied on their instructors' feedback in the form of written comments and/or grades. Jun's first interview provides an example of how students used instructor feedback in their assessment of their texts and goals, seemingly to an extent that overshadowed their own self-assessments:

> Interviewer: Did you achieve these goals? How? Or why not?
> Jun: According to the mark he, she [the instructor] gave me, maybe no. I don't know. […] [The instructor] said the ideas are quite good, and the meaning is deep enough, and.. just I have to work hard on organization.   (Jun, Interview 2)

The extent to which the students deferred to their instructors' evaluations of their writing may, however, have been an artefact of our data collection. Most of the students brought to our interviews drafts of their writing that their instructors had already commented on or marked (18 out of 22 samples), and several students reported that they had discussed their writing with their instructors before the interview (particularly in Phase 1).

In Phase 2, instructors rarely provided detailed feedback on students' papers, and so the students often had to rely on grades alone when assessing their instructors' judgements of their writing and goal attainment. The importance of instructors' feedback in supporting students' (self-) assessment of their texts and goal attainment was clear in cases where no feedback had been given. In such instances, some students were unable to assess their own performance or goal attainment. Qing, for instance, was unable to judge the quality of his text and goal attainment, a task that he felt was "up to the professor":

> Interviewer: Did you achieve the instructor's goals?
> Qing: Ym… kind of. I don't know yet.
> Interviewer: What about your own goals?
> Qing: My own goals is to meet the professor's requirement.
> Interviewer: So did you achieve this goal?
> Qing: I believe so, but I haven't got the mark yet, so I don't know yet.
> Interviewer: How well did you achieve your purpose?
> Qing: How well? I just wrote down whatever I know. How well is up to the professor … Maybe I need more on the discussion. Maybe I need to explain more.

Maybe some part in the result, the people might not understand. So the discussion is the part that I explain to them, so maybe I need more. I am not sure.

(Qing, Interview 4).

Interestingly, students in Phase 1 tended to apply self-assessments and instructors' feedback to different aspects of their writing. Students relied on self-assessments when assessing the knowledge and ideas in their writing, but tended to appeal to their instructors' feedback when assessing the rhetoric and, particularly, language of their papers. The result was that the students usually evaluated their knowledge and ideas positively, but evaluated their language, and, to a lesser extent, rhetoric, negatively. For example, Jun readily self-evaluated the content of his paper but relied on the instructor's feedback to assess his rhetoric (organization, coherence) and language (grammar). While Jun's evaluation of the content of his paper was generally positive, his evaluation of language and rhetoric was negative, although the instructor's assessment during the interview was highly positive. Even in the few cases where she pointed out some problems in language, the instructor considered these to be minor issues that did not interfere with meaning. Indeed it seems that ESL instructors' focus on language (and rhetoric) in their comments on papers in Phase 1 led several students to believe these aspects of their writing were weak. In turn, these students interpreted the absence of instructors' comments on knowledge and ideas as indicating that they had written these aspects of their texts successfully.

A second point is that instructors' feedback seemed to play a mediational role, supporting students' self-assessments of their goal attainment and texts. Many students accepted their instructors' feedback as reflecting their own perceptions of their writing and used it when assessing their goal attainment and texts. For example, Hong felt in Phase 1 that her instructor's comments on her paper were "same as my feeling […] I think everything she said is true". Kazuko also found the instructor's feedback "useful" because it focused on language (vocabulary), an area that she felt she had not yet mastered. Likewise in Phase 2, Yi appreciated his instructor's comments: "Actually the comments weren't really nice, but I like it. All the thing they said is true." In some cases, this perceived agreement between teacher and student assessment led the students to confirm their beliefs or misconceptions about writing.

However, students did not always accept their instructors' comments at face value; in many cases they seemed to challenge the comments or react to them negatively. Several students were critical of instructors' comments, indicating an ability to take an active role in evaluating and responding to judgements about their own writing. For instance, WenZhen in Phase 1 interpreted her instructor's feedback as related mainly to local linguistic errors or mistakes (e.g., tense, punctuation, vocabulary, articles), but considered these aspects "minor" because they did not affect her intended meaning. Other students found some feedback unclear or too general to guide their revision, while others were not able to infer their instructors' intentions from such feedback:

> I think she didn't give me very much response. She just say um.. actually, you… you did not a bad job about something. In grammar it has some problems, but it's very interesting content. That's all. … She told me to find the mistake by myself and rewrite those…and correct mistakes. And last night I did that.
>
> (Yi, Interview 2)

There were fewer negative reactions to instructors' feedback in Phase 2, mainly because this feedback was mostly in the form of a final grade. In addition, while students were encouraged to revise and resubmit their written work in the ESL course, rewriting was not usually encouraged or permitted in the university courses (see Chapter 4).

Attributions. In assessing their goal attainment, several students referred to such factors as goal properties (e.g., difficulty), contextual constraints (e.g., task difficulty, time constraints), and internal factors (e.g., L2 ability, carelessness) to explain their writing performance. For example, Kazuko considered structural complexity, "smoothness' of her writing, and appropriate "use of references" when assessing her goal attainment and text in Phase 2. She reported that she could neither attain these aspects, particularly paraphrasing, nor assess her performance of them adequately. Kazuko attributed this failure to her low proficiency in English and to the fact that the goal itself was difficult to achieve (i.e., goal property):

> Kazuko: Because it's English. I mean, I shouldn't say it's because of language proficiency, but I think it's difficult to describe subtle nuances in English. It's a very subtle thing, but I thought it was very difficult. […] I don't have to use exact words from the references, but I often use exact phrasing. It's because I don't have sufficient English proficiency.
> Interviewer: Do you mean you copy words?
> Kazuko: Yes, nearly. I sometimes feel difficulty because of my powers of expression.   (Kazuko, Interview 4)

WenZhen, on the other hand, attributed her failure to achieve her goal in Phase 2 and the language mistakes she made to both carelessness and time constraints. Sarah also attributed the poor quality of her text in Phase 1 (e.g., incorrect tense) to carelessness and to the difficulty of the task, specifically the reading which she found "challenging […] because it was about economy". Finally, Hong explained that one of the reasons for her inability to achieve her goal is that the reading was not interesting. As pointed out above, some of the participating instructors also considered task difficulty (e.g., Linda in Phase 1) and student L2 proficiency and time constraints (e.g., Mary in Phase 2) when assessing students' texts.

Personal standards and involvement. Four students seem to have employed particularly high personal standards when assessing their texts and goal attainment. These students were sceptical as to whether they had achieved either their own or their instructors' goals for the assignments, despite their instructors' positive evaluations of their texts. The main reason for the discrepancy between student and instructor assessments in these cases seems to be that the students held high, though often also vague, standards of achievement. For example, in Phase 1 Hong felt that she achieved the goal of the assignment but was not satisfied with her essay:

> Interviewer: You mean the idea is ok. but the way you write is not perfect? Hong: Yes. The idea is ok, the grammar is ok, not big error like this. But when I read it, just uh a paragraph, nothing. You cannot be, you cannot find this kind of writing is charming or is exciting. It's interesting or something? no feeling for it. […] Um, but I don't know how to make it beautiful…
> Interviewer: So basically you think you achieve the purpose, just the writing, that's not expressed that perfect.
> Hong: Yes. In my mind I think I just finished the assignment, I finish the homework, but I didn't get uh the uh my purpose of improve it, I just can correct my grammar errors, I can use some suitable vocabulary, and I can grasp the other information from the article, I can respond my opinion, but that's all. […] So I said I just finished my homework very well, but I didn't write it very well.
>
> (Hong, Interview 2)

Hong indicated her dissatisfaction with the essay with reference to making the essay "beautiful", a goal she said she did not attain. Rihoko and Kazuko also reported that they did not achieve their goals in their papers for either ESL or university courses, but in both cases the instructors praised the students' papers. Thus, in response to the interviewer's comment that Rihoko's self-rating of her writing did not reflect Leeane's (Rihoko's ESL instructor) assessment that her text was "fabulous", Leeane responded that she could "remember this person being extremely hard on herself" and that "that kind of harshness reflects the complexity of [Rihoko's] ideas and how she wants her personality and her ideas to be reflected in her writing." These students seem to perceive high standards that they often could not articulate clearly, which might explain their inability to attain them. It is also possible that differing cultural beliefs and expectations about self-evaluation were at work here (as discussed further in Chapter 8).

Two students (Kazuko in Phase 1 and Xin in Phase 2) showed high emotional engagement with their writing during the prompted recalls. When asked why she thought she performed well in her paper, Kazuko explained that she was able to express her ideas clearly because she felt strongly about them. According to her, she was able to talk about very specific aspects, such as starting the essay in a way that attracts the reader ("This kind of like way to start is so attractive"). She also showed an awareness of rhetorical requirements and an ability to flout what she believed to be a convention in order to express her opinion effectively:

> Yes, I was so satisfied with this sentence, because this sentence is the way I feel, exactly how I feel. [Why do you think you were able to say it so nicely in this sentence, and not so nicely in others?] I don't know? [What do you think it will take you to write always in sentences like this?] Maybe, uh, I think I the better have very strong, strong, strong opinion, or, uh, I don't know, anything in terms of strong things. That if I don't have, maybe the sentence becomes so weak, I guess. [So you think that when you are trying to express a really strong opinion that you can write it well.] Yeah.   (Kazuko, Interview 2)

Summary

In sum, the present analyses – though hampered by limitations in the quality, extent, and comparability of the naturalistic data – shows that the present ESL students and their instructors usually had explicit goals for the completion of writing tasks and could usually evaluate whether or not these had been achieved to their personal satisfaction. Most often students' goals for writing were simply to complete a task focused on their ideas and knowledge and their sense of their instructors' expectations. The students' references to instructionally oriented goals increased in frequency and in quality as they progressed from ESL to university courses. Sometimes, the goals of the students and instructors corresponded, particularly where students appropriated or reinterpreted the goals that their instructors had set for their learning or where instructors had made their instructional goals notably explicit, particularly for content-oriented goals in university courses. But other times, their mutual goals did not correspond, suggesting that students and instructors were engaged in different or divergent activity systems. A variety of reasons for such dissonance appeared, including the diversity of possible criteria by which writing can be assessed or improved, students' (mis)understanding of instructors' criteria for evaluation or their not knowing about them (because of limited feedback on their writing), the attributes or properties of the goals or the quality of students' engagement with the tasks, and certain students' unusual or high personal standards for their writing.

CHAPTER 7

The language of intentions for writing improvement: A systemic functional linguistic analysis

Michael Busch

How exactly is a goal expressed? Our efforts to code transcripts of students discussing their goals for writing improvement inevitably led us to take a particular stance on this fundamental question about intentionality. As described in Chapters 2 and 3, we developed a coding scheme that provided a formal definition of an intention about writing improvement. In applying the coding scheme, statements such as "I'm trying to improve my grammar, especially tenses" were easily recognized as intentions. But other expressions of intentions were more subtle and so proved difficult to categorize reliably. For example, statements such as "I want to know how to reduce the sentence in order to make effective essay" constitutes a statement of desire. Likewise, the statement "It is important to… make it clear what kind of clause it is" expresses a statement of value. As many previous analyses of goals have recognized, statements of intention also involve statements of desire, belief, ability, hypothetical situations, and future-directed actions. Adding to this difficulty in our data were learners' uses of their second language, differing perceptions of intentional action, cultural influences, and language proficiency.

Coding for intentions in discourse data necessarily relies on interpretations of participant's uses of language. So I approached our coding in respect to linguistic categories such as single lexical items, phrases, and speech acts. But, more interestingly, verbal expressions also indicate relationships between conceptualizations of intentional action, as psychological constructs, and the linguistic options through which people realize their understanding of these constructs. To this end, the present analysis was conducted after our initial coding was completed as an effort to document the conceptual and linguistic complexities related to propositional statements of intentions. I have sought to understand better the language of intentions, believing that conceptual issues (e.g., links between agency, intention, and action, delineating individual actions, and inferring causality) relate to participants' expressed meanings. Particularly, I wanted to determine an empirically grounded data set of lexicogrammar that students had used to describe their intentions. I wanted to succinctly define psychological constructs and goal-directed activities as well as to provide information that may be useful for future inquiry and have pedagogical applications (e.g., in helping L2 students or teachers to define learning goals). Three research questions guided this analysis:

1. What are the kinds of linguistic realizations of intentions that ESL learners expressed when asked about their goals for writing improvement?
2. What is the relationship between a conceptual framework of goals and the linguistic realization of these concepts?
3. How does an awareness of linguistic realizations of intention inform our knowledge of goal-oriented learning activities and contribute to more refined methods of identification of goals?

Method

The present analysis draws its data from 90 interviews of 45 adult learners of English who described their goals for writing improvement at the beginning and end of an advanced-level ESL composition course (i.e., Phase 1 of our data collection, see Appendix A). We identified 1,475 passages of the interview transcripts for statements containing a participant's goal (or multiple goals if they existed within one passage). The length of each passage varied, but nearly all consisted of several clauses with some sections stretching out over one and a half pages of text. Once a participant's stated goal was identified, coders determined the developmental force of the goal – dilemma, intention, or outcome (as described in Chapters 2 and 3) – and classified the passage accordingly. The coded goals in Phase I included 116 dilemmas, 918 intentions, 191 outcomes, and 250 passages in which coders could not identify the developmental force. The focus of the present analysis is only on the statements coded as "intentions" because in these statements learners most distinctly had an object of the goal in mind and often referred to plans or actions they were undertaking to carry them out, and they were the most prevalent in these data. As explained in Chapter 2, statements of outcomes or dilemmas also involve goals in varying states of progression or developmental force over time, but may, in the case of outcomes, already have been obtained, satisfied, finished, or even given up, or in the case of dilemmas be more like a dilemma, conflict, or uncertainty.

Within each passage classified by coders as an intention we conducted a second round of coding that involved searching for a *core statement of intention* (CSI). A CSI consisted of at least one main clause and was defined by relying on our definition of an intention as "the expressed belief and/or desire of the learner and subsequent creation, deployment, and regulation of plans in order to move toward the goal" (cf. Chapter 2). In other words, passages categorized as an intention during Phase I were further analyzed for at least one main clause that represented the participant's expressed intention to act on a goal. The propositional statement was operationalized as having at least one of five components found in our definition of an intention in order to be considered a CSI: an antecedent desire, belief, object of the goal, plan, or action in progress.

I classified the CSI into various lexicogrammatical forms using an initial apriori, inductive method (Lofland & Lofland, 1995; Manning, 1982; Miles & Huberman, 1994; Silverman, 2001; Strauss, 1987) that involved a search for recurring grammatical patterns, lexical items, and rhetorical structures. For example, verbs of conation and statements (e.g., "My goal is…") comprised the initial classification groupings of CSI. As the analysis continued, CSI categories expanded to include linguistic realizations of intentions above the clause. Subsequently, clause complexes, speech acts, and multi-clause rhetorical structures were added to the analytical scheme.

To classify and describe CSI as a formal linguistic system I employed a systemic functional linguistic (SFL) approach (Halliday & Matthiessen, 1999, 2004). SFL may be glossed briefly as a theory of functional language use in which various systemic features are tied together through organizing principles pertaining to syntagmatic and paradigmatic relations, realization of meaning into expression and content planes, and metafunctions of language use. Syntagmatic organization is accomplished through a rank scale of morpheme, word, group, and clause, while paradigmatic organization is created through systems of meaning potential that take into account all possible choices of what lexis and grammar could potentially appear within one quantum of meaning. Realization of meaning is achieved by the stratification of phonetic and phonological expression into lexicogrammatical and semantic content. The fourth organizing principle is the division of language use into metafunctions, two of which, the experiential and logical, play a primary role in helping to identify CSI. The experiential metafunction involves the deployment of language to represent the external world, centering on what may be considered traditional grammatical categories of processes (verbs), participants (subjects), and circumstances (adjuncts) related to processes. The logical metafunction builds logical relations among various elements through taxis and logico-semantic relations. Discourse analysis of the data using SFL was limited to 1) word, group, group complexes, clause, and clause complexes, 2) location of systems of meaning potential, 3) the linking of semantics with lexicogrammar, and 4) experiential and logical metafunctions relevant to the signalling of intentions.

Results

The ways in which students indicated an intention were diverse, ranging from a single lexical verb to more elaborate multi-clause discourse. A simple yet comprehensive division of propositional statements emerged from the data by classifying them as either a CSI or a reply to a question posed by the interviewer. In the following I describe the lexicogrammar of each kind of CSI according to a systemic functional analysis, followed by examples taken from participants' interview transcripts, an explanation for classifying the propositional statement as an intention, and any other relevant information needed to understand the theoretical context of the lexicogrammar. After accounting for the various types of CSI found in the transcripts, a similar description of the replies to a question will be presented. Following the presentation of CSIs and replies to a question, I discuss other means of conveying intentions, above and below the clause.

Propositional statements

The simple clause. The most basic lexicogrammar of CSI was a simple clause with the learner as first participant (subject) and a verb in the present in present (present progressive) tense, which was also the unmarked form:

> I am working on vocabulary based on the reading that I have that... that we discuss on... in our class.

Less frequently used was the simple past or present tense. Examples of processes of single lexical items were *correct, do, focus, help, improve, learn, miss, notice, practice, prefer, read, remember, start, study,* and *use.* The phrasal verbs *figure out, make an effort, pay attention to, think about,* and *work on* were also used by students to express an intention. Each of the simple clauses was categorized as a CSI because the process used by the participant demonstrated an action in progress or a generalized description of an ongoing action.

Expansion. The second kind of lexicogrammatical structure of statements of intention was a variety of hypotactic verbal group complexes involving three types of logico-semantic relations related to expansion: elaborating, extending, and enhancing. Hypotactic verbal group complexes, also known as cantenative verbs, have at their core a chain of two or more verbs in a sequence with the first verb, termed the primary group, in the finite form. The secondary verbal group in the sequence is always non-finite and assumes the form of either perfective (*to* + verb), imperfective (*+ing*) or, in the case of *do, done* (Halliday, 1994, p. 278). The primary group elaborates the unfolding of the process (e.g., *begin, continue,* or *try*), while the secondary group represents the central meaning of the clause. If, however, there are three or more verbs chained together, the final infinitive carries the experiential meaning of the clause.

Two systems of organization, taxis and logico-semantic relation, are central to understanding the characteristics of verbal group complexes found in CSI. Taxis refers to the interdependency of two or more elements as they form a relationship of equality (parataxis) or subordination (hypotaxis). Logico-semantic relations is the relationship of two or more verbs through either *expansion* of meaning or *projection* of an idea or verbal expression. When the primary process expands its meaning to the secondary process, the logical relation is one of three types. The secondary process may *elaborate* on the meaning of the primary process by clarifying, restating, providing greater detail, exemplifying, and so on; *extend* its meaning through addition or subtraction of new information, offering an alternative; or *enhance* its meaning by qualifying circumstances of time, place, manner, cause, or condition. Projection is the logical relation of a primary process of saying or sensing followed by an idea or other metaphenomenon that exists in a different order of reality. For example, a verbal process would be followed by a locution (quoted speech or reported facts) and a mental process paired with an idea (proposition or proposal).

Taxis and logico-semantic relations proved to be an efficient means of identifying a CSI verbal group complex taxonomy since every relation of hypotaxis was to be found in the data. However, as a side note, one of the forms, paratactic verbal group complexes, were not considered significant enough to warrant analysis because they occurred as the result of participants rephrasing or repeating the verbal group:

> When I learn a new vocabulary I like to create, make a sentence to help, to help me to memorize this vocabulary, this word.

The first type of hypotactic verbal group complex used by participants were those of time phase elaboration:

> I start to, start to study for TOEFL.

Examples from the data consisted almost exclusively of the verb *start* which, according to Halliday and Matthiessen (2004), has an inceptive meaning. They have proposed that some time phase elaborations are of a durative, "going on" quality, using processes like *keeps on* or *goes on*, but these possibilities were absent from the data. Conceptually, time phase elaboration was considered a CSI because it indicated that the participant had initiated an action of some kind toward an object.

The second type of hypotactic verbal group complex involved what most would consider to be a central concept of intention. Participants used extending hypotactic verbal group complexes with the primary process composed of a verb of conation to indicate an inclination or drive to act. The most prominent form of extending hypotactic verbal group complexes of conation were those with the primary process of *try* in the unmarked present in present or simple present tense and only one participant as subject:

> I'm trying to improve my grammar, especially tenses.

Verbs of conation demonstrate an intention via actions already taken. Evidence of conation as intention was based on participants' statements that the action was in progress.

Within the same set students expressed four other forms of conation. Hypotactic verbal group complexes of potentiality, *can do* and *be able to do*, showed a resemblance to modality in that participants communicated their potential abilities to do something and since they also communicated an inclination to act that occurred in the past or was ongoing, these statements were classified as a CSI:

> I remember some sentences or some phrases, so I can use it sometimes in my writing.

The next hypotactic verbal group complex of conation, *have to (do)*, also has a sense of modality and is in fact described by Halliday and Matthiessen (2004) as such. Participants who used conation-modality complexes articulated a belief that they were required to take some sort of action in order to improve their writing:

> I have to know the structure of how to write a report and what kind of language is academic enough for reports.

The final conative hypotactic verbal group complex type was the reussive *help/ enable to do*, in which participants indicated that they received additional assistance from something or someone, usually the teacher, or knew how to do something through the help of a mediating figure or element:

> The teachers help us to write by giving us... a lot of text. We study a lot of texts and we find the words.

Two other processes appearing in the conative-reussive form were *motivate* and *influence*. The unmarked construction of the clause was causative with two participants, the first participant being the initiator and the second participant, the student, as actor. Again, like the conative *try to*, there was an indication that the participant had taken action or was describing a generalized, on-going activity, so these were categorized as CSI.

Along with the logico-semantic systems of elaboration and extension were the enhancing, cause: purpose types with the participant as subject expressing a means to an end:

We use MSN to check the homework.

Other primary processes expressed by students were *look for, read,* and *practice.*
The unmarked form comprised a three-participant causative construction of the
learner as initiator (we), an actor (MSN), and a goal (homework). Enhancing,
cause:purpose type hypotactic verbal group complexes were coded as CSI because
they indicated that the student engaged in purposeful behaviour by using a mediating object to achieve an outcome. As with the other two kinds of verbal group
complexes, elaborating and enhancing, the primary and secondary processes in
the enhancing types are considered to represent a single process with two events.
It should be noted that this analysis is controversial (Butler, 2003; Fawcett, 1996,
2000a, 2000b). An alternative analysis of the three-participant causative is to
say that it is not a verbal group complex, but a clause complex instead with two
separate processes and participants (Huang, 2000; Yang, 2004). Additionally, the
traditional view has been that the second process serves as a complement of the
first verb in the form of an embedded non-finite clause (Huddleston et al., 2002).
An example of the difficulty in categorizing hypotactic verbal group complexes of
the enhancing type as verbal group complex or clause complexes may be seen in
the following:

I read newspapers to have more fluency.

This is a marked form of the enhancing, cause: purpose type with only one participant, the learner, two processes (verbs), and two events, *reading* and *improved
fluency.* The issue is whether *reading* and *improved fluency* occur simultaneously as one happening or in serial. I have followed Halliday and Matthiessen's
(2004) description. According to their view, the role of the primary process in
the enhancing type is to modulate the meaning of the secondary process in a way
similar to a circumstantial element, of which there are potentially many types of
modulation available to participants to describe intentions, such as time (e.g., *tend
to do*), manner (*insist on doing*), cause: reason (*happen/remember to do*), contingency (*get to do*) and accompaniment (*help with/ do with*). These modulation types
are considered to be part of a single happening representing two events because
of the tactic and logico-semantic relationships that go beyond the apparent structural aspect of constituency. One process is subordinate (hypotactic) to another
and logically related in a way that qualifies the relationship through time, place,
manner, cause, and so on. A second, more compelling argument made by Halliday
and Matthiessen is to take into account the "flow of events" and the potential
options speakers have to organize their descriptions of these events with different
grammatical devices, among the most efficient of these being "single events realized by simple verbal groups" in clause complexes (p. 521), but other means of
organizing the flow of information, such as verbal group complexes representing

two events, are available to express nearly the same meaning. Thus, even though the processes of *read* and *to have more fluency* could be expressed in a clause complex, the speaker has fused them together using different resources (taxis and logico-semantic relations).

Projection. The third kind of CSI expressed by learners was projection, the representation of speech and thought by a speaker who uses verbal or mental processes to project a locution or idea that then becomes a different linguistic representation with a separate ontological status, what Halliday and Matthiessen (2004) referred to as a "metaphenomenon...of a different order of reality" (p. 441). Like expansion, projection is organized through taxis and logico-semantic relations, but unlike expansion, speech and thought can be construed as a hypotactic verbal group complex or clause complex. Three aspects of projection make up its system: 1) level of projection identifies the projected element as locution or idea, 2) mode of projection describes the interdependency of the process (taxis) and the projected element as a quote or report, making the two potential choices quote: paratactic or report: hypotactic, and 3) the speech function of the projection describes a proposition in finite form that involves the exchange of information or a finite/ non-finite proposal dealing with the exchange of goods and services. Together with taxis and logico-semantic relations the three aspects of projection combine to create several potential systems of meaning.

Within the data set six systems of projection were articulated by participants as CSI, although for the sake of clarity it is useful to point out before proceeding that all CSI using projections shared some common characteristics: all had a mental process operating as the primary process that, in turn, projected ideas in a report: hypotactic relationship, and all were proposal speech functions.

The first of the six systems, desideration, involved the verbs *want, like, would like*, and *prefer* as primary processes with the projected element functioning as an idea realized in a hypotactic verbal group complex or hypotactic clause complex. The unmarked form of *want* contained one participant, the learner, and the second process in perfective aspect:

> I want to improve my vocabulary in my writing.

Marked forms of *want* included two participants in a clause complex:

> Sometimes I, when I finish my writing, I want...somebody fluent at English to help me to review it and help me to correct the, the grammar.

This statement again raises issues about its validity as a verbal group or clause complex. What distinguishes the statement as a clause complex is the projected element's status as a proposal and metaphenomenon having a second participant and corresponding process. *I* and *somebody fluent at English* function as first and second participants while *want* and *to help me to review it* operate as corresponding processes. A second observation to be made is that regardless of the lexicogrammar of the CSI a tactic relationship (report: hypotactic) still remains between the two clauses. In contrast, other desiderative processes appeared only as a verbal group complex:

> I would like to explain more with numbers.

> I like to write about personal experience.

> I try to improve it (grammar), but now I prefer to write many joint sentences.

Following desideration was the projection of need, in which the unmarked form was the verb *need* used with one participant, the learner, in a verbal group complex:

> While I'm writing, I need to acquire more vocabulary, more synonyms cause maybe you write something, then you need… You don't want to be s--, to be repetitive.

Verbs other than *need* did not appear and no clause complexes were employed by learners. In projecting need participants expressed a belief that they were compelled to take action for some reason. The rationale for classifying need as well as the other systems of desideration as a CSI is based on an observation dating back to Aristotle (Aristotle, Brody, & Rowe, 2002) that belief/desire is the root of intentional action (Goldman, 1970; Mele, 1997; McCain, 1998). Davidson (1986), in supporting Aristotle's position, explains that even though belief or desire may not necessarily lead to an intention to act, they are, by their co-occurrence as events, in a relationship with intentional action, making them inseparable from intention and so effecting each other. Davidson also pointed out that it is through beliefs and desires that agents rationalize their intentions, subsequently revealing purposes and avenues for actions.

The next system of projection, expectation, differed in its lexicogrammatical composition, occurring as both verbal group complex and clause complex with learners using the verb *hope* to express a desire to act:

> I hope to write some… like uh… a thesis.

> At the end of this course I hope I will review the most basic grammar parts or rules, so I will be able to use them in English.

The latter statement is an example of an unmarked clause complex with the learner referring to herself in both first and second participant slots. The first clause *I hope* contains a mental process followed by the reporting of an idea, *I will review the most basic grammar parts or rules, so I will be able to use them in English*, in a hypotactic relationship, thus creating a report: hypotactic clause complex.

Participants' expressions of expectation, like desideration, is a belief in close relation to intention; therefore I classified it as a CSI.

The fourth system of projection was intention, consisting of the verbs *intend* and *plan* as primary processes in a verbal group complex:

> I can't use a word naturally or influ-- or fluently, so I intend to go to the library to borrow some writing book to have a glance at that, many people's essay.

> In the future, I'm planning to write something about politics or about my opinion about history or something like that, especially my country.

As with verbs of conation, *intend* and *plan* come closest in meaning to what may be perceived as CSI, although surprisingly the two statements cited above were the only two examples of a projection of intention found in the data. A text search of the transcripts showed that *intend* occurred in the data twelve times and that learners who used the word used it in the context of describing their future plans for study or a career.

The next system of projection, quote: paratactic clause complexes, differs from previously described projections in two significant ways. Learners articulated two separate participants in each clause, as would be expected in a clause complex, but more interestingly the mental processes of cognition, *think*, and perception, *find*, were followed by a quoted thought (Halliday & Matthiessen, p. 456) in the form of an interrogative. Second, the projected element constituted a proposition rather than a proposal:

> First of all I'm thinking. I'm thinking now I've... what will be the first paragraph, the second, the third?

> Sometimes when I read something, I find, I find "Oh, this is very useful."

Halliday and Matthiessen (2004) observed that native speakers of English use quote: paratactic clause complexes (glossed as "I said to myself..."), but usually with verbal processes:

> This combination of a verbal process with reporting... is the normal way of representing what people say, in most registers of English today. The opposite combination, that of a mental process with quoting, is also found, although considerably more restricted (p. 456).

For non-native speakers the restriction is less of an issue since they tend to use mental processes with quoting for circumlocution (Bialystok, 1990). As for the rationale behind classifying report: hypotactic clause complexes as CSI, they were coded as such because learners use them to verbalize the actual thought processes that they experienced while acting on a goal. In the two statements above learners demonstrated a focus of attention on an object and a mode of planning by mentioning an inceptive action or (in the latter statement) by portraying the object as personally valuable.

The last system of projection, report: hypotactic clause complexes, shares many of the same characteristics as quote: paratactic clause complexes in that there are two separate participants and the mental processes of *think* and *find* are used to project the second clause. However, the projected clause functions as a proposal rather than a proposition and, most notably, the projected element has a paratactic relationship with the first clause:

> In writing class, I find adjective clauses are very difficult for me... Restrictive or unrestrictive...?

Report: hypotactic clause complexes exemplify CSI because they show that the learner is consciously aware of a goal and is taking an inceptive action to achieve it by working out which course of action to take.

Replies to a question

Replies to a question (RQ) involved the interviewer asking students directly what their goals were for writing improvement. The student typically responded with a short answer, sometimes elaborating on it or, in other instances, being encouraged by the interviewer who probed for further information. Questions were almost always based on the standard interview protocol we used (see Appendix C), and the answers from these questions comprised about one-third of the goals coded as intentions. Direct questioning constituted an important part of the interview data, yielding the most information about participants' goals in comparison to other means. Five types of RQ appeared in the data: simple affirmation, simple affirmation with an explanation, nominal group, *I think* + nominal group, and an existential clause. Simple affirmations, in which the student replied in the affirmative to a question such as the following about grammar, were followed by a series of interviewer questions aimed at soliciting further information:

Interviewer: Are you trying to improve your grammar in your writing?
Student: Yes.
Interviewer: Yes.
Student: Definitely.
Interviewer: O.K. What grammar would you like to improve?
Student: Whatever I learn. The tense sometimes. I.. It's not that I don't know, but sometime I forget and practice is different than theory. Sometime I know something but when I have to- when I write, sometime I write too fast.
Interviewer: O.K. How are you trying to improve your grammar? Like your tenses, for example.

Student: Just that don't, try to don't write too fast and pay more attention to my verbs. Sometime I, in my mind I translate from Spanish because it help me to... to know.

Simple affirmations followed by an explanation usually contained the affirmation and then either a simple declarative sentence, *that's why, that's the reason,* or *because*:

Interviewer: Can you tell me how you are improving vocabulary?
Student: Yes. I have the book, the vocabulary book, New Oriental School, word 3000, so I read word.
Interviewer: So you try to memorize some words every day.
Student: Yes, because there are not only the word, also have example sentence. It's good.

The nominal groups that comprised RQs consisted of a single word or phrase:

Interviewer: What grammar would you like to improve?
Student: Grammar? Gerunds.
Interviewer: Gerunds, um-hum.
Student: How to use participles.

In some instances the nominal group was preceded by the phrase "I think: "

Interviewer: Are there any special types of writing that you want to do (e.g., description, exposition, narrative, etc.)?
Student: I think maybe the description. Description.
Interviewer: And why is that?
Student: I think the description is very, is very hard for the word choice. Sometimes you like, you describe a desk and you have to choose some words, it's used for the desk. I think it's hard for me now.

Lastly, some participants replied by using an existential clause:

Interviewer: Is there anything specific that you are now trying to learn or improve in your writing in English?
Student: You mean some difficulty?
Interviewer: Anything specific that you are trying to improve?
Student: Sometimes there are some noun clauses, I don't know where can I put some, in which part I can put them in the sentence.

The distinguishing feature of students' RQ, in comparison to CSI, is that they contained one or more objects of a goal but did not include information about additional aspects of their intentions until after the interviewer had prompted further or the students themselves offered more details. RQs were coded as intentions according to the goals framework because they consisted of at least one of the five components (belief, desire, object, plan, or action in progress) deemed essential to our construct of an intention.

Other means of conveying intentions

While CSI and RQ were the most conspicuous linguistic realizations according to the definition of intention that we had developed, they were not the only ways that students expressed intentions. In addition to propositional statements, students also utilized particular communication strategies to convey meanings that could only be identified by moving away from clause level analysis of propositional statements to consider more contextualized meanings (Widdowson, 2004). In the mind of many discourse analysts this implies consideration of pragmatics, but pragmatic meaning was not always the case since some indicators of intentions were found below the clause and contributed to the cohesion of the discourse as a whole. A further observation based on the transcript data is that participants conveyed these meanings in some cases to augment CSI and RQ, so they were not easily reducible to one clause whereby the intention was realized in the lexico-grammatical elements themselves.

The more locally contextualized meanings related to intentions fell into two categories that I have labelled discourse strategies and discourse themes. I further categorized discourse strategies as rhetorical structures involving strings of clauses and cohesive elements (Halliday & Hasan, 1976; Stoddard, 1991) consisting of adverbials, prepositional phrases, and nominal groups.

Discourse strategies. The first of the discourse strategies was the rhetorical structure of inductive reasoning:

> Like write the essay, this essay, I know there...I should give disagree or my opinion is disagree this sentence or agree with this sentence. But I, if I uh make sure my points, uh why I disagree about this, or I agree about this, I should give some examples to confirm others, to persuade others. But I can't just say I agree with it. It's right. I should give some specific examples to confirm others and... make others agree with my opinions. So this I need to search some example.

The significance of inductive reasoning in expressing intentions lies in the initial confusion that one may feel in reading passages like the above in which the student has used parallelism, repetition, and an elaborate listing of reasons (or in other interviews lists of events and actions) and the insertion of "so" clauses that in all instances in the data appeared at the very end of the turn. An explanation lies in the use of inductive reasoning as a culturally preferred form of discourse organization (Kirkpatrick, 1993; Scollon & Scollon, 2001; Young, 1994), perceived by some ethnic groups to be the appropriate rhetorical structure based on literary tradition. In contrast, deductive reasoning with the statement of intention placed at the beginning followed by supporting information may be thought of as "child-like, rude, or uncivilized" by some second language speakers (Fitzgerald, 2003, p. 87). Thus, cultural background has the potential to play a role in how students communicate intentions and what they perceive as important antecedents to intentional action. Indeed, the background circumstances themselves may be important to the student's own reasoning in taking actions.

A second strategy involved the rhetorical structure of hypothetical situations and elements of grammatical cohesion consisting of the conditional conjunctive adjuncts *if* and *then*:

> If I get an assignment and don't know much about it, or if I write something and I don't know, in this case, I search for information through the Internet.

The common thread among the two kinds of discourse strategies was a generalized event beginning with an "if-then" clause followed by the details of the hypothetical action. Learners hypothesized about what they would do if faced with a problem and then reported on what they believed were their previous actions or what they did as a matter of practice. No reference to an actual event was made, raising a methodological issue in examining what learners actually do when they set out to write in contrast to what they believe they do. An argument can be made that hypothetical situations provide an insight into students' beliefs about their performance and goal-directed activities because the learners are offering their own personal perspectives.

A third discourse strategy employed described recurrent actions, particularly those actions in which the object of the goal was the study of language or rhetoric/ genres. Recurrent actions are important because they are a simple and direct means of identifying intentions, showing that students are aware of purposely performing an activity on a routine basis. Students used four types of cohesive elements to characterize recurrent actions:

1. circumstance of extent, e.g., "I bought a visual dictionary about design and architecture. From time to time I read it and I can learn some words."
2. circumstance of manner, e.g., "If I study grammar… continuously, maybe later, maybe it's easy to see… after study."
3. modal comment adjunct, e.g., "I always focus on the grammar that they [authors] use, and also connectors… connector words, and like commas."
4. temporal conjunctive adjunct, e.g., "Whenever I finish my essay, I check which sentence can be combined. Then I use some clauses to combine the sentences."

Circumstantial elements of extent (*from time to time, every day, every morning, nowadays*) and manner (*continuously*) indicated duration, frequency, or a unit of measure, while modal comment adjuncts (*sometimes, usually, often, always*), and conjunctive adjuncts (*whenever, once again*) indicated usuality or temporal relations with previous meanings in the text (glossed as "then").

The final strategy found in the data was *try to* + *infinitive* used by students in a series of clauses:

> Every time I try to improve my spelling. I try to memorize spelling of certain words. I try not to use dictionaries very often. Every time I try to reduce use of dictionary, so just memorize those words.

At first glace, this particular use would appear to be a CSI, but because of the extent of its repetition in the discourse, it was clear students were communicating something else. In the present statement, *try to* + *infinitive* operates as a temporal-type conjunctive adjunct to indicate a series of linked actions. In support of this analysis another conjunctive adjunct, *then*, frequently preceded *try to* + *infinitive* in the data, lending additional evidence that it functions as a kind of secondary cohesive device.

Discourse themes

Similar to speech acts or speech functions, what I have designated as discourse themes clustered around thematic content rather than the locutionary force associated with speech acts (Austin, 1962; Levinson, 1983; Mey, 2001; Searle, 1969) or the delicacy of clause-level speech functions in a system of mood as is typical of SFL analysis of spoken discourse (Eggins & Slade, 1997; Martin, 1992; Sinclair & Coulthard, 1992). To identify these utterances as either speech acts or speech functions was beyond the scope of this analysis. Instead, I identified utterances that had a wider pragmatic meaning simply by theme and then corresponding lexicogrammar. The result was four discourse themes classified as expressions of utility, importance, lack of knowledge, and difficulty. Each had a distinctive register, confirming their place in their respective categories.

Students used expressions of utility to state the usefulness of an object or action:

> Sometimes I draw a map. It is useful to organize my thoughts.

In nearly all cases these expressions consisted of a relational: attributive process (copula) and adjectives (*useful, helpful, effective, worthwhile*) or nominal groups (*good/ best way, best method*). In contrast, expressions of importance involved a balance of relational: attributive and relational: identifying processes:

> I think choosing words is very important, especially because I, I don't know about the right, the appropriate, appropriate words.

Students articulated an intention by explaining what they felt was important for them to do or draw their attention to in order to improve their writing.

Expressions of lack of knowledge involved participants stating in negative terms ignorance or inability in various aspects of the writing process:

> If I found some vocabulary which I don't know, I usual put down a note and then find dictionary and find sentence about that word and write down in my notebook and see it.

The lexicogrammar of expressions of a lack of knowledge were the most diverse of the four discourse themes, each containing either an embedded clause, such as in the statement immediately above, or simple clauses with relational: attributive, relational: identifying, or cognitive processes (e.g., *know*). As previously mentioned, each of the expressions was given in negative terms. Other examples included "I can't get it," and "My skill is not very good." Expressions of difficulty addressed problems with various aspects of writing but in very specific terms. Students were explicit in what their problems were and how they could go about remedying them:

> If I see sentence, I can't break it down, like subject, verb. It's really hard to see.

Expressions of difficulty consisted of relational: attributing processes and the adjectives *hard* and *difficult*. It is important to note that both expressions of difficulty and lack of knowledge or ability differ from the developmental force of dilemma (as described in Chapter 2) in that the student has an awareness of how to address the situation. In the case of what we have called dilemmas, students are unsure of themselves and are at a loss as to what steps to take to resolve their problems.

Discussion

The kinds of linguistic realizations expressed by learners about their intentions for writing improvement were diverse and complex, going far beyond a simple clause with a single lexical verb. These realizations of intentions can be classified according to their lexicogrammar and discoursal meanings as simple clauses, hypotactic verbal group complexes related to logico-semantic relations of expansion and projection, paratactic and hypotactic clause complexes of projection, replies to questions about intentions in the form of simple affirmations with or without explanation, nominal groups, *I think* + nominal group, and existential clauses. Realizations of intentions were also identified below the clause in the cohesive elements of conjunctive adjuncts, modal comment adjuncts, and circumstantial elements of extent and manner, and above the clause in the rhetorical structures of inductive reasoning, hypothetical situations, and in the pragmatic expressions of utility, importance, lack of knowledge, and difficulty.

To understand the nature of the relationship between a conceptual framework of goals and the linguistic realizations of these concepts, it is first necessary to review our framework and the requisite psychological construct. For our study we conceived of intentions as part of a theory of action in which an agent acts towards an object through mediating artefacts. The antecedent intentions of the agent who acts toward an object are based primarily on desires and/ or beliefs about the object, which are then put into practice by using plans. The key components of our construct of an intention can be reduced to belief, desire, object, plan, and action in progress. At least one of the five components was found in each of the passages coded as an intention. While this may appear to be reductionist, it is in fact plausible to have only one of the components and no others. For example, it is entirely possible for a learner to have an intention without a goal in mind or to have a intention to act on a goal without an underlying desire or belief (Bratman, 1997; Harman, 1976; Mele, 2001; Searle, 1983). A second point that emerges about the relationship of concept and linguistic realization concerns register (Halliday & Hasan, 1985). As the CSI, RQ, and communication strategies show, statements of intention are linked to particular linguistic forms. Psychological constructs have a unique, identifiable linguistic register. Such linguistic forms may vary considerably, as is evident from this analysis, but identifying the relationship between construct and linguistic realization provides for a succinctly defined construct resulting in a more reliable identification of the phenomena being studied.

How does awareness of linguistic realizations inform our knowledge of goal-oriented learning activities? The simple answer is that identification of register helps to further refine both theories of intentions and methodology. It is clear from the present analysis that not only beliefs and desire are important to learners as they set goals for writing improvement, but also what they find useful, valuable (important), difficult, or lack in understanding. While belief and desire are discussed at length in the philosophy literature on intentions, only recently have philosophers come to realize that how the pragmatic aspects of an agent's statements plays a role in the interpretation of intention (Knobe, 2003; Mele, 2003). Another example of how knowledge of register contributes to better understanding of intention was found in the ways in which participants used various hypotactic verbal group complexes. In some CSI, particularly three-part causatives, the link between agent, intention, and goal is made clear, but in other CSI, such as in some desideratives, there is only mention of an agent and the object. The link between agency, intention, and activity is not always obvious in students' statements about their goals, so they could be prompted to clarify these to their own advantage and understanding. Knowledge of the various conceptual components of an intention on the part of a researcher or teacher in asking students about their goals for writing would lead to more effective questioning as well as identification of intentions.

CHAPTER 8

Goals, motivations, and identities of three students writing in English

Tae-Young Kim, Kyoko Baba, and Alister Cumming

In this chapter we extend our analyses of students' goals for writing improvement in two directions. Theoretically, we interpret students' goals for writing improvement as a dynamic interplay between their motivations and senses of identities as expressed in samples of their academic writing and interviews. Empirically, we present data from an additional, third year of data collection in the context of university studies. But to attain these perspectives we concentrate on the cases of just three students. We describe how the three learners individually motivated themselves, created and adjusted attainable learning goals, and gradually came to express identities, in their writing, as ESL learners and as functioning, novice members in the written discourse of their communities of academic study. As such, the analytic framework in this chapter diverges from the methods (described in Chapter 2) we developed for the main study to account for group trends in learners' goals for writing improvement. Here we adopt a more interpretive, socio-historical, and personalized set of case-study accounts to describe how the three students each uniquely and progressively developed their goals and their writing in English.

Goals, motivation, and identity

Writers' representations of themselves are elusive and complicated. For this reason Cherry (1988) recommended studying them from different angles and from a multidimensional perspective. We have tried to do so in the present chapter. We assume that goals reflect students' motivations, which in turn express and construct their identities. Goals and motivations are integral to the construction of identities because they involve a person's expectations or desires for who the person wants to be in the future. From the perspective of activity theory (Leont'ev, 1979; Engeström, 1999) people's goals are focal representations, in the context of actions and situations that form an activity system, of their motivations for long-term development. These are shaped by the sociohistorical contexts of their lives, arising from their past experiences and in view of an expected future. A situational perspective on motivation similarly links individual learners' behaviors to their unique situations (Paris & Turner, 1994). Situational motivation is "contextualized", "unstable", and "construct[ed] in a given situation or in general will change over time, and is malleable" (Hickey, 1997, p. 183).

Numerous theories of language and literacy learning have adopted these perspectives to focus on the construct of identity and the processes of socialization. Norton [Peirce]'s (1995, 1997) term "social identity" is particularly relevant to the population of ESL learners in the present research. Norton (1997, p. 410) defined identity as "how people understand their relationship to the world, how that relationship is constructed across time and space, and how people understand their possibilities for the future." Identity is not a single subjective mental position, but rather a co-existence of senses of selves (Davies & Harré, 1990; Ivanič, 1998; Norton, 1995, 1997, 2000). Ochs' (1993, p. 288) theories of language socialization elaborated on this mutual interaction between identit(ies) and discourse, proposing that people establish identit(ies) relative to particular communities through "socially recognized, goal-directed behavior" while adopting various stances (i.e., socially recognized points of view or attitude).

An ESL learner's social identity is continually claimed, negotiated, and re-positioned within the activity systems of the discourse communities in which the person engages. An ESL writer's identity develops through multiple interactions in diverse contexts, such as with other students, instructors, acquaintances, and family members. Through participation in academic activities – like attending classes, socializing with other students, taking part in personal activities or entertainments, and writing course assignments – ESL learners invest in, create, and expand their unique (academic) discourse communities, wherein their identities are initially projected and later re-created. Norton's (1995) term, investment, links motivation, language socialization, and identity through the mental, emotional, and behavioral efforts to use a second language in perceived legitimate social milieus. Drawing on Bourdieu (1977, 1982), Norton observed the cultural capital associated with prestige languages, such as English, in which immigrants and sojourning students of English invest. A student's motivation for improving ESL writing abilities can be understood as a prudent investment to obtain and retain linguistic capital represented by academic writing skills in English. By developing more of this linguistic or academic literacy capital an ESL writer also becomes a functioning member of a particular discourse community, for example, the institutional system of a university and of a broader academic discipline.

Writers' identities

Ivanič (1998) established a framework for analyzing university students' projections of their senses of their selves in their writing through four aspects of identity, as: (a) autobiographical self, (b) discoursal self, (c) self as author, and (d) possibilities for self-hood. We adopted this framework for the present analysis, while recognizing that these categories tend to overlap and interact, providing indications, rather than absolute definitions, of selfhood as it appears in a sample of discourse.

Drawing on Goffman (1959), Ivanič (1998) defined autobiographical self as a representation of how writers present their identities in real life including their previous life histories, ways of thinking, points of views, and ideologies in texts. The *autobiographical self* changes according to the development of a person's life history. In some academic disciplines, writers are encouraged to reveal their autobiographical selves, whereas other disciplines shun personal expressions. We use the term autobiographical self to refer to the students' experiences, interests, ideas, opinions, and commitments. *Discoursal self* is an image of the writer that emerges in a specific text. Writers may intentionally manipulate indications of their discoursal self to achieve specific purposes, but these may also be projected unconsciously. Indications of a discoursal self do not necessarily reflect the writer's social identity, but may relate more to the norms or expectations of written genres in particular contexts. *Self as author* is concerned with attitudes of authority (i.e., the extent to which the writer wants to appear authoritative in expressing knowledge). In academic writing, writers can appeal to authority by citations to established authorities or sources on a topic, they can claim their authority by "presenting the content of their writing as objective truth", or they can personally indicate their own "responsibility for their authorship" (Ivanič, 1998, p. 26). Ivanič and Camps (2001) also pointed out that the authorial stance in texts hinges on the dynamics of power relations between the writer and the reader. That is, the more self-assured and epistemologically certain the writer is, the greater power he or she holds or may wish to exert over the reader. In *possibilities for selfhood*, Ivanič (1998) proposed that there are various ways for writers to present themselves in texts. Writer's identities are multifaceted, and depending on the discourse community, writers emphasize one aspect of their identities over others in their writing. Ivanič argued that possibilities for self-hood are constructed in social contexts each time students write. Even in a discourse community that seems to have restricted rules for written genres, there is always room to negotiate identities and express them in different ways in writing.

The four types of writers' identities may be evident in texts. However, Ivanič cautions that expressions of identities in texts do not necessarily correspond with writers' real identities (in other contexts or any absolute sense). Writers may present themselves in texts in ways that internalize their future aims ("aspiring selves"), or they may restrain from presenting part of their selves ("desired identities"). To guide our analyses of the intricate relationship among goals, motivations, and identities, we posed three research questions: (1) How did each student express, in their writing samples and interviews, their autobiographical selves, discourse selves, selves as author, and possibilities for self-hood? (2) What changes in goals for writing, motivations, and identities did the three participants demonstrate in relation to their sociocultural contexts and their perceived communities? (3) How might their communities have influenced their goals, motivations, and identities?

Method

We focus on three East Asian students – Kazuko and Rihoko from Japan and Jina, a Korean – who we interviewed over a three-year period. (See Table 8.1 below and Appendices A, B, and C.) The first two interviews were conducted in English with subsequent interviews done in the native language of the participants, of which we share native-speaking membership in, respectively, Japanese (Baba) and Korean (Kim) societies. In addition to the data collection described in Chapter 2, we conducted fifth and sixth interviews individually with the three students in the autumn then the winter of 2004 (but gathered writing samples only in the fifth interview, and Rihoko did not participate in the sixth interview). Below we cite interview numbers and corresponding essay numbers from these interviews (e.g., Essay 1 was part of Interview 1). As elsewhere in this book, extracts from interviews that appear in italics below were originally spoken in Japanese or Korean, and we have translated them here to English; underlined extracts appeared in students' written texts (rather than in their interviews).

Each participant had six years of formal English study at secondary schools in their home country prior to starting the ESL program. Kazuko obtained a bachelor's degree in Japan and began another undergraduate degree program in her late 20s, whereas both Jina and Rihoko were younger (in their early 20s), and their highest previous degrees were a high school diploma. Kazuko and Rihoko held international student visas, whereas Jina was a landed immigrant in Canada (a point we elaborate on below, and which made her unique in our sample of students). Kazuko majored in political science and planned to return to Japan after completing her degree in Canada. In the third year of our study, Kazuko changed her program to an honor's degree. Rihoko majored in architecture in her first year of university studies but changed to chemistry in her second year. Rihoko was not

Table 8.1. Summary of the three participants' writing samples

		Year	Program	Field of study	Type of writing	Title	General features of each writing sample
Kazuko	Essay 1	2001	ESL	NA	Narrative	My new class mate, XXXX	An essay introducing one of her classmates to the class
	Essay 2	2001	ESL	NA	Expository	Bravo!! Multiculturalism!!	An essay on some virtues of multiculturalism in Canada
	Essay 3	2002	1st year at univ.	Political Science	Expository	Country profile: Issues of Japanese political system	An essay on problematic issues of democracy in Japanese political system
	Essay 4	2003	1st year at univ.	Political Science	Expository	Issues of Japanese media: Why they are not democratic?	An essay on some problems in Japanese media with regard to freedom of speech
	Essay 5	2004	2nd year at univ.	Political Science	Argumentative	Was Socrates guilty of impiety?	An essay on Socrates' philosophy, analyzing his thoughts and Athenians' misunderstanding of him
Rihoko	Essay 1	2001	ESL	NA	Expository	No title	A summary of an article on U.S. eugenics and Rihoko's comments on eugenics
	Essay 2	2001	ESL	NA	Expository	No title	An essay on the Palestinian problem and suggests a solution for it
	Essay 3	2002	1st year at univ.	Architecture	Description	The project for Eaton's college street	An analysis of architectural features of a building in a North American city
	Essay 4	2003	1st year at univ.	Architecture	Description	Expression of materials	An analysis of characteristics of an architect by illustrating one of the buildings that he designed
Jina	Essay 1	2001	ESL	NA	Description	The Walkerton tragedy	Summary of a tragedy about water contamination
	Essay 2	2002	ESL	NA	Expository	No title	Summary of an activist's anti-slavery work and Jina's evaluation on the activist's behavior
	Essay 3	2002	1st year at univ.	Economics & Commerce	NA	No title	Lecture notes with formula, graphs
	Essay 4	2003	1st year at univ.	Economics & Commerce	Description / Narrative	No title	Two samples: detailed description of a portrait of a woman, explanation of a Korean proverb with narratives of personal experience
	Essay 5	2004	2nd year at univ.	Economics & Commerce	NA	Midterm exam paper	Multiple choice, filling the gap test for English word origins
	Essay 6	2004	3rd year at univ.	Economics & Mathematics	NA	No title	Lecture notes with formula, graphs

sure if she would return to Japan after completing her degree. Before coming to Canada, Jina had completed one year in business administration at a university in Korea, where she majored in economics and commerce. She hoped eventually to get a job in Canada. During the course of the interviews Jina worked part-time at a restaurant and then at her university's international student centre.

We present our analyses in respect to Ivanič's (1998) four aspects of writers' identities, analyzing various linguistic features (such as lexical, syntactic, and rhetorical choices), in the three students' essays, following Ivanič (1998) and Ivanič and Camps (2001). We also draw on data from interviews to describe the students' long-term goals, motivations, and life histories.

Findings

Kazuko

During the pre-university ESL program, Kazuko's writing was primarily a means to express her thoughts and at the same time to obtain course grades. Articulating her opinions and making strong claims in her writing was her dominant goal. She preferred to foreground her opinions in her writing, and if she could not do so, she thought that the quality of her writing declined: "*I think I, the better have very strong, strong, strong opinion...That if I don't have it, maybe the sentence becomes so weak*" (Interview 2). Kazuko's motivation to present an autobiographical self in her writing in English was implicit in her selection of topics for essays and her approach to writing. Whenever possible, Kazuko chose topics that interested her. She had a profound consciousness of being Japanese, so she wrote about the Japanese political system (in her third essay) and Japanese media (in her fourth essay).

Autobiographical self. Kazuko expressed her autobiographical self – particularly her life-experiences, interests, and opinions – vividly in the first two essays she wrote in the ESL program. For example, in her second essay about multiculturalism in Canada, instead of describing general features of multiculturalism, Kazuko focused on her personal sense of the importance of multiculturalism, citing its impact on her personal life: "*Multiculturalism is a, to understand as a culture, is important thing... to deal with someone, to deal with the others, so just I wanted to mention that second opinion that why I think multiculturalism is helpful for my life*" (Interview 2).

In her essays for university courses, Kazuko's expression of her life experiences were not quite so straightforward, but her belief in writing as a means of self-expression became deeper as she proceeded with her undergraduate studies:

Writing is a way to present my feelings and opinions. Before [entering the university], speaking was more important, and I did not recognize its significance. But now writing is very important in not only academic essays but also letters and e-mails. While writing essays at the university, I noticed that this is a good means [to express myself]. ... Writing makes my opinions even clearer. I think it is also a matter of my identity. To be able to express my opinions explicitly is to express my own identity in writing.   (Interview 6)

To this end, in her university essays, Kazuko continued to use first-person "I" and to state her opinions, though sometimes in a peculiar way, as we observe in the next section.

Kazuko also demonstrated her intent to shape her identity, particularly her autobiographical self, in her writing through a firm commitment to her major in political science. Kazuko's interest in political science was rooted in her life experiences. She had been profoundly influenced by her late father who had long been involved in political activities in Japan and whose death seems to have motivated her to pursue an honors degree. In Canada, Kazuko was intrigued by the phenomenon of multiculturalism in Canadian society, wondering what policies prompt a situation in which multiculturalism is *"working too well"* (Interview 6). From this perspective, studying political science was a crucial part of Kazuko's autobiographical self, evident in her active use of personal voice in all her academic writing. In turn, studying and writing about political science related directly to Kazuko's future goals as she intended to develop a career in this field. For this reason, Kazuko's expression of her autobiographical self in her course assignments represented efforts to invest herself in academic writing and the discipline of her studies.

Discoursal self. There was a qualitative difference in Kazuko's expression of her discoursal self between her writing in the pre-university ESL program and in her later academic courses. In her university essays, Kazuko presented herself as belonging to an academic discourse community. For example, she appealed to authority by citing publications, which she never did in her two pre-university essays. The number of citations in her writing gradually increased over the period of our data collection. To establish objectivity in her essays, Kazuko also cited the results of surveys to support her claims. Likewise, her lexicon shifted to words and phrases specific to her academic major (e.g., *public hearings, judicial system, Diet, Proportional Representation System*) as well as words of Greco-Latin origins (e.g., *proclaims, abolish, disregard, prohibit, expulsion*). She also used categorical present tense verbs to add authoritative tones to her writing, for example, "has" in Essay 3 and "is deeply influenced" and "allows" in Essay 4:

In conclusion, the Japanese political system has three major problems such as the unsuitable limitation of people's participation in politics, the chaotic independence

> among the three powers and the unequally electoral system.   (Essay 3)
> First of all, Japanese media is deeply influenced by political power, which allows
> their government to control information.   (Essay 4)

A unique characteristic of Kazuko's academic essays was that her personal voice
suddenly emerged from time to time in her texts, appearing in phrases such as "I
strongly believe" (Essay 3) or "I'm unable to see any improvement in Japanese
media from when Japan was autocracy before the World War 2" (Essay 4). On
the latter phrase, Kazuko's teaching assistant commented, "Isn't this an overstate-
ment?" Such idiosyncratic ways of expressing her opinions in academic writing
marked Kazuko as a novice in this discourse community. Other such indications
were her uses of colloquial expressions common to the register of speech rather
than formal written discourse, such as abbreviated forms like "aren't," "isn't," or
"can't"; she sometimes chose general words rather than more specific words (e.g.,
"people" instead of "citizens"); and she made excessive numbers of citations in
her writing.

Self as author. Kazuko was self-expressive as an author. As observed above,
she frequently used the first person singular pronoun in her university essays,
primarily to underscore her opinions but also to guide readers to the organization of a paper. Kazuko's uses of phrases like "I would like to argue" or "moving
on, I would like to discuss" indicated that she was "reader-considerate" (Ivanič &
Camps, 2001). She also used plural person pronouns, such as "we," "us," "you,"
suggesting that as an author Kazuko was positioning herself alongside her potential readers and trying to draw them into her arguments. Put differently, Kazuko
did not entirely rely on an authoritative stance to strengthen the credibility of her
arguments. She also used rhetorical questions to influence her potential readers:

> How many languages have you heard in Canada?   (Essay 2)

> For example, why would many Athenians consider him as impious?   (Essay 5)

Possibilities for selfhood. Kazuko was learning to be a legitimate member
of her academic discourse community, but at the same time she wanted her
personal voice to be prominent in her writing. Her attempts to express her beliefs
and opinions sometimes resulted in sentences that seem awkward for academic
writing. But Kazuko gradually established an awareness of the inappropriateness
of some of her ways of expressing herself. When asked about sources for her
writing Kazuko explained, "*I would like to involve my own ideas... However, it is
this research paper that doesn't allow me to do so. I would like to, I like including my
ideas, but that is not allowed*" (Interview 4). In addition, Kazuko faced inconsis-
tencies in academic conventions and the policies of certain professors about uses
of the first person pronoun in her writing:

Basically I like to use "I", but some professors tell us not to do so. If I am allowed to use "I", I use it several times and I express my opinion. If I cannot use "I", I write for the audience. Not for specific someone, but people in general.   (Interview 5)

Kazuko's inclination to emphasize her opinions and ideas conflicted with her emerging sense of what is appropriate for writing in her academic discourse community. Kazuko was in the process of understanding the boundaries of, while also establishing practices for, expressing her own legitimate voice in this discourse context.

Rihoko

Rihoko's essays contrast sharply with Kazuko's. Throughout her essays, including the ones she wrote in her ESL classes, she maintained an academic or detached tone. Rihoko never displayed her experiences or her interests in her written texts, nor did she use the first person singular pronoun. In these respects, Rihoko took a more authoritative stance in her essays than Kazuko did. Rihoko seemed to have a particular image of "academic discoursal self" in her mind which she believed "correct and ideal" and felt comfortable with. The difference between Rihoko's and Kazuko's writing may be that Rihoko opted to stick to her "ideal discoursal self" regardless of practices or norms favored in her field of studies, whereas Kazuko was more flexible in her orientation towards academic writing. Rihoko was not motivated to write about any particular topics as Kazuko was. According to Rihoko, she changed her major from architecture to chemistry because she could not compete with English native speakers in terms of writing quality or expectations. For Rihoko, obtaining good grades and graduating from university seemed more important than writing about what most interested her or expressing her thoughts and ideas (tendencies that we frequently observed in Kazuko's writing and interviews).

Autobiographical self. No trace of Rihoko's autobiographical self – as past experiences, interests, or ideas/opinions/commitments – appeared in her essays. Rihoko seemed to intentionally separate her identity, or what she thought to be her identity, and her "real self" from her academic writing. Rihoko believed that eliminating indications of her identity from her writing would lead to the scientific objectivity required in the realm of academia:

Identity of my country or my own personality? When I do academic writing, I cannot use words with my own feelings or biases or prejudices, right? So I am trying not to show my identity. I was told not to do so.   (Interview 3)

Rihoko's hesitancy to highlight her opinions or interests can be attributed to her personality as well. She admitted being cautious about making strong claims in her essays because she was not sure whether she was allowed to do so. Additionally, during the interviews Rihoko seemed to select words carefully and be attentive to what she was saying even in her mother tongue. She never appeared opinionated, and she avoided subjective explanations. Another possible reason for Rihoko's reluctance to express her personal identity in her academic writing is that her field of study (and thus her writing for or about that field) did not occupy a special place in her identity as it did for Kazuko. For Rihoko the motivation for writing essays came from external obligations such as graduation and course grades rather than from intrinsic desires for self-expression. Even Rihoko's field of her major did not seem important to her. As mentioned above, Rihoko switched her major from architecture to chemistry, and earlier (in Interviews 1 and 2) she told us she was intending to major in biology.

Rihoko's lack of expressions of an autobiographical self in her writing and her conformity to academic conventions in her essays may be related to her personal experiences. Before coming to Canada, Rihoko failed to gain admission to a university in Japan. That experience had had a considerable impact on her life, which she mentioned repeatedly throughout the interviews. Instead of making another attempt to enter a Japanese university, Rihoko decided to choose the more challenging option of earning a degree at a foreign university (in Canada):

> Interviewer: *What personal or family incidents have affected your life as an English learner most, for example, marriage, divorce?*
> Rihoko: *Not particularly. If anything, my failure in entering a university [in Japan], rather than family incidents.*
> Interviewer: *That's all right. So it was the largest incident for you?*
> Rihoko: *Yes.*
> Interviewer: *Then you didn't want to study English?*
> Rihoko: *No. Failure is frustrating, isn't it? I felt like doing something challenging, and then I went abroad.*
> (Interview 5)

Because Rihoko's motivation was to graduate from a Canadian university she made every effort to accommodate her perceptions of written academic discourse in English to attain that goal.

Discoursal self. Rihoko's commitment to academic-writing conventions appeared in various features of her writing. In all her essays she avoided using first or second person pronouns, even in places she could have used them. She wrote, "one must consider discrimination" instead of "we" (Essay 1), "observers wonder what make the conflict difficult to settle" instead of "you", "we", or "I" (Essay 2). Even when she emphasized her own claims, Rihoko avoided phrases such as "I believe" or "I think". Rihoko also used many categorical present tense verbs to achieve an academic tone in her writing, such as "discrimination sometimes results in" (Essay 1), and "Canada's diverse ethnic makeup is reflected in architecture at a certain place" (Essay 3). Other academic features in her essays were the frequent use of modals, complex grammatical structures (especially phrasal structures), nominalizations, and passive voice. Another strategy Rihoko adopted to place herself in the discourse of her academic discipline, architecture, was to insert many adjectives into her essays. Her third essay written in the first semester in university was replete with adjectives (e.g., in the first paragraph, 23 out of 248 words were adjectives). Many of the adjectives she used were subjective and aesthetically value-embedded (e.g., *beautiful, splendid, pleasurable*): "However, the podium, a piece of the project, give such an exquisite appearance that one could not help envisaging how gorgeous it would be, if the project of the department store had been completed." (Essay 3).

In her fourth essay, Rihoko employed fewer adjectives, but instead she increased the number of words specific to her academic major (e.g., *podium, perimeters, columns, scones are conjugated in a stripe pattern*). These changes in her lexical usages reflect the efforts that Rihoko was making to adapt herself to the register of the academic discourse community, or to put it more critically, how susceptible she was to her proximal environment.

Self as author. As noted above, Rihoko seldom displayed her autobiographical self directly in her writing. This resulted in an "authoritative" tone and a sense of exerting a certain power over the reader. One exception appeared in her first essay: "Sadly, such discrimination sometimes results in unreasonable events when people are driven by anxiety or frustration" (Essay 1). The use of "sadly" here may represent Rihoko's emotional state, but its personal effect quickly disappears with the subsequent categorical present-tense verb "results in." Nonetheless, Rihoko was not completely negligent about her potential readers. Like Kazuko, Rihoko sometimes used rhetorical questions to engage her potential readers. Moreover, she used many hedges to lower the certainty of her claims, including adverbs like "perhaps" and "presumably" and the modals "can" and "might."

Possibilities for self-hood. One of Rihoko's problems was how to include her subjective impression in her writing about architecture while also maintaining a perspective of objectivity. Rihoko wanted to avoid expressing her personal voice in her texts, but detailing her own impressions was mandatory for her course requirements. As observed above, Rihoko did such things as making strenuous efforts to insert value-laded adjectives into her university essays. But eventually Rihoko ceased to explore the possibility of aligning her self-hood with discoursal practices in the field of architecture. She changed her major to chemistry, thinking she would not be required to expose her personal self in academic writing in English and believing that studies in chemistry were likely to produce better grades.

Jina

Jina's identity as an ESL writer related to her degree of comfort expressing her thoughts. She often compared her comfort level writing in Korean to oral communication. She attributed her discomfort writing in English mainly to her lack of English vocabulary and sentence structures, which produced a disjuncture between her intended thoughts and her capacities to express them in English texts:

> Interviewer: *Do you think your writing in English is different from your writing in Korean?*
>
> Jina: *Yeah, of course. Because limited, because of limited vocabularies. And even though I write, I write vocabularies or I use right vocabularies or right structure, it can be slightly different from what I meant.*   (Interview 2)

Like Rihoko, Jina tried to follow the specific conventions of academic writing in her program in economics. But virtually all her writing for university courses consisted of mathematical formulas, visual graphs, and charts. Perhaps because of this, at the time of the fourth interview, Jina was not fully satisfied with her English writing proficiency, so she decided to take a non-credit writing course designed for non-native English speaking undergraduate students. Her fourth writing samples, a narration and description from this course, were strikingly similar to those she produced in her pre-university ESL course.

Autobiographical self. Jina expressed her autobiographical self clearly in her second essay in the ESL program. Writing on the topic of human slavery and an activist's effort to buy back slaves, Jina composed an essay with two parts, a summary and a response. The first section described the activist's efforts, whereas the second part contained many judgmental remarks. Jina used such phrases as "I think" and "in my opinion" to express her condemnation of the activist's behavior: "I think Vogel's [the activist's name] actions are not appropriate in a long term. In my opinion, giving money to poor parents is more effective than to slave traders to prevent slavery." (Essay 2) As this extract shows, Jina's tone was evaluative, reflecting her past academic knowledge about the topic of slavery and its economic system. However, in her writing for economics courses Jina's free expression of such evaluations, reflecting her autobiographical self, disappeared. This transition seemed to reflect Jina's academic goal of adhering to the academic conventions required in her major.

Jina's past experience as an immigrant was another influence, and one that subsequently distinguished her from Kazuko and Rihoko. When asked why she decided to study in an English-dominant country like Canada, Jina replied:

When I meet Korean immigrants who live here, firmly rooted here, I think the first generation all has the same jobs – convenience store or self-employed business, more or less small business. Without proper education, however fluently they can speak English, in most cases, the second generation will have the same job. Because they've seen their parents' jobs when they were very young. (laugh) So they think it would be much easier to continue on with their parents' family business rather than getting a white-collar, office job. If they didn't get much education, they almost always think like that. In my case, I'm not sure if I am going to stay here or go back to Korea. Anyway, if I get more education, I think I will have many opportunities to actualize my real self. Otherwise, I have no choice but getting a job in a convenience store… It is a great motivator for me.   (Interview 5)

Jina's motivation to learn English and obtain a university degree was to improve her socioeconomic status. Throughout the interviews, Jina expressed her intention to secure an office job in the future, emphasizing the importance of getting good grades for such employment. Writing in English was not a means of expressing herself, but rather was a way to obtain excellent course grades. As a consequence, the writing samples Jina brought to our interviews were lecture notes, exam questions and answers, and supporting charts and graphs. None showed any indication of her autobiographical self.

Discoursal self. Jina, however, proved to be a persuasive author, as shown in these statements from her pre-university essays in the ESL program:

> But this is triggering a controversy. Some people think adding chlorine will keep water out of bacteria or viruses, while others think it will make water more hazardous with the possible risk of cancer or health problems.   (Essay 1)

> Human trading is a hard and complicated problem to be rooted out at once. Although the solution is a makeshift, this is the second best solution.   (Essay 2)

Like Kazuko and Rihoko, Jina relied on categorical present tense verbs to convey the objectivity and logic of her judgments. Another strategy Jina used to make her discoursal self prominent in her writing was the inclusive first person plural pronoun "we":

> Furthermore, we can't certain that freed slaves aren't enslaved again.   (Essay 2)

Jina's strategy for denoting her discoursal self, however, changed drastically in her university writing. Her assignments in economics mainly involved the use of formulas and calculations, so Jina turned to using domain-specific lexical phrases (e.g., *quantity demand, quantity supplies, price elasticity, price ceiling,* and *equilibrium prices*).

Self as author. Jina's writing for her undergraduate major mostly involved exam papers or note-taking primarily intended for her personal reference, typically about a variety of mathematical formulas and calculations. There was no room in these writing tasks for the concept of self as author, as Ivanič (1998) defined it, as the degree to which an author exerts an impression on a potential reader.

Possibilities for selfhood. Nonetheless, Jina expressed a strong desire to write logical and persuasive essays throughout our six interviews.

> Interviewer: *Do you have distinct topics that you want to write about in English and in Korean?*
>
> Jina: *Generally speaking, yes. Because the topics that I want to write in Korean are relevant for Korean readers, and those that I want to write in English will be topics that I want Canadians to know about Korea. For example, I'm thinking of such topics as why Korean universities lack international quality. On such topics I think I can make some conclusions. I would like to write on such topics for newspapers in Korean.*
>
> (Interview 6)

Jina's differentiation of writing for Korean or Canadian readers hints at a wholly different context in which Jina opted to resolve the dilemma of expressing herself in writing: personal Internet websites.

> *I wrote in English lots of times in my Internet homepage. I guess I wrote about my personal thoughts or feelings in English a lot there. I have two homepages. One is Daun, and this is open to everyone. So in that homepage, I rarely express my private feelings. The other one is called "Sayworld". In that homepage, only some very close friends of mine can even see my very personal feelings or thoughts. In this case, I think I wrote in English a lot.*
>
> (Interview 6)

For one website, Jina mainly wrote in Korean and the content of her writing was less personal. For the other website, Jina frequently used English, and the content of her writing was more emotional (e.g., involving topics such as love or hatred toward another person). In this way, Jina established an emotional outlet to fulfill her need of self actualization in a context that was not available or relevant to her academic studies.

Discussion

The academic writing of all three students, in the transition from pre-university ESL to university degree programs, reflects their unique academic contexts and personal histories, experiences, and beliefs. Differences in expressing their writer's selves increased as they advanced through their different academic programs. In Kazuko's case, zeal for her major upheld her strong tendency to express her autobiographical self. In Jina's case, the nature of her major prohibited the expression of personal voice in her university writing (so she sought to do so in her personal space on the Internet). Rihoko believed that academic writing should not reveal any personal voice, so the disparity between her belief and the written assignments required for her undergraduate major induced her to change her major to chemistry. Casanave (1995, p. 108) reported similar cases of graduate students changing their academic major after taking a course because they did not feel ownership in the discipline. She attributed these cases to the fact that the students failed or did not choose to "construct contexts for writing."

These students' expressions, developing uses, or repressions of Ivanič's (1998) four categories of a writer's identity represent their desires and struggles to acquire membership in their respective academic communities. These processes of participation in academic communities relate directly to identity negotiation because identity is "concerned with the social formation of the person" (Wenger, 1998, p. 13). When newcomers to a community notice features of the community that are foreign but also crucial to obtain in-group membership (Giles & Johnson, 1981), newcomers tend to negotiate their identities in the new community in regards to these features. As Sfard and Prusak (2005) have argued in respect to immigrants from the former Soviet Union to schools in Israel, their learning focuses on closing the gap between their "actual" and their "designated" identities. This interrelationship between writers' identity negotiations and processes of entering academic discourse communities has been well documented in studies of both L1 (e.g., Dysthe, 2002; Herrington, 1992; Hull & Rose, 1990; Ivanič, 1998; Prior, 1998; Wilder, 2002) and L2 writing development (e.g., Angelil-Carter, 1997; Belcher, 1994; Gentil, 2005; Ivanič & Camps, 2001; Leki, 2001a; Spack, 1997). For example, Angélil-Carter (1997) described problems faced by an ESL undergraduate student because his primary writing experience had previously been to write letters to his friends from prison. The student resisted academic writing because it "suppress[es] his self, his 'soul,' as he called it" (p. 279), and thus experienced an arduous process in establishing his identity as a writer of academic discourse.

Kazuko and Rihoko experienced similarly cumbersome and painful processes of coming to participate in their academic communities, notably when they were required to write lengthy essays in their limited English without much background knowledge or experience in their disciplines. Whether they stuck to the same academic community (as Kazuko did) or sought a more congenial one (as Rihoko did), they were attempting to acquire a new voice as a writer in that larger context. The three students' maturity or cognitive/affective development as a social being may have also influenced their perceptions of and commitments to their discourse communities as well as their construction of relationships between themselves and their social environments (Kohlberg, 1969; Kohlberg & Mayer, 1972; Norton, 2000). Kazuko, who had more and longer life experiences, seemed to have conceived a clear career path and so incorporated learning in the discourse community into her identities and life. The two younger students, Jina and Rihoko, had vaguer ideas about university studies, and so positioned themselves as merely acquiring some tools for success in whatever undefined future careers they might have.

From the perspective of Locke and Latham (1990), the three students' behavioral patterns of writing can be understood as on-going processes of goal setting and adjustment to unique sociocultural factors. Locke and Latham (1990) maintained that the success of learning goals depends on the goals' specificity and perceived difficulty. The more specific and concrete the goal, in view of optimal difficulty, the more successful the learner will be in his or her field of learning (Locke, 1996). As Kazuko and Jina illustrated, their past experiences such as paternal influences or perceptions of other immigrants' unsuccessful careers in Canada influenced their initial setting of goals for academic achievement. But their more specific goals for writing improvement arose from their interactions with their academic communities. In this regard, Wenger (1998, pp. 173–174) drew a useful distinction between three ways of belonging to a community of practice – engagement, imagination, and alignment – which he defined as:

- Engagement – active involvement in mutual processes of negotiation of meaning;
- Imagination – creating images of the world and seeing connections through time and space by extrapolating from our own experience; and
- Alignment – coordinating our energy and activities in order to fit within broader structures and contribute to broader enterprises.

For Rihoko, her imagined academic community did not correspond to what her academic program really required. There was a non-alignment. She found it difficult to engage herself. Rihoko perceived that she should omit her personal voice in her writing – as a way of participating legitimately in her imagined academic community – but the norms of the community actually required her to express her own judgments and opinions, which Rihoko was not, as an author, prepared to do. So she changed her academic major. In terms of Norton's (1995) metaphor of investment, Rihoko had to find a new market in which to invest her linguistic capital. In contrast, both Kazuko and Jina seem to have imagined communities which did not differ much from those that existed in the academic communities of their majors. Able to engage themselves in relevant academic discourse and to align themselves in the communities, Kazuko and Jina gradually acquired in-group membership. From Norton's (1995) concept of investment, we can see that Kazuko had ideal conditions to encourage her further investment in revealing her identity in her academic writing because of the close correspondence between imagined communities and existing communities. For Jina, a huge gap existed between her pre-university ESL writing assignments and those assigned in her university courses, but she readily conformed to the new writing conventions of her major and gradually adjusted herself to her imagined academic community. She did so even though this investment involved repressing her expression of personal identity.

The personal agency of each of the three participants is important here (McKay & Wong, 1996). The differences in their academic contexts do not in themselves explain the different ways in which Kazuko, Rihoko, and Jina sometimes expressed and at other times repressed their identities in their English writing. For example, Kazuko's personal determination to express herself in her academic writing related fundamentally to her being a mature university student, her past educational experiences, her home culture, and her paternal influence.

The interplay among the three participants' writing goals, motivations, and identities emphasizes the importance of rules and community from the perspective of the components of an activity system (Engeström, 1999). The students conceptualized the rules of academic writing conventions in respect to the imagined communities as well as the existing communities of their university courses. Discrepancies in rules between imagined and existing communities sometimes resulted in students conforming to a rule (Jina) and other times relinquishing the actual community (Rihoko). At these points the role of personal agency intervened. Only when the participants felt secure in placing themselves as legitimate members of their perceived existing communities, not their imagined communities, could they establish the precondition for negotiating their expressions of their identities as writers in English. At that point, it was the learner's personal agency that decided the possibility and extent of further investment in linguistic capital through the development of academic writing abilities in English.

CHAPTER 9

Variations in goals and activities for multilingual writing

Guillaume Gentil

In this chapter I re-examine the framework and findings of the research study into goals for ESL writing improvement presented in Chapters 2, 3 and 4. I do so in light of a parallel study that I conducted at the same time as Phase 2 of that study and while collaborating with the others involved in this book. I investigated students' goals for multilingual writing improvement in a different but nearby context – in a bilingual English-French university also in central Canada. By shifting the focus from an ESL program and English-medium university (as in the other chapters in this book) to goals and contexts for bilingual and multilingual writing my parallel study extends the results of the main study reported in this book. My analyses reveal sources of variation in goals and activities for writing improvement that may not be evident from a focus solely on ESL writing. By the same token, this perspective exposes some of the social conditions that may shape individual learners' goal formations and goal achievements.

A key theoretical assumption that I make is that individual learners' goals are intersubjectively negotiated and socially constructed within social discourses that themselves construct symbolic and material relations of power between social groups. In monolingual contexts, the competing interests that underlie the socio-discursive construction of individual goals may be masked or not be clearly identifiable. For instance, in the context of an ESL program within an English-medium university, goals for ESL writing improvement may vary according to individuals, but the overall desirability of improving writing in English is generally assumed by the ESL students and their instructors. The social importance and dominance of English is taken for granted and uncontested. Implicit in this assumption is a symbolic and material order wherein written competences in English are necessary for academic and professional success. Also implicit in this assumption is the acceptance of the inequities that this social order produces and reproduces between those students who come to university already equipped with strong ("native" or "native-like") English language competences and those (ESL) students who do not.

In bilingual or multilingual contexts, in contrast, there are alternative options for individual development of literacy in particular languages, reflecting differences in power relations associated with each language as well as issues of individual agency, as I have demonstrated in Gentil (2005). Rather than assuming that writing improvement in English is paramount, one has to ask in a bilingual or multilingual context why people want to improve their writing abilities in particular languages in the first place: Why English and not French, Spanish, Vietnamese, or Chinese? Moreover, do learners want to improve the same aspects of their academic writing in one language or another? Do they take the same or different actions to improve their writing in each language? Why? How can variations be explained in terms of the sociolinguistic contexts and social conditions of goal formulation and goal achievement for writing improvement in a particular language?

In this chapter I attempt to answer these questions by reflecting on the results of my investigation (described in detail in Gentil, in preparation). I adopt a different vantage point, both empirically and theoretically, from that presented in other chapters in the book, despite fundamental similarities in our foci on goals for writing improvement. I take a critical hermeneutic case study approach, drawing on theories of situated activity, biliteracy, and critical linguistics (Bourdieu, 1982; Gee, 1996; Heller, 2002; Hornberger, 2003; Wertsch, 1998) to conceptualize participants' motivations, goals, and activities for writing development within broader institutional and societal contexts. I begin the chapter by briefly describing the participants and methods of my research then discuss five key sources of variation in goals for writing improvement that emerged from my comparison of the findings of the two studies. I suggest that these five points have theoretical and educational implications to extend the framework of goals for second-language writing presented in Chapter 3 to other contexts and for uses of this framework as an educational resource for teachers and students to negotiate learning goals.

Context, participants, and methods

I focused my research on comparing goals for writing improvement between language contexts in a bilingual English-French college rather than, as in the main study in this book, between a pre-university intensive ESL context and a university context a year later. I gathered data for one academic year (the fall and the winter term) as students simultaneously took second-language-writing courses and subject-area courses (through the medium of their first or second and sometimes third language). The participants included two ESL and two FSL (French as a Second Language) instructors, and eight of their students recruited from their second-language writing classes. Among these students, three were

French-dominant (recruited from the ESL writing classes) and five were English-dominant (recruited from the FSL writing classes). The labels "French-dominant" and "English-dominant" are more appropriate than "mother-tongue-French-speakers" or "mother-tongue-English-speakers" because many of these students were trilingual and had not necessarily learned English or French as their first languages. However, most of these students reported greater academic and conversational fluency in either English or French as a result of their being schooled in either one of Canada's official languages. In fact, all students had been in Canada for several years and some reported stronger proficiency in English or French than in their heritage language. No students assessed their proficiency as being equal in English and French, and all declared either English or French as being more dominant.

As in the main study presented in this book, my data included (a) semi-structured interviews with students about their goals for writing improvement (in English, French, and other languages if applicable), (b) samples of their writing (in English, French, and other languages if applicable) in courses, and (c) stimulated recalls concerning goals for the writing samples. I collected parallel interviews and stimulated recall data from their instructors in addition to interviewing them about the content and aims of their courses, requesting course outlines, and observing some of their classes. I obtained further insights into language practices at the College through documentary data (e.g., course calendars). My fieldnotes (e.g., on the relative uses of English, French, and other languages on bulletin boards and signs on campus) provided further insight into the language practices of the College. Although I did not interview any subject-area instructors, I did collect samples of the students' writing from their subject-area courses along with written feedback from their instructors, and I discussed these with students during their interviews where possible.

Variation in the contexts of goal formation and achievement

The results of my inquiry suggest five sources of variation in the contexts of students' goal formation and achievement:

1. Students' objects of goals for writing improvement varied according to the language in which they had learned to write and the language they were aiming to improve

A striking finding that emerged from my study is that the students' goals for writing improvement varied according to languages. The English-dominant students consistently focused their goals for writing improvement in FSL courses on language, especially vocabulary development, lexicogrammatical accuracy, and stylistics. In contrast, the French-dominant students' goals for ESL writing improvement centred on the expression and organization of ideas, such as how to structure and sustain an argument in a philosophical essay, or more generally how to develop an argument and find counterarguments. One interesting case was a student I have called Giselle. She was considered by the College as anglophone and hence was placed in a second-year FSL writing course. However, she considered herself to be an English-French-Chinese trilingual because she had a French-speaking mother and a Chinese-speaking father. She felt misplaced in the FSL course because unlike most other students, she spoke French at home (in addition to Chinese with her father and English with her siblings) and had completed her schooling in French immersion, that is, studying through both French and English. Unlike her FSL classmates, and more like the students in the ESL class, Giselle's goals for writing improvement in French were not focused on language but on the development of her ideas and arguments.

2. Students' contexts for achieving their goals also varied according to the language in which they had learned to write and the language they were aiming to improve

The contexts that the French-dominant students described for acting on their goals for ESL writing improvement were both their ESL classes and their English-medium subject-area courses (e.g., philosophy or psychology). In contrast, the English-dominant students' contexts for acting on their goals for FSL writing improvement were mostly FSL language classes and, for the most advanced students, other courses in French literature and French linguistics. Giselle, again, was an interesting case. She was the only student that I recruited for the study from an FSL writing class who described her goals for writing improvement in French in the context of a French-medium subject-area course she was taking outside the French department, namely a second-year course in women's studies. The other four FSL students did not take subject-area courses in French outside the French department. In contrast, the ESL students all took subject-area courses in English outside the English department, though none of them took courses in English literature. In addition, the French-dominant students reported that they used English frequently outside the College. In contrast, the English-dominant students rarely used (and never wrote in) French outside their French classes, except Giselle who mostly used English for her social life but spoke some French and some Chinese at home with her parents.

3. Students tended to view themselves as the main originators of their goals for writing improvement, but the variation of their goals and contexts for goal achievement according to languages suggests other potential origins of these goals

As in the main study in this book (see Chapters 3 and 4), the students I interviewed saw themselves as the main originators of their goals for ESL or FSL writing improvement. However, if these goals originated in individual students, there is a need to explain the extent to which these goals were largely shared goals among the English-dominant students for FSL (in their common focus on language improvement) and among the French-dominant students for ESL (in their common focus on argumentation and the expression of ideas), and the sharp contrast between these two groups' sets of goals. The English-dominant students' goals for FSL were eerily congruent, in their very formulations, with the goals that their FSL instructors voiced for them. For instance, one student referred to her need to learn how to correct "serious mistakes" by quoting the very words ("corriger les fautes graves") that her instructor had used in class and in the course's grading scheme. The students generally agreed with their FSL instructors when they emphasized, in the interviews and in the classes I observed, the importance for the students to improve basic grammar ("grammaire de base"), vocabulary, and style. Similarly, the French-dominant students' goals for ESL were generally congruent with their instructors' goals for them. However, because the French-dominant students took second-language as well as subject-area courses in English, their goals for ESL writing improvement did not always match the goals of their ESL instructors precisely. Rather, if they described a goal for writing improvement in the context of a subject-area course assignment, they tended to align their goals with the perceived expectations of their subject-area professor as inferable from the feedback and the instructions they had received on the assignment. For instance, after her professor of philosophy commented that her introduction to her first essay was "weak," one aspect of essay writing that a student I call Tania aimed to improve was how to introduce her essays. Improving introductions was not a focus of Tania's ESL instructor's goals for her or for the ESL writing course generally.

The commonalities among the students' goals and their instructors' goals for them point to the interpersonal, intersubjective nature of goal formation. These students' goals for writing improvement in their second language appeared, to borrow Bakhtin's phrase, to be partly their own and partly their instructors'. The power the College had vested in the instructors to assess and grade students' writing further explains the students' tendency to align themselves with their instructors' goals and expectations for them. Further, when students identified a mismatch between their instructors' goals for them and their own goals, the students unsurprisingly tended to align themselves with the goals of the instructor who would mark the assignment at hand.

Thus, students' goal formulations reflected in part their interpretations of the local exigencies of writing tasks in specific course contexts. In the present study, these exigencies varied somewhat across subject-area and second-language courses for the ESL students. For most FSL students, on the other hand, the expectations and goals of their instructors for French writing varied little across the FSL and subject-area courses because all the courses they took in French were administered by the French department. Moreover, their instructors in that department generally emphasized the importance of stylistic appropriateness and grammatical accuracy whether the course focused on language per se or literature or linguistics. However, students' goal formulations occasionally also reflected their perceived language needs and abilities independent of their immediate course contexts. For instance, Giselle did not embrace her FSL instructor's goals for her – to experiment with more complex sentence structures and further develop her style and vocabulary – because she believed that overall her command of French grammar was "pretty good" and much better than that of her FSL classmates. Rather, based on her personal assessment of her language learning needs, Giselle's primary goal for her French writing achievement was to improve on how to introduce, develop, and conclude an argumentative essay. Giselle justified that goal in the context of the written assignments (extensive, theoretically-informed critical summaries and research papers) she had difficulty completing for the second-year course in women's studies she was taking. However, rather than formulating different goals for writing improvement in the context of the different exigencies of her FSL writing course assignments (mostly short narrative and expository pieces), Giselle kept to her primary goal of improving argumentation structure and rejected her FSL writing instructor's goal for her, presumably because her own goal better reflected her self-assessed language learning needs.

In some cases, students also appeared to mobilize their own goals for second-language writing improvement, and strategies for acting on them, across writing tasks and course contexts. For instance, learning how to organize and develop an argument was not a goal for ESL writing improvement that Tania expressed when she discussed her assignments in the ESL course, even though this was one of the main course objectives of her ESL instructor, Ann. A possible reason for this divergence is that Tania had little difficulty in structuring her research paper for the ESL course according to Ann's suggested template. However, in Tania's philosophy course, learning how to organize and develop her essays became a key objective as she struggled to understand and meet her professor's rhetorical expectations. As Tania described her effort to figure out her professor's expectations in a recall interview with me, she used the very metalanguage ("thesis statement," "supporting point," "paraphrase," and "claims") that Ann had provided in her ESL course. Tania's change in her goal formulations suggests that students may be receptive to their second-language writing instructors' goals for them, even though they may not always acknowledge their instructors' goals as being (already partly) theirs during an interview. Rather, students may highlight or downplay goals, expressly formulating them and consciously attending to them or keeping them in the back of their mind, as exigencies arise in specific contexts of writing.

In sum, these students' goals for writing improvement appeared to be both subjectively and intersubjectively negotiated and appropriated. Once communicated more or less explicitly by instructors to students, through course outlines, written and oral feedback, and class lectures and discussions, the students interpreted these goals within their evaluative perspectives and subjectivities, and variously appropriated or resisted them. In this respect, goals may be part of what Bourdieu (1980) called "habitus," a "system of durable and transposable dispositions, structured structures predisposed to function as structuring structures, that is, as generative and organizing principles of practices and representations" (p. 88, my translation). Goals are "structured structures" as schemata that reflect the social conditions of their appropriation (for instance, the power relation between the instructor who formulates a course objective and the student whose grade depends on meeting this objective). They are structuring structures in that once formulated they orient students' actions for learning, for instance, predisposing them to attend to particular aspects of their writing (at the expense of other aspects). Lastly, they are "durable and transposable dispositions" because, once appropriated, they can be transposed from one activity context to another.

4. Even though students tended to situate their goals for writing improvement within the immediate contexts of their second-language and university classes, the fact that their goals and contexts for goal achievement varied according to the language points to less visible social contexts of influence

The French-dominant students situated their goals for ESL writing within the context of their ESL courses in the department of English as well as in the context of English-medium subject-area courses in other departments. The English-dominant students generally (with the exception of Giselle) situated their goals for FSL writing within the context of their FSL and other courses in linguistics and literature at the department of French studies. How can this difference be explained? Despite the College's official commitment to the equal status of English and French as languages of instruction – a commitment that is reflected in the

College's bilingual curriculum, bilingual signs, and bilingual administrative and student services – a closer examination of the College's language practices revealed an asymmetry between English and French on campus. The College calendar lists more subject-area courses in English than in French in most departments, with the obvious exception of the French department. Indeed, in some departments like economics, philosophy, and women's studies, over 70% of the courses listed were in English. Moreover, whereas many foundational and core courses were offered in both English and French, many specialization courses were available only in English. In sum, in most subject areas, completing a Bachelor's program only in English appeared to be easier than completing a comparable program only in French. On the other hand, FSL courses greatly outnumbered ESL courses. In addition, English clearly predominated on the campus's language landscape: The majority of flyers, notices, and posters pinned on departmental and student-run bulletin boards were in English. This greater visibility of English in turn suggests that English dominated student's social and academic life on campus.

In other words, the students' contexts of goals for second language writing improvement reflect the language ecology of the College, that is, the relative use and status of English and French in the curriculum and on campus. It appears that the College provided more opportunities for the ESL students to take subject-area courses in English and practice their English outside the English department than for the FSL students to take subject-area courses in French and practice their French outside the French department. The College's language ecology also appeared to inform the teaching orientations that underlay the FSL and ESL instructors' goals for their students. Indeed, the ESL writing instructors' goals were informed distinctly by an orientation to English-for-Academic purposes. Their primary course objective was to help prepare their students for academic studies in their respective subject areas, and consequently the ESL instructors tended to focus their instructional goals on research-based argumentative essay writing and proper documentation of sources rather than on the grammar and vocabulary of English. Given that all the ESL students who participated in the study were taking English-medium subject-area courses outside the English department, it certainly made sense for them and their instructors to focus their educational goals on the improvement of writing for the purpose of academic studies in other disciplines. In comparison, the FSL writing instructors' goals were informed by a belletristic orientation. Their primary course objective was to help prepare their students for the study of French literature and French stylistics in the Department of French. Consequently they tended to focus their instructional goals on French language and style, literary descriptive and narrative writing, and only secondarily (at the most advanced levels) on argumentative writing (as an introduction to literary analysis). Of note, FSL writing courses were reserved for the students who planned to major or minor in French. Students in other programs were directed to FSL courses with a greater emphasis on oral communication. All the FSL students who participated in my study were completing a major or a minor in French. It therefore made sense for (most of) them to focus on vocabulary, style, and grammar, as these dimensions of writing were considered foundational for French literary studies.

In short, although the instructors and the students, respectively, tended to see themselves as the main originators of their teaching or learning goals, their individual goals in fact reflected their more or less conscious understanding of the curriculum. The language instructors' goals for their students were also partly influenced by language placement policies and practices in that their instructional goals were expected to follow the recommended syllabus of the course level into which their students had been placed. When students felt misplaced in a course, their learning goals did not match their language instructors' goals for them. For example, Giselle's goals for French writing improvement might have been more aligned with her French instructor's goals for her if she had been placed in a first-language academic writing course (available on campus) rather than an intermediate second-language writing course.

The students' and instructors' individual or interpersonally negotiated goals for writing improvement must therefore be situated within the broader context of curricular structures and practices. Moreover, the College's curriculum can in turn be understood as an institutional response to a regional and societal context where English dominates. Situated in Ontario, the College must maintain its bilingual character within a predominantly English-speaking province (according to the 2001 Census of Canada, over 88% of Ontario residents use English at home vs. fewer than 5% who use French, and over two thirds of those who reported using French also reported using English). Whereas the College successfully recruits English-speaking students from Ontario and other English-speaking provinces, attracting French-speaking students from Québec has become more difficult in recent years in part because tuition in Ontario has become much higher than in Québec. As a result, the majority of incoming students can take subject-area courses in English upon arrival at the College, but they need instructional support in French, if only to satisfy the minimum bilingual requirement of the College. I was told that many English-dominant students satisfy this requirement by completing two language courses in their second language at the second-year level and shy away from subject-area courses in French (beyond the required courses in French literature and French linguistics if they major or minor in French). In contrast, fewer students were directed to ESL classes upon admission, and among them, most eagerly completed a significant part of their subject-area studies in English. The College responds to the needs and wants of its student population by offering a battery of FSL courses for general proficiency or further French literary studies and a smaller ESL program for academic studies in English.

Maguire's (1994) notion of "nested contexts" helps to capture the simultaneous influence of many contextual layers on an individual's goals and actions for literacy and language learning, including the institutional and societal contexts of learning. When they situated their goals for second-language writing beyond immediate classroom contexts, the students typically related their goals to long-term career aspirations. But their career plans reflected their more or less conscious understanding of their future job prospects given their social situation and linguistic capital. The ESL students were well aware that mastery of English would be important in their future careers regardless of their occupations, and they consequently invested in all the English language learning opportunities they could find on and off campus. Their goals and activities for ESL writing improvement were thus informed by an instrumental orientation to the English language; they saw English as a resource for academic studies and future work, and defined their goals accordingly. Given that, for academic studies, the mastery of English lexicogrammar was generally of lesser importance (in the grading schemes of the writing assignments) than the ability to use English for making sustained and complex arguments, so the ESL students were understandably more inclined to focus their goals for ESL writing improvement on argumentation than on language. When they did formulate goals related to language accuracy, ESL students were motivated by concerns over projecting a professional image in their future work-related writing. In contrast, the FSL students were aware that French would be useful for certain professions such as language teaching and translation, but less useful or unnecessary for other professions in the Ontario context. These students were therefore predisposed to perceive French as a language of study for the purpose of teaching or of cultural enrichment, and so to focus their goals and activities for FSL improvement within that orientation. Arguably, lexicogrammatical accuracy may be of prime importance for language professionals.

5. The responsibilities for individual learners' goal achievement should be extended to include all educational stakeholders, including program administrators, policy makers, curriculum planners, and educators, as well as their public and corporate partners

All the students I interviewed generally assumed primary responsibility for achieving their goals for second-language writing improvement, and usually blamed themselves for not achieving their goals, although they sometimes criticized their instructors for unjustified or unclear expectations. However, if we view educational goals as situated within various nested contexts of opportunities and possibilities, responsibilities for goals cannot be easily attributed to single individuals. If students fail to accomplish their goals for second-language improvement, who is to blame? For instance, Giselle's goal to learn how to structure sustained theoretical arguments in French proved difficult to achieve as she struggled to compose critical summaries and research papers in her women's studies course. Perhaps such a goal might have been easier to reach had the curriculum been designed differently. For example, an advanced French writing course designed to prepare students for academic studies in women's studies (i.e., an adjunct or sheltered course) or across the curriculum (i.e., a general French-for-academic-purposes course) might have been more enabling for her than the intermediate FSL writing course in which she had been placed. Organizational arrangements between the second-language and subject-area curricula offer a space of possibilities and constraints for individual goal formulations and attainments. Some organizational arrangements may be more enabling than others for students and instructors to formulate and achieve certain goals; hence curriculum planners share some responsibility in the goal definitions and achievements of students and instructors alike.

In particular, the different distribution of subject-area and second-language courses in French and in English made it more likely for the students and instructors not only to pursue but also to achieve different kinds of goals for second-language writing improvement in French and in English. The ESL students generally agreed with their ESL instructors that grammar and vocabulary development were not as important as learning to write from sources and organize a sustained argument. Moreover, their subject-area curriculum provided opportunities for the ESL students to practice research-based argumentative essay writing in English. The FSL students generally agreed with their FSL instructors that they should improve on their grammar and vocabulary, and that they should pay particular attention to "basic grammatical principles" such as subject-verb agreement and noun-adjective agreement as well as other aspects of French morphosyntax (e.g., gender). But several FSL participants in my study appeared to have lingering difficulties with French morphosyntax despite a systematic focus on form and error correction in their FSL courses over several years at the College and in high school. Such a mismatch between target goals and actual performance created linguistic insecurity among some participants. For example, although his written and oral French was generally lexicogrammatically accurate, a student I call Charles was so concerned over every mistake he could make that he questioned whether his French would be "good enough" to teach the language in the future. Very well aware of her recurring "serious mistakes" ("fautes graves") that were flagged in red on her papers, another student, Sophie, reported that she had lost in high school and at college the sense of confidence and fluency she had earlier gained as a writer of French in elementary and middle school. The question again arises: If both the FSL students and their instructors agree that improving on lexicogrammatical accuracy is an important goal to pursue, who is to blame if that goal is not met?

The issue of grammar correction has been widely debated in the second-language writing and second-language acquisition literatures (e.g., Ferris, 2003; Spada, 1997; Truscott, 1996). At the College, the ESL instructors were closer to the view that error correction is mostly unnecessary because language errors are part of the process of language learning and should disappear as learners move through developmental stages; excessive emphasis on error correction can even be detrimental because it can undermine language learners' confidence and motivation. The FSL instructors were more inclined toward the opposite view that error correction is necessary and desirable to prevent the fossilization of errors. Regardless of the side they take on this issue, language educators overwhelmingly agree that the greater the opportunities for exposure to and use of a second language, the greater the chances for second language development; the greater the opportunities for speaking, reading, and writing in a second language in a variety of academic and non-academic contexts and genres, the greater the chances for second-language writing development (Hornberger, 2003). It seems that the College afforded fewer opportunities, or incentives, for the FSL students to study and write academically in French than for the ESL students to study and write academically in English. Not only were French-medium subject-area courses fewer than English-medium subject-area courses, most FSL students were reluctant to take elective French-medium subject-area courses. A reason often invoked was that their Grade Point Average (GPA) could be compromised if students took subject-area courses in French because of their lower command of the language of instruction and examination. The ESL, French-dominant students were more willing to take the risk of studying in their weaker language, English, and had little choice but to do so when the courses they wanted to take were available only in English. As a result, they were more likely to benefit from opportunities for achieving their goals for second-language writing improvement – indeed, for improving even on aspects of writing that were not explicit and conscious objects of learning goals.

In sum, the organization of the curriculum appears to have been more enabling for the French-dominant students to attain goals for second-language writing improvement in ESL than for the English-dominant students in FSL. This differing enablement can be illustrated by comparing the strikingly divergent learning trajectories of two of the College's graduates that I also interviewed, Jean and Janos. Jean was a French-mother-tongue student born and schooled in a French-speaking area of Québec where English was seldom spoken or heard except in the ESL classroom (three hours a week). In his first year at the College, Jean was admitted to an early advanced ESL class and took subject-area courses in French only. However, he took subject-area courses in English as early as in his second year at the College, seized every possible opportunity to use English on and off campus, and graduated with a Certificate of Excellence in Bilingualism. Born in Hungary but schooled in English-dominant Ontario schools from a young age, Janos's exposure as a teenager was limited to core French instruction in secondary school (three hours a week). At the College, Janos was admitted to a French beginners' course and struggled to complete the College's minimum bilingualism requirement, a second-year course in French. Janos did not take any subject-area courses in French, and he reported using French less and less on campus, as his francophone schoolmates became more fluent in English. At the time of my interview, two years after graduation, Janos reported that he was barely able to speak French, let alone to write it, and he regretted that all the years he had spent learning French had been a "kind of waste."

Arguably, Jean and Janos bear some personal responsibility for establishing and meeting their learning goals for oral and written development in French or English as a second language. However, if the curriculum at the College provided a mediating context that oriented and variously enabled the goal formulation and attainment of learners and their instructors, then curriculum developers and program administrators also have a share of responsibility for individual learners' goal definitions and goal achievements. For instance, Gee (1996) compared the educational goals of instructors and students in a dual-track English school in the U.S. Gee found that the High-track English and Social Science instructors and their students aimed for developing critical thinking skills ("to think critically – to analyze – ask questions" p. 39); the Low-track instructors and their students emphasized the ability to use reading as a tool (to fill out forms, write a check, and to follow directions). In other words, the organization of the curriculum into two tracks informed the instructors' expectations and goals for their students, who in turn aligned themselves with their instructors' goals for them. Although the College that I studied did not officially have separate streams for English-dominant and French-dominant students, the systematic placement of students into ESL or FSL courses and other curricular arrangements tended to place the English-dominant and French-dominant students on different learning paths. As a consequence, the French-dominant students were more likely than the English-dominant students were to set and attain higher-order learning goals in their second languages.

This being said, institutional and individual goals for second language writing improvement at the College were also defined in response to the broader societal contexts of education. The particular predisposition or habitus that learners developed toward a particular language reflects their more or less conscious understanding of the symbolic and instrumental value of a competence in that

language in a given linguistic market (Bourdieu, 1982). Thus, the French-dominant students were more predisposed than were the English-dominant students
to aim for and achieve second-language writing improvement, arguably because
of the perceived higher status and use of English compared to French as languages
of professional written communication in Ontario and elsewhere. If this is so,
then, language policy makers and all the public and corporate social actors that
play a role in valuing French and English linguistic capitals have also a bearing on,
and correlative responsibility for, the goal definition and attainment of second-
language learners of French and English.

Implications for theory, research, and pedagogy

The analyses and results of this study extend the framework for describing goals
for ESL writing improvement presented in Chapter 3 and subsequent chapters of
this book. The conceptual foundations of this framework rest on goal theories in
educational psychology and on activity theory. Educational psychologists (e.g.,
Austin & Vancouver, 1996; Locke & Latham, 1990) have tended to view goals as
established, formulated, monitored, and achieved by individuals in response to
contextual features in their environments; thus, goals are seen primarily as the
product of individual mental activity. Although individuals are acknowledged to
interpret and interact with their environments, self-regulated learning is understood to originate in and be the responsibility of individuals. Activity theorists
(Engeström, 1987, 1999; Leont'ev, 1972, 1978; Vygotsky, 1978) emphasize the
fundamentally mediated and situated nature of individual goal-directed action.
They have tended to view goals as subjectively and intersubjectively defined. That
is, while reflecting his or her own intentions, an individual's goal formulations also
"refract," in Bahktin's terms, the goal formulations and orientations, values, and
beliefs of others, including teachers, parents, and institutionalized others (e.g., the
mandated curriculum). Activity theory in no way invalidates the characterizations
of goals by educational psychologists as appearing in phases, as having domain-
specific content, and as having structures (as described in Chapter 1). But activity
theory helps us to understand that the content, structure, and development of
individual learners' goals are mediated – informed and enabled – by various
symbolic and material contexts of activity. Engeström (1987, 1991b) for instance
elaborated on the social dimensions of learning activities by viewing goal-directed
learning as mediated by the discourse norms and labor rules of the communities
and institutions within which learning takes place. In the present chapter, I have
tried to show how the organization of the curriculum and the division of labor
between the instructors and the students, notably the power relations between

them, influenced the individual and interpersonal negotiations of learning goals within the classrooms I observed and in which these people acted.

What I hope this chapter has made salient as well is the importance of adding a critical dimension to the framework by drawing on social theory and critical sociolinguistics (e.g., Bourdieu, 1980, 1982; Giddens, 1984; Heller, 2002; Kögler, 1996). Such a dimension is necessary to expose, in Giddens' terms, the unattended social conditions and unintended social consequences of individual intentional actions. Despite learners' tendency to conceive of their goals within their immediate activity contexts as expressions of their personal intentions and as claims to their individual responsibilities, this chapter has attempted to account for some of the unattended contexts of their goal-directed actions. Some of these contexts were evident in my comparison of goals for writing improvement in English and in French because it became apparent that the nature of goals for writing improvement in one language or another reflected the symbolic and instrumental value of that language for academic study, work, or social life on campus and beyond. However, it is important to understand these unattended symbolic and economic contexts of goal formulation and goal attainment even when considering only one language because, as Giddens has argued, individuals may unwittingly reproduce inequitable social structures and orders at their own expense through their intentional actions as they overlook the social conditions and social consequences of their actions. Thus, an exclusive focus on goals for ESL writing improvement diverts attention away from the fact that any effort expended on learning English is likely to result from (and in) the increasing hegemony of that language in North America and in the world, a hegemony that typically works at the expense of speakers of other languages (see, e.g., Gentil, 2005). Thus, to benefit students and their instructors truly, explicit goal formulations should move from the mere identification and ranking of objects of intentional learning to a critical consideration and awareness of the social conditions and social consequences of goal formulation and goal attainment.

Section III. Implications

CHAPTER 10

Implications for pedagogy, policy, and research

Alister Cumming

The preceding chapters of this book have demonstrated that goals are a valuable focus for understanding ESL students' efforts to improve their writing in English for academic purposes. We have shown how the principal features of these goals can be described systematically (in Chapters 1, 2, 3 and 7) and analyzed longitudinally to document group trends in writing development (in Chapters 3, 5, and 6) as well as individual, cultural, and contextual differences in and influences on them (in Chapters 3, 4, 5, 8, and 9). Our research was situated in a specific educational setting that is crucially consequential for many learners of English around the world – the transition between intensive ESL studies and the first year of academic programs at universities. The purpose of the present chapter is to discuss the findings of this research in view of their implications for pedagogy, university policies, and future inquiry on ESL writing in academic contexts.

Our main research result is a theoretically informed and empirically substantiated framework (presented in Chapters 2 and 3) to describe the characteristics of goals that adult ESL learners have to improve their writing for academic studies. Among the particular characteristics of goals for ESL writing improvement are that such goals have:

- a certain *force* (most often a clearly formulated intention but sometimes also in the form of a problematic dilemma that could lead to an intention or as the outcome of a goal that was previously realized),
- an *object* of the goal (related to the second language, rhetorical or genre features, composing processes, acquiring new ideas or knowledge, learning or transferring abilities, affective states about writing, and/or issues of identity or self-awareness about writing),
- specific *actions taken* to realize the goal (involving seeking assistance from instructors or others such as student peers, friends, or family; self-regulation of one's own behavior; uses of tools or resources; studying; reading; and/or altering conditions for writing),
- a *context* in which the goal is acted upon (such as ESL or academic courses, work settings, homes, tests, and/or with family members),

- a relation to long-term *aspirations* (such as university studies, career objectives, and/or passing tests or certifications), as well as
- certain *origins* (in students themselves, instructors, other students, family members, and/or work) and perceptions about
- ongoing *responsibilities* for achieving the goal (residing in the student, instructors, student peers, or other people such as friends or employers).

A second major finding from our research is that these goals have multidimensional realizations. The students we interviewed all had multiple, interacting, and interrelated sets of goals for their writing improvement. None had just a single goal that they obsessed over, and even those who focused on certain categories of goals (such as grammar, vocabulary, or writing specific genres such as essays) expressed a large number of specific goals related to each of these categories. The students' instructors, likewise, had multiple goals for their students' writing improvement (as described in Chapters 4 and 6). Instructors focused their teaching and expectations for students' achievement on a range of goals for writing that included and combined specific linguistic, rhetorical genre, and content knowledge. Each of these dimensions of writing featured in all of the courses we studied, though their relative emphasis shifted as students progressed from ESL or bridging courses – which tended to highlight goals related to English usage, rhetorical genres, or composing skills – to mainstream university courses, which tended to assume that students already had attained English language and composing abilities, and so needed to perform specific rhetorical genres to display or express their conceptual knowledge.

If we conceive of learning to write in English at university as an activity, then we see that many goals of diverse but related kinds feature in many interacting activity systems concurrently for any one student, writing task, instructor, course, or program. Perceptions of these goals may coincide or diverge between and among students and instructors (as demonstrated in Chapters 6 and 9). Nonetheless, many of the goals that ESL students have for their writing improvement originated from the goals and activities that their instructors had established for them, setting crucial contexts and opportunities for the actions, responsibilities, and long-term aspirations associated with their achievement in writing. In this regard, a disappointing finding from our research (and for the literacy experiences of the participating students) was that many (but not all) first-year university courses required little in the way of extended writing beyond exams, quizzes, and lab reports, and so provided limited opportunities for students' continued writing development.

A third major finding is that students' goals for ESL writing improvement tend to persist for long durations and to transfer across learning contexts. Collectively, the ESL students participating in our research expressed similar frequencies of types of goals for writing improvement near the beginning and near the end of their ESL courses (as we already demonstrated in Cumming, Eouanzoui, Gentil & Yang, 2004) and then, a year later, in their first year of university studies (as shown in frequency tables in Chapter 3). So, these goals are, to some extent predictable, at least within these particular university contexts. The resilience (and thus value) of these goals was particularly evident in instances where students observed that their goals (and strategies or orientations to writing arising from them) transferred from ESL to the mainstream university courses. For instance, some students recounted how they applied heuristics for planning, drafting, or editing their writing, which they had developed initially in ESL courses, to their writing assignments in university courses, even to wholly new genres such as lab reports that the students had not previously encountered (see Chapters 5 and 8). At the same time, writing and languages are so inherently complex, and take so long to master, it seems reasonable to conclude that many goals integral to ESL writing improvement may take periods of years to achieve in a variety of contexts for language, literacy, and academic studies, not within the confines of a single semester-long course. Such expectations for ESL university students' writing development correspond to Cummins' (1984) oft-cited estimate that ESL learners in schools take 4 to 7 years to reach age-appropriate norms on standardized tests.

Individually, however, we could identify clusters of students who oriented themselves towards certain types of goals or actions related to them. We also identified students who retained certain types of goals for two years or more, whereas others altered their goals within the same period (as shown in the dual-scaling analyses in Chapter 3 or for the Chinese students in Chapter 5). So, despite overall similarities among the students' goals for ESL writing improvement, there were also many individual differences (as would be expected from students with diverse cultural, experiential, and linguistic backgrounds). Examining the personal histories of individual students can start to explain the unique conceptualizations and trajectories of specific students' goals for writing improvement (as demonstrated in Chapter 8). Many variables must influence the qualities, intensity, and nature of these goals – as tensions between competing aims – at the level of individual cases and across sociolinguistic situations (as argued in Chapter 9). Even when goals for writing improvement persist for lengthy durations, their precise qualities are not static but rather change with contexts of literacy, personal senses of affect and identity, and other processes of individual development and socialization. Although university courses and instructors play a critical role in providing the opportunities for learning associated with ESL writing improvement, many personal elements also figure in students' formulations of their goals and means of acting on them, including relations with family members, friends, neighbors, and employers (both past and envisioned for the future) (as documented in Chapters 3 and 5).

These findings provide answers to the three research questions (presented in Chapter 1) that guided our research: First, we have established a framework for describing the characteristics of ESL students' goals for writing improvement. Although developed in just one setting, our framework applies to students' as well as instructors' goals, and seems robust enough to extend to other contexts as well (but doing so, and evaluating such applications, is a step for future research). Second, we have determined that ESL students' goals are closely but not exclusively related to the goals that their instructors in ESL and university courses have and enact for students' writing improvement. Perhaps most fundamentally, we have seen that goals provide a valuable focal point to analyze learning, teaching, curriculum, writing, and assessment together, rather than as separate activities.

The third aim of our inquiry, however, is less clearly resolved. We tried to identify the changes that appeared in students' goals for writing improvement during their transition from ESL to mainstream university courses. We observed tendencies for some (but not all) students in their university courses, compared to their previous ESL courses:

- To focus on reading as an activity for writing improvement, especially to learn discipline-specific vocabulary,
- To occupy themselves with the immediate demands of writing assignments for particular university courses (rather than aiming to develop writing skills in general or in reference to abstract career goals or passing proficiency tests),
- To be concerned with the transfer or applications of their writing abilities to new genres and tasks,
- To expand their contacts with Canadians for assistance with their writing, for example, in providing help with or proofreading written assignments, and
- To rely less on their instructors for assistance with their writing, often because university instructors were not readily accessible for this purpose (in the ways that ESL instructors had been).

But overall, we observed more continuities than differences across our four points of data collection, indicating gradual adaptations rather than dramatic changes among individuals and across educational contexts. We speculate that these tendencies arise from the characteristics of goals for ESL writing improvement described above: the complex nature of goals, their multidimensional and interacting realizations, their embeddedness in educational and other social contexts, their resilience that permits diverse adaptations, their inherently personal qualities, and individual variability. These tendencies appear to be fundamental reasons why people's orientations to their writing seem to develop progressively over time rather than alter radically, even for students learning to write in a second language in new cultural contexts with varying demands for academic literacy.

Implications for pedagogy

Our research has made clear that ESL students and their instructors have many types of goals for students' writing improvement, and these goals feature centrally in their thinking about writing activities, instruction, and improvement. So we cannot claim novelty in asserting the importance of goals for writing pedagogy. Rather, our recommendations for educators are to make explicit – and to capitalize pedagogically on – the nature, value, and use of goals for teaching, learning, and assessment.

The educational implications of our research align with ideas already articulated in goal theory, self-regulated learning, and activity theory (reviewed in Chapter 1) though for domains other than ESL writing improvement. Fundamentally, learning the complex abilities of writing in a second language requires students to regulate and progressively improve their own learning processes and performance by making strategic uses of their own behaviors, relevant resources, and other people to help them do so. This conceptualization aligns, in turn, with the promotion of autonomous or self-directed learning by second-language educators such as Dam (2001), Dickinson (1987), Holec (1981), or Wenden (1991). Concepts related to goals, such as strategies (Oxford, 1990), address some of the heuristics useful for acting on goals productively, as does task-based learning (Skehan, 1998) in addressing the relevant conditions for ESL writing practice.

But goals encompass a broad, profound, and individually relevant perspective on learning processes, literate behavior, and real-life activity systems. Moreover, we have shown that adult students and ESL and university instructors alike have and act on goals for writing improvement and can talk readily about them, to varying degrees of explicitness. So the pedagogical question is not how to generate, teach, or justify goals (as has often been suggested, for example, in applications of communication or learning strategies to education in second languages, e.g., Oxford, 1990). The question for educators is how to help students progressively and appropriately articulate, refine, act on, monitor, achieve, and then extend and transfer to new contexts their own personally-relevant goals for ESL writing improvement.

An obvious way to do this is to have goals for writing improvement (and related processes of self-regulated learning) feature centrally in curricula, instructional activities, writing tasks, and assessments. Our framework (in Figure 3.1) to describe the characteristics of goals for writing improvement provides an explicit set of criteria that instructors can prompt their students to use to specify their own personal goals and then to refine, monitor, evaluate, and extend their progressive achievement of these goals over the period of a course. These processes can be performed individually in respect to students' subsequent drafts of their own writing and to similar types of compositions, in comparison to and discussion about similar efforts by peers or more skilled writers, and in individual consultations with and feedback from instructors. Action research studies such as Cumming (1986) or Hoffman (1998) have already documented ESL writing instructors applying this approach, based on goal theory, as the organizing principle for ESL writing courses in university contexts in Canada and New Zealand, respectively. Studies of self-assessment have likewise recently developed and evaluated various methods and frameworks for the diagnostic self-assessment of second-language writing abilities (Alderson & Huhta, 2005; Ekbatani & Pierson, 2000; Little, 2005; Ross, 1998).

Some basic principles of instructional design along these lines are for instructors to:

- Design curricula to make the setting and monitoring of individual goals for writing improvement a central focus for students while they write and perform assigned or individually chosen activities;
- Provide frameworks and models to help students determine relevant goals and factors associated with them (e.g., our framework for goals in Figure 3.1 or more general proficiency criteria, such as Council of Europe, 2001);
- Prompt students to specify precisely the goals they want to achieve in their upcoming writing tasks as well as the range of actions they will take to do so;
- Model multiple ways of achieving these goals, for example, in respect to language and rhetorical features of compositions (e.g., through text analysis), composing processes (e.g., by thinking aloud and through demonstrations and practice of heuristics such as outlining, mind-mapping, or proofreading for common personal errors), and collaborative processes (e.g., through peer-level analyses and discussions of drafts of compositions, or consultations with others such as friends, native speakers of the second language, or family members) (cf. Cumming, 1995);
- Facilitate students' systematic self-assessment and personal record-keeping of their goals, their uses of relevant resources, their successes in achieving the goals, the constraints they perceived on doing so, and their intended extensions of the goals;

- Respond to and evaluate students' writing directly in reference to the goals students have individually specified, both in respect to drafts of compositions and to subsequent series of related writing tasks (e.g., through portfolios), as well as more general criteria for effective writing (cf. Ferris, 2003); and
- Assign series of writing tasks that are sufficiently similar to (but also slightly different from) each other to permit students to practice achieving and transferring their goals to successive contexts, that involve multiple stages of drafting texts to permit students to approach and evaluate their goals repeatedly for the same task, and that incorporate varied resources that impact on writing development such as extensive reading or consultations with experts about specialized topics to acquire new vocabulary and genre familiarity (cf. Cumming, 1986; Grabe, 2003).

The contribution of our present research is in providing a framework to describe and track such goals for ESL writing improvement, based on systematic empirical research and applications of relevant theories about learning and instruction. As such, our major findings about goals for writing improvement (discussed in the opening section of this chapter) are worth reiterating for their applications to classroom pedagogy. First, goals for ESL writing have distinct characteristics. The characteristics described in our framework are worth familiarizing students with so they can place their tacit awareness of their goals into a coherent perspective and so they do not overlook, in stating or monitoring their goals, some of their integral features.

Second, goals have multidimensional and multiple realizations. Students cannot realistically expect to achieve, in the context of one course, all of the goals they might have for writing improvement, so they will need to select a few of the most important and attainable goals on which to focus their learning and writing. At the same time, students should address goals at varied levels of discourse and through diverse actions, because these interact and interrelate, rather than attending just to one aspect of writing or one mode of activity. A related issue is that instructors and students alike should make explicit their goals for writing improvement, so as to avoid serious incongruities or misinterpretations in their respective expectations (e.g., of the sort described by Block, 1994). The prevalence and profundity of goals is that they readily make a focal point for bringing together, and negotiating if necessary, the otherwise disparate functions of teaching, learning, and assessment. For this reason, it is important for instructors to make explicit the purposes of writing assignments, provide relevant models of past student performance on writing tasks, and direct feedback on and evaluation of students' writing to these purposes and students' individual goals and abilities. This instructional responsibility is as important for ESL instruction as for instructors in mainstream university courses (see Chapters 4, 5, and 6; Ferris, 2003). In situations where mainstream university instructors may not perceive their roles (or abilities) to involve writing instruction, per se, then writing centers, bridging courses, and tutorial or editing services can provide relevant resources to help ESL students achieve their goals for writing improvement (Brinton, Snow & Wesche, 2004; Leki, 2001b; Stoller, 2004, as we discuss further below in respect to curriculum policies). Importantly, students have to write – frequently and purposefully – in their courses to experience opportunities to develop their writing abilities, act on the goals they have, learn how to participate in this form of discourse activity, and understand and take ownership of their academic knowledge (Langer & Applebee, 1987; Russell, 1995, 1997a; Sternglass, 1997).

Third, the persistence, predictability, and individual nature of goals need to be acknowledged. Instructors might expect some students to attend to, refine, and extend the same goals for writing improvement over the period of years. Professional writers certainly do (Plimpton, 1963). Other students might dismiss or fulfill their goals within a few tasks, and adopt new goals to replace them. Some students will be oriented to certain types of goals and actions or resources to achieve them (as our dual-scaling analyses reveal in Chapter 3). The difficulty of learning certain grammatical features of English or academic prose is relatively predictable, and so making them the focus of learning goals may seem instructionally trivial or, conversely, overly consequential as markers of identity in ESL students' texts. Some students (such as Rihoko, as described in Chapters 3 and 8) may seem highly idiosyncratic in their goals and ways of writing, related to their personal experiences and expectations. All these matters attest to the integrally personal nature and strength of goals and of written communication. Individual differences, contextual variability, and continuity as well as change are to be expected. These are the reasons that students, themselves, must necessarily define their own goals to achieve in their writing as well as their personal means for doing so. The role of instruction must necessarily be to encourage, support, and where possible enhance these processes.

A question arises, however, about motivation. The students participating in our research were all highly motivated to improve their writing abilities in English, well before we encountered them (as described in Cumming, Kim & Eouanzoui, in press). They enrolled in the intensive ESL course for this reason and because they had the financial means and time to do so. Like other successful students of second languages (e.g., Dornyei, 2003) or literacy (e.g., Wang & Guthrie, 2004), their intrinsic motivation (and goals deriving from it) would probably have led them to improve their writing in whatever relevant contexts they found themselves. A major question for instruction, then, is how goal-oriented pedagogical approaches might apply to students who intrinsically lack motivation to improve their writing or may even, such as subjugated minorities, have reasons to resist doing so related to historical or socio-political forces beyond their personal control (cf. Canaga-rajah, 2004; Hidi & Harackiewicz, 2000; Gibson & Ogbu, 1991)?

Two issues intersect here. One is, can the motivation to improve one's writing be taught, or at least educationally fostered? Might goal-oriented pedagogies be a way to capitalize on personal needs for self-expression and the development of self-confidence and identity that other orientations to writing or language instruction might neglect? Might students who lack motivation or opportunities to improve their language abilities through inter-personal interactions be able to learn to control their language production, learning processes, and social status more constructively while writing than in other settings for communication in a second language (cf. Cummins & Sayers, Moll, 1989; Rueda & Moll, 1994)? The other issue is the uniqueness of writing compared to other modalities of communication. Are the lengthy durations, commitments to expression of the self, and rhetorically circumscribed contexts of writing particularly conducive to reflection, planning, and self-assessment of progressive achievements? Is writing different, in these respects, from teaching other language skills such as speaking or reading that occur more rapidly and are embedded more integrally in social interactions? These are questions which are important to address in future inquiry that extends beyond the relatively elite situations of students who can afford the time and expense of attending intensive ESL programs and universities in foreign countries.

Implications for university policies

Our research set out to study goals. But by situating this study in the interface between ESL and freshman university programs, and by using a naturalistic case study design to focus on ESL students' writing improvement, we have also addressed several policy issues in these contexts. First and foremost, this research has veri-fied (if only indirectly) the value of intensive ESL studies in preparing students from overseas to perform subsequently in their university studies. Although most of the students in our research had the requisite scores on English proficiency tests to have permitted them to enter university programs in Canada without undertaking ESL studies, there is ample evidence from our research that what these students learned in the ESL program helped them to prepare for the writing and other academic demands they later encountered in mainstream university courses. Specifically, the goals the students formulated and activities they pursued in the ESL program established ways of approaching writing and learning that transferred to diverse types of academic activities later. We did not study students who had not taken the intensive ESL program, so we cannot evaluate precisely how they might have fared in their university studies without such prior preparation. But we can observe that all of the students in our research succeeded in their first year of university studies, obtaining competent to high grades in their courses and remaining relatively satisfied with their own performance.

Second, we also observed the value of bridging courses in the first year of university studies in helping some students to continue to focus on developing their writing in English while they concurrently eased their ways into university courses that tended not to treat language or writing as explicit foci for instruction. In turn, several university instructors we interviewed pointed to the value of writing centers, tutorial supports, or editing services for helping ESL students individually to improve their writing and English. But in point of fact, these students were too preoccupied with the immediate demands of their course assignments, readings, and other academic tasks to have the extra time to plan for or to take advantage of such services. We concur that such services can be helpful and policies to fund and organize them are needed, particularly in culturally diverse universities such as in the Toronto area. But a policy with more potential for coherence, subject matter relevance, and impact on advanced literacy development at universities would involve all university instructors assuming responsibilities for writing development in the context of their academic courses, as suggested by Russell (1997a), Bazerman and Russell (2003), or advocates of Writing Across the Curriculum. Some university instructors and curricula do, for example, provide explicit instructions for discipline-relevant writing tasks, models of past successful performance on these tasks, and evaluation criteria for task fulfillment based on professional standards. As attested in Chapter 5, students looked for such elements in their academic courses, finding them helpful when they were provided, but sadly they seldom found they were provided. Where these orientations to disciplinary writing are not provided, then bridging courses of the kinds described in Chapter 4 seem to be a suitable introductory context for students entering their first year of university.

A related policy issue was the limited amounts and types of writing required in many mainstream university courses (as Leki, 2003, has suggested may be the case in other North American universities). The prevalent response we received from students in Phase 2 of our study was that writing did not figure much in their mainstream courses except for exams, quizzes, or lab reports. Some felt, as a consequence, that the writing abilities they had developed during the ESL program were withering away in a kind of "lose it if you don't use it" phenomenon. Some courses did provide extensive written assignments, however, which students such as Hong or Jun (described in Chapter 5) capitalized on to their advantage, while other students may have shied away from such courses because of their perceived limitations in their English or time commitments. But the fact is that students' writing development requires that they write. There did not appear to be any explicit policies at the two universities we studied to ensure that extended writing was taking place in freshman courses (other than through exams), though such policies could usefully have been developed.

A final policy issue is whether coordination may be desirable or even feasible between ESL and university mainstream instructors. We studied a situation where the programs of ESL and of academic studies operated separately from one another. The ESL instructors seemed savvy about the expectations for writing that their students would encounter in their subsequent university studies, and they shaped the writing activities in their ESL courses to these expectations. In turn, the instructors of bridging courses taught their courses in faculties (of arts or of engineering) with cognizance of the demands that their colleagues had of students for writing in academic courses in these fields. Such awareness and transitions from ESL to bridging to mainstream university courses seem desirable, to be sure, but it would be difficult to envision how much further coordination between ESL, bridging, and academic courses would be organized in these universities. In this respect, we recognize the value of Fishman and McCarthy's (2001) argument that composition and discipline-specific academic courses perform different functions and offer qualitatively different learning opportunities, particularly for ESL or other minority background students.

Implications for future inquiry

Although a guiding purpose of this book is to describe and promote the value of goals for ESL writing improvement, the present research is but a preliminary step in understanding this phenomenon. Other contexts of literacy and second language education warrant investigations in respect to students' and instructors' goals – around the world, with different learner and age groups, and in respect to diverse languages and contexts for writing development. Explicit pedagogical applications of goal theory, self-regulated learning, and activity theory need to be documented and evaluated for their impact on second-language literacy and their inherent sources of situational variation. A theoretical perspective on how goals can unify learning, teaching, curriculum, and assessment in various contexts for ESL literacy education remains to be articulated. The present research and book have nonetheless, we hope, provided some new insights as well as bases for future inquiry. There are three interrelated issues that we, at least, would like to know more about in future inquiry: (a) the systematic application of major theories to analyze naturally occurring situations of learning and pedagogical practices and policies for ESL writing education; (b) the value and challenges of multi-method, longitudinal, cross-contextual research incorporating the perspectives of students and of instructors about writing development; and (c) tensions between conceptualizations of goals for writing development as stable constructs or as individually constructed, culturally embedded practices.

In addition to the obvious recommendation that we should make – that future research needs to study goals and second-language writing education in various contexts – there is the larger question of applying well established theories (e.g., of learning, teaching, literacy, or intergroup relations) systematically to analyze and elucidate these phenomena. As Silva (2005) has observed, most research on ESL writing has been patently empirical (rather than theoretically oriented) in its investigations of particular cases of student groups, text types, conditions for composing, or instructional contexts. Researchers have said, here is a key aspect of ESL writing and a situation in which it appears. What can we see, under close analysis, here? Others, taking a comparative or quasi-experimental approach to debatable pedagogical issues, have asked, is x different from or more effective than y? How and to what extent? What evidence emerges under controlled or survey conditions? Much useful documentation has emerged from these approaches to research. But they can be self-limiting. Moreover, they beg for explanations that extend beyond the situation(s) investigated. ESL writing is not a self-contained field. Rather, it is a uniquely complex set of circumstances that involve issues common to education, literacy, psychology, sociology, and communication broadly. For these reasons we cannot expect a single, all-embracing model or theory of second-language writing to be constructed in its own right. Indeed, that may be empirically impossible (as demonstrated in Cumming & Riazi, 2000). But we should expect theories from relevant domains to help explain and inter-relate, for particular purposes, key aspects of second-language writing education (Cumming, 1998; Grabe, 2001). We encourage others, in future inquiry, to under-take more theoretically-guided inquiry from diverse orientations to understand second-language writing more fully.

A second, related issue concerns the value and challenges of multi-method naturalistic inquiry (e.g., Burke Johnson & Onwuegbuzie, 2004). The complexity of second-languages, of writing, and of education calls for multiple perspectives on these phenomena, to be sure. But there are many ways of mixing research methods and many such methods to call upon as well as complicated issues of research design, sampling, analysis, and interpretation. We opted in the present research for a longitudinal, case-study design, primarily involving parallel sets of interviews with volunteer students and their instructors, supplemented by stimulated recalls, analyses of sample compositions and documents, and classroom observations. These perspectives provided insights from multiple perspectives, purposeful samples of people and writing, and over different points in time and location. They helped us to state with confidence certain things about ESL students' and instructors' goals for writing improvement as well as their relations to their beliefs, writing, and teaching.

But organizing these multiple ways *into* our data did not assure our ways *out* of them. We encountered various analytic and interpretive challenges, which may be instructive for other researchers addressing similar matters. As with all longitudinal research, we had the assurances of continuity among our student participants but also two commonplace problems. One was attrition: Only 15 of 45 students continued in the second year of the project, most of whom were Chinese, limiting and perhaps biasing the representativeness of our sample. The second problem was uncertainty about contextual and historical change: To what extent did the students' goals or writing develop or did their situations for writing and studying just differ? A second challenge was in interpreting our results. We found our major analyses mainly consisted of (a) comparing frequencies of categories of goals as stated in interviews and (b) writing case study profiles of individuals. Neither analytic technique was particularly innovative though each complemented the other. Applying dual-scaling to the categorical data helped to identify relevant clusters of variables, but the results of the scaled plots were so complex as to be puzzling and did not, in themselves, explain reasons for the clusters, occurrences, or differences. We tried time-series plots, as well, but found they showed trends less clearly than simple bar charts did, and they would have required another year or two of data samples to model, evaluate, or predict temporal trends precisely.

Our interviews documented people's perceptions of their goals for writing improvement, all right, but they did not get us far into describing the activity systems in classrooms and other contexts in which these goals functioned. To describe these precisely would have required indepth ethnographic observations (which in fact Yang, 2006, has pursued in analyses of the Chinese students doing group projects in Commerce courses). Likewise, our comparisons of stimulated recalls by students and their instructors about their achievement of goals did reveal some of their mutual perspectives on these achievements (in Chapter 6). But we did not get as close as we might have to demonstrating how students' perspectives on their goals related to their instructors'. That, too, probably would have required extensive observations as well as other kinds of interviews than we did conduct. Moreover, we relied on processes of naturalistic, self-selected sampling for these data: Students selected texts that were often not equivalent to one another, and instructors chose to comment on only some of their students' writing, which resulted in much missing data. Collectively these limitations in our research methods do not, in sum, undermine our results. In some respects, they assert the ecological validity of the approaches we did take. But they do suggest that future research will want to consider new ways of addressing some of these dilemmas.

A final issue – with theoretical as well as methodological dimensions – is how future inquiry might conceive of goals for writing improvement. Our analyses present two diverging viewpoints, as well as some intermediary perspectives between them. Our main analysis, presented in Chapter 3, puts forward a taxonomic framework, based on extensive analyses of a relatively large data set of students as well as instructors, interviewed under structured conditions and verified by inter-coder reliability checks with multiple coders. This perspective is informed by an eclectic range of goal and activity theories but was derived, in a grounded manner, from the interview data we gathered. The framework is suitable to describe group trends in goals by categorizing their chief characteristics. Related perspectives are adopted in Chapter 6, but oriented to Pintrich's (2000b) definitions of goals as standards for achievement, and in Chapter 7, oriented to Halliday and Matthiessen's (1999, 2004) functional systemic linguistic theories.

At the opposite extreme is the hermeneutic perspective advocated in Chapter 9, and adopted in some aspects of our case study accounts in Chapter 8. This perspective assumes that each expression of a goal needs to be interpreted uniquely in respect to a particular person, occasion, and context (both present and retrospectively). From this viewpoint, the personal development of an individual's goals for writing improvement can be traced, but derive uniquely from that person's history, experiences, contextual relations, and intentions. Importantly, expressions of goals cannot be considered stable because they represent processes of negotiation, and even of individual challenge, to power relations and discourses about them. So attempting to establish group trends in the development of goals imposes normative standards on the uniquely personal, negotiated, and situational features of an individual's ever-changing situational relations.

These divergent perspectives represent – in Jones, Turner and Street's (1999) terms, discussed in Chapter 1 – the range of predominant theories about literacy as either skills, academic socialization, or academic literacies. Are goals a form of skill, trait, or knowledge with their own integral but changeable status? Or are goals socially constructed artifacts of discourse and so transitory and utterly relative? A challenge for future research will be to try to reconcile or distinguish further these macro/normative and micro/relative perspectives. Like most dichotomies, there are truths in both perspectives as well as complementary purposes that either viewpoint might serve. For pedagogy, there is value in instructors considering each of their student's goals uniquely, to provide personal guidance, but there are also needs to identify trends among groups or whole classes of students as a basis for instructional decision making. For research, all depends on the purpose. Aggregating people's goals for writing may be necessary to describe, diagnose, or evaluate performance, achievement, or potential in valid and equitable ways. In turn, considering goals individually, as negotiated processes in relation to socio-historical phenomena, may be necessary to understand personal cases or development. Most of the research in this book has assumed the stability of goals while acknowledging their relation to, and origins in, socio-historical and educational circumstances. Future researchers will have to decide which of these conceptualizations of goals they wish to pursue or, if like us, they want to accept these fundamental dualities.

References

Alderson, J.C., & Huhta, A. (2005). The development of a suite of computer-based diagnostic tests based on the Common European Framework. *Language Testing, 22*, 301–320.

Ames, C. (1987). The enhancement of student motivation. In M. L. Maehr, P. R. Pintrich, D. E. Bartz, M. Steinkamp, J. G. Nicholls, D. A. Kleiber, & C. Ames (Eds.), *Advances in motivation and achievement: Enhancing motivation* (pp. 123–148). Greenwich, CT: JAI Press.

Ames, C. (1992). Classrooms: Goals, structures, and student motivation. *Journal of Educational Psychology, 84*, 261–271.

Angelil-Carter, S. (1997). Second language acquisition in spoken and written English: Acquiring the skeptron. *TESOL Quarterly, 31*, 263–287.

Angelova, M., & Riazantseva, A. (1999). "If you don't tell me, how can I know?" A case study of four international students learning to write the U.S. way. *Written Communication, 16*, 491–525.

Anscombe, G. E. M. (1957). *Intention.* Oxford: Basil Blackwell.

Archibald, A. (1994). *The acquisition of discourse proficiency: A study of the ability of German school students to produce written texts in English as a foreign language.* Frankfurt: Peter Lang.

Aristotle (Broadie, S., & Rowe, C. J. Eds. and trans.) (2002). *Aristotle: Nicomachean ethics.* Oxford: Oxford University Press.

Astington, J.W. (1999). The language of intention: Three ways of doing it. In P.D. Zelazo, J.W. Astington & D.R. Olson (Eds.), *Developing theories of intention: Social understanding and self-control* (pp. 295–315). Mahwah, NJ: Erlbaum.

Atkinson, D. (2002). Toward a sociocognitive approach to second language acquisition. *Modern Language Journal, 86*, 525–545.

Atkinson, D., & Ramanathan, V. (1995). Cultures of writing: An ethnographic comparison of L1 and L2 university writing/language programs. *TESOL Quarterly, 29*, 539–568.

Austin, J. L. (1962). *How to do things with words.* Cambridge, MA: Harvard University Press.

Austin, J. T., & Vancouver, J. (1996). Goal constructs in psychology: Structure, process, and content. *Psychological Bulletin, 120*, 3, 338–375.

Bailey, K. (1999) *Washback in language testing.* TOEFL Monograph 15. Princeton, NJ: Educational Testing Service. http://ftp.ets.org/pub/toefl/Toefl-MS-15.pdf

Bandura, A. (1986). *Social foundations of thought and action.* Englewood Cliffs, NJ: Prentice Hall.

Bardovi-Harlig, K. (1997). Another piece of the puzzle: The emergence of the present perfect. *Language Learning, 47*, 375–422.

Barkhuizen, G. (1998). Discovering learners' perceptions of ESL classroom teaching/learning activities in a South African context. *TESL Quarterly, 32*, 85–108.

Barton, D., & Hamilton, M. (1998). *Local literacies.* London: Routledge.

Basturkmen, H., & Lewis, M. (2002). Learner perspectives of success in an EAP writing course. *Assessing Writing, 8*, 31–46.

Bazeley, P., & Richards, L. (2000). *The NVivo qualitative project book.* Thousand Oaks, CA: Sage.

Bazerman, C. (1988). *Shaping written knowledge: The genre and activity of the experimental article in science.* Madison, WI: University of Wisconsin Press.

Bazerman, R., & Russell, R. (2003). *Writing selves, writing societies.* http: //wac.colstate.edu/ books/selves_societies.

Belcher, D. (1994). The apprenticeship approach to advanced academic literacy: Graduate students and their mentors. *English for Specific Purposes, 13,* 23–34.

Belcher, D., & Connor, U. (Eds.) (2001). *Reflections on multiliterate lives.* Clevedon, UK: Multilingual Matters.

Bell, J. (2002). Narrative inquiry: More than just telling stories. *TESOL Quarterly, 36,* 207–213.

Bereiter, C. (2002). *Education and mind in the knowledge age.* Mahwah, NJ: Erlbaum.

Bereiter, C., & Scardamalia, M. (1987). *The psychology of written composition.* Hillsdale, NJ: Erlbaum.

Bereiter, C., & Scardamalia, M. (1989). Intentional learning as the goal of instruction. In L.B. Resnick (Ed.) *Knowing, learning and instruction: Essays in honor of Robert Glaser* (pp 361–392). Hillsdale, NJ: Erlbaum.

Bereiter, C., & Scardamalia, M. (2005). Technology and literacies: From print literacy to dialogic literacy. In N. Bascia, A. Cumming, A. Datnow, K. Leithwood & D. Livingstone (Eds.) *International handbook of educational policy, Vol. 2* (pp. 749–761). Dordrecht, Netherlands: Springer.

Berkenkotter, C., & Huckin, T. (1995). *Genre knowledge in disciplinary communication: Cognition/culture/power.* Hillsdale, NJ: Erlbaum.

Berkenkotter, C., Huckin, T. & Ackerman, J. (1988). Conventions, conversations, and the writer: A case study of a student in a rhetoric Ph.D. program. *Research in the Teaching of English, 22,* 9–45.

Berkenkotter, C., Huckin, T. & Ackerman, J. (1991). Social context and socially constructed texts: The initiation of a graduate student into a writing research community. In C. Bazerman & J. Paradis (Eds.), *Textual dynamics of the professions* (pp. 191–215). Madison, WI: University of Wisconsin Press.

Bialystok, E. (1990). *Communication strategies: A psychological analysis of second -language use.* Oxford: Blackwell.

Block, D. (1994). A day in the life of a class: Teacher/learner perceptions of task purpose in conflict. *System, 22,* 473–486.

Bosher, S. (1998). The composing processes of three southeast Asian writers at the post-secondary level: An exploratory study. *Journal of Second Language Writing, 7,* 205–241.

Bourdieu, P. (1977). *Outline of a theory of practice.* Cambridge, UK: Cambridge University Press

Bourdieu, P. (1980). *Le sens pratique* [Practical sense]. Paris: Éditions de Minuit.

Bourdieu, P. (1982). *Ce que parler veut dire: L'économie des échanges linguistiques* [Language and symbolic power: The economics of linguistic exchanges]. Paris: Fayard.

Braine, G. (1995). Writing in the natural sciences and engineering. In D. Belcher & G. Braine (Eds.), *Academic writing in a second language: Essays on research and pedagogy* (pp. 113–134). Norwood, NJ: Ablex.

Braine, G. (2002). Academic literacy and the nonnative speaker graduate student. *Journal of English for Academic Purposes, 1,* 59–68.

Bratman, M. (1997). Two faces of intention. In A. R. Mele (Ed.), *The philosophy of action* (pp. 178–203). Oxford: Oxford University Press.

Bridgeman, B., & Carlson, S. (1984). Survey of academic writing tasks. *Written Communication, 1,* 247–280.

Brindley, G. (1998). Outcomes-based assessment and reporting in language learning programs: A review of the issues. *Language Testing, 15,* 45–85.

Brinton, D., Snow, M.A., & Wesche, M. (2003). *Content-based second language instruction* (rev. ed.). New York: Harper and Row.

Britton, J., Martin, T., McLeod, N., & Rosen, H. (1975). *The development of writing abilities.* London: Macmillan Education.

Burke Johnson, R., & Onwuegbuzie, A. (2004). Mixed methods research: A research paradigm whose time has come. *Educational Researcher, 33*(7), 14–26.

Busch, M. (2002). *Manual for data collection and coding: Goals in writing project.* Unpublished manuscript. Toronto: Modern Language Centre, Ontario Institute for Studies in Education of the University of Toronto.

Butler, C. S. (2003). *Structure and function: A guide to three major structural-functional theories* (Vols. 1–2). Amsterdam: Benjamins.

Canagarajah, S. (2004). Multilingual writers and the struggle for voice in academic discourse. In A. Pavlenko & A. Blackledge (Eds.), *Negotiation of identities in multilingual contexts* (pp. 266–289). Clevedon, UK: Multilingual Matters.

Carson, J. (2001). Second language writing and second language acquisition. In T. Silva & P. Matsuda (Eds.), *On second language writing* (pp. 191–199). Mahwah, NJ: Erlbaum.

Casanave, C. (1992). Cultural diversity and socialization: A case study of a Hispanic woman in a doctoral program in sociology. In D. Murray (Ed.), *Diversity as resource: Redefining cultural literacy* (pp. 148–180). Alexandria, VI: TESOL.

Casanave, C. (1995). Local interactions: Constructing contexts for composing in a graduate sociology program. In D. Belcher & G. Braine (Eds.) *Academic writing in a second language: Essays in research and pedagogy* (pp. 83–110). Norwood, NJ: Ablex.

Casanave, C. (2002). *Writing games: Multicultural case studies of academic literacy practices in higher education.* Mahwah, NJ: Erlbaum.

Casanave, C. (2005). Narrative in L2 writing research. In P. Matsuda & T. Silva (Eds.), *Second language writing research: Perspectives on the process of knowledge construction* (pp. 17–32). Mahwah, NJ: Erlbaum.

Cheng, L., Myles, J., & Curtis, A. (2004). Targeting language support for non-native English-speaking graduate students at a Canadian university. *TESL Canada Journal, 21*, 50-71.

Cherry, R.D. (1988). Ethos versus persona: Self-representation in written discourse. *Written Communication, 5*, 251–276.

Chiseri-Strater, E. (1991). *Academic literacies: The public and private discourse of university students.* Portsmouth, NH: Boynton/Cook Publishers.

Cole, M. (1996). *Cultural psychology: A once and future discipline.* Cambridge, MA: Belknap Press.

Connor, U. (1996). *Contrastive rhetoric: Cross-cultural aspects of second-language writing.* New York: Cambridge University Press.

Connor, U., & Kramer, M. (1995). Writing from sources: Case studies of graduate students in business management. In D. Belcher & G. Braine (Eds.), *Academic writing in a second language: Essays on research and pedagogy* (pp. 155–182). Norwood, NJ: Ablex.

Cope, B., & Kalantzis, M. (Eds.) (2000). *Multiliteracies: Literacy learning and the design of social futures.* London: Routledge.

Council of Europe. (2001). *Common European framework of reference for languages: Learning, teaching, assessment.* Cambridge: Cambridge University Press.

Cumming, A. (1986). Intentional learning as a principle for ESL writing instruction: A case study. In P. Lightbown & S. Firth (Eds), *TESL Canada Journal*, Special Issue 1, 69–83.

Cumming, A. (1989). Writing expertise and second-language proficiency. *Language Learning, 39*, 81–141.

Cumming, A. (1990). Metalinguistic and ideational thinking in second language composing. *Written Communication, 7*, 482–511.

Cumming, A. (1992). Instructional routines in ESL composition teaching. *Journal of Second Language Writing, 1*, 17–35.

Cumming, A. (Ed.) (1994). *Bilingual performance in reading and writing*. Amsterdam: John Benjamins/Language Learning.

Cumming, A. (1995). Fostering writing expertise in ESL composition instruction: Modeling and evaluation. In D. Belcher & G. Braine (Eds.), *Academic writing in a second language: Essays on research and pedagogy* (pp. 375–397). Norwood, NJ: Ablex.

Cumming, A. (1998). Theoretical perspectives on writing. *Annual Review of Applied Linguistics, 18*, 61–78.

Cumming, A. (2001a). The difficulty of standards, for example in L2 writing. In T. Silva & P. Matsuda (Eds.), *On second language writing* (pp. 209–229). Mahwah, NJ: Erlbaum.

Cumming, A. (2001b). Learning to write in a second language: Two decades of research. In R. Manchon (Ed.), *Writing in the L2 classroom: Issues in research and pedagogy*, special issue of *International Journal of English Studies, 1*, 2, 1–23.

Cumming, A. (2003). Experienced ESL/EFL writing instructors' conceptualizations of their teaching: Curriculum options and implications. In B. Kroll (Ed.), *Exploring the dynamics of second language writing* (pp. 71–92). New York: Cambridge University Press.

Cumming, A., Busch, M., & Zhou, A. (2002). Investigating learners' goals in the context of adult second-language writing. In S. Ransdell & M. Barbier (Eds.) *New directions for research in L2 writing* (pp. 189–208). Dordrecht, Netherlands: Kluwer.

Cumming, A., Eouanzoui, K., Gentil, G. & Yang, L. (2004). Scaling changes in learners' goals for writing improvement over an ESL course. In D. Albrechtsen, K. Haastrup & B. Henriksen (Eds.), Writing and vocabulary in foreign language acquisition, Special Issue of *Angles on the English-Speaking World, 4*, 35–49. Copenhagen: Museum Tusculanum Press, University of Copenhagen.

Cumming, A., Kim, T., & Eouanzoui, K. (In press). Motivations for ESL writing improvement in pre-university contexts. In P. Boscolo & S. Hidi (Eds.), *Academic writing and motivation*. Amsterdam: Elsevier.

Cumming, A., & Riazi, A. (2000). Building models of adult second-language writing instruction. *Learning and Instruction, 10*, 55–71.

Cummins, J. (1984). *Bilingualism and special education: Issues in assessment and pedagogy*. Clevedon, UK: Multilingual Matters.

Cummins, J., & Sayers, D. (1995). *Brave new schools: Challenging cultural illiteracy*. Toronto: OISE Press/University of Toronto Press.

Currie, P. (1993). Entering a disciplinary community: Conceptual activities required to write for one introductory university course. *Journal of Second Language Writing, 2*, 101–117.

Csizer, K., & Dornyei, Z. (2005). Language learners' motivational profiles and their motivated learning behaviour. *Language Learning, 55*, 613–659.

Dam, L. (Ed.). (2001). *Learner autonomy: New insights*, Special Issue of *AILA Review, 15*.

Davidson, D. (1984). *Inquiries into truth and interpretation*. Oxford: Oxford University Press.

Davidson, D. (1986). *Essays on actions and events*. Oxford: Oxford University Press.

Davies, B., & Harré, R. (1990). Positioning: The social construction of selves. *The Journal for the Theory of Social Behaviour, 20*, 43–63.

Davis, B., Scriven, M., & Thomas, S. (1987). *The evaluation of composition instruction* (2nd ed.). New York: Teachers College Press.

Dennett, D. (1981). True believers: The intentional strategy and why it works. In A.F. Heath (Ed.), *Scientific explanations* (pp. 556–568). Oxford: Oxford University Press.

Dickson, P., & Cumming, A. (Eds.) (1996). *Profiles of language education in 25 countries.* Slough, UK: National Foundation for Educational Research.

Dickinson, L. (1987), *Self-instruction in language learning.* Cambridge, Cambridge University Press.

Donato, R., & McCormick, D. (1994). A sociocultural perspective on language learning strategies: The role of mediation. *Modern Language Journal, 78*, 453–464.

Dörnyei, Z. (Ed.). (2003). *Attitudes, orientations, and motivations in language learning.* Malden, MA: Blackwell.

Dysthe, O. (2002). Professors as mediators of academic text cultures: An interview study with advisors and master's degree students in three disciplines in a Norwegian university. *Written Communication, 19*, 493–544.

Eggington, W., & Wren, H. (1997). *Language policy: Dominant English, pluralist challenges.* Amsterdam: John Benjamins.

Eggins, S., & Slade, D. (1997). *Analyzing casual conversation.* London: Cassell.

Ekbatani, G., & Pierson, H. (Eds.) (2000). *Learner-directed assessment in ESL.* Mahwah, NJ: Erlbaum.

Engber, C. (1995). The relationship of lexical proficiency to the quality of ESL compositions. *Journal of Second Language Writing, 4*,139–155.

Engeström, Y. (1987). *Learning by expanding: An activity-theoretical approach to developmental research.* Helsinki: Orienta-Konsultit.

Engeström, Y. (1991a). Overcoming the encapsulation of school learning. *Learning and Instruction, 4*, 243–259.

Engeström, Y. (1991b). Activity theory and individual and social transformation. *Activity Theory, 8/9*, 6–17.

Engeström, Y. (1999). Activity theory and individual and social transformation. In Y. Engeström, Y., Miettinen, R., & Punamáki, R. (Eds.), *Perspectives on activity theory* (pp. 19–38). Cambridge: Cambridge University Press.

Engeström, Y., & Miettinen, R. (1999). Introduction. In Y. Engestrom, R. Miettinen, & R. Punamaki (Eds.), *Perspectives on activity theory* (pp. 1–16). Cambridge, UK: Cambridge University Press.

Engle, R., & Conant, F. (2002). Guiding principles for fostering productive disciplinary engagement: Explaining an emergent argument in a community of learners classroom. *Cognition and Instruction, 20*, 399–483.

Faigley, F., & Hansen, K. (1985). Learning to write in the social sciences. *College Composition and Communication, 36*, 140-149.

Fawcett, R. P. (1996). A systemic functional approach to complementation in English. In M. Berry, C. S. Butler, R. P. Fawcett & G. Huang (Eds.), *Meaning and form: Systemic functional interpretations* (pp. 297–366). Norwood, NJ: Ablex.

Fawcett, R. P. (2000a). In place of Halliday's 'verbal group: ' Part 1: Evidence from the problems of Halliday's representations and the relative simplicity of the proposed alternative. *Word, 51*, 157–203.

Fawcett, R. P. (2000b). In place of Halliday's 'verbal group: ' Part 2: Evidence from generation, semantics, and interruptability. *Word, 51*, 327–375.

Feez, S. (1998). *Text-based syllabus design.* Sydney, Australia: NCELTR Publications, Macquarie University.

Ferrris, D. (2003). *Response to student writing: Implications for second language students.* Mahwah, NJ: Erlbaum.

Fishman, S., & McCarthy, L. (2001). An ESL writer and her discipline-based professor: Making progress even when goals don't match. *Written Communication, 18,* 180-228.

Fitzgerald, H. (2003). *How different are we? Spoken discourse in intercultural communication.* Clevedon: Multilingual Matters.

Fontana, A., & Frey, J. (2000). The interview: From structured question to negotiated text. In N.K. Denzin & Y.S. Lincoln (Eds.) *Handbook of qualitative research* (pp. 645–672). Thousand Oaks, CA: Sage.

Fretz, C. (2003). *Goals, revisions, and teachers' comments: Case studies of five adult ESL writers.* Unpublished M.A. thesis, Department of Curriculum, Teaching and Learning, University of Toronto.

Gass, S., & Mackey, A. (2000). *Stimulated recall methodology in second language research.* Mahwah, NJ: Erlbaum.

Gee, J. (1996). *Social linguistics and literacies: Ideology in discourses* (2nd ed.). Bristol, PA: Taylor & Francis.

Gentil, G. (2005). Commitments to academic biliteracy: Case studies of francophone university writers. *Written Communication, 22,* 421–471.

Gentil, G. (in preparation). Goals and activities for multilingual writing: Case studies of students and instructors in a bilingual college. Manuscript, Carleton University, Ottawa.

Gibson, M., & Ogbu, J. (Eds.). (1991). *Minority status and schooling: A comparative study of immigrant and involuntary minorities.* New York: Garland.

Giddens, A. (1984). *The constitution of society: Outline of the theory of structuration.* Cambridge: Polity Press.

Giles, H., & Johnson, P. (1981). The role of language in ethnic group relations. In J. C. Turner & H. Giles (Eds.) *Intergroup behaviour* (pp. 199–243). Oxford, UK: Basil Blackwell.

Gillette, B. (1994). The role of learner goals in L2 success. In J.P. Lantolf & G. Appel (Eds.) *Vygotskian approaches to second language research* (pp. 195–213). Norwood, NJ, Ablex Publishing.

Goetz, J., & LeCompte, M. (1984). *Ethnography and qualitative design in educational research.* Orlando, FL: Academic Press.

Goffman, E. (1959). *The presentation of self in everyday life.* New York: Doubleday.

Goldman, A. I. (1970). *A theory of human action.* Englewood Cliffs, N.J.: Prentice-Hall.

Goldstein, L. (2004). Questions and answers about teacher written commentary and student revision: Teachers and students working together. *Journal of Second Language Writing, 13,* 63–80.

Grabe, W. (2001). Notes toward a theory of second language writing. In T. Silva & P. Matsuda (Eds.), *On second language writing* (pp. 39–57). Mahwah, NJ: Erlbaum.

Grabe, W. (2003). Reading and writing relations: Second language perspectives on research and practice. In B. Kroll (Ed.). *Exploring the dynamics of second language writing* (pp. 242–263). New York: Cambridge University Press.

Grabe, W. & Kaplan, R. (1996). *Theory and practice of writing: An applied linguistic perspective.* Harlow, UK: Longman.

Graham, S., & Harris, K. (1994). The role and development of self-regulation in the writing process. In D. Schunk & B. Zimmerman (Eds.), *Self-regulation of learning and performance: Issues and educational applications* (pp. 203–228). Hillsdale, NJ: Erlbaum.

Grant, L., & Ginther, L. (2000). Using computer-tagged linguistic features to describe L2 writing differences. *Journal of Second Language Writing, 9,* 123–145.

Guba, E., & Lincoln, Y. (1983). *Effective evaluation.* San Francisco: Jossey-Bass.

Hale, G.., Taylor, C., Bridgeman, B., Carson, J., Kroll, B., & Kantor, R. (1996). *A study of writing tasks assigned in academic degree programs.* TOEFL Research Report 54. Princeton, NJ: Educational Testing Service.

Halliday, M.A.K. (1994). *An introduction to functional grammar* (2nd ed.). London: Edward Arnold.

Halliday, M. A. K., & Hasan, R. (1976). *Cohesion in English.* London: Longman.

Halliday, M. A. K., & Hasan, R. (1985). *Language, context, and text: Aspects of language in a social-semiotic perspective.* Geelong, Australia: Deakin University Press.

Halliday, M. A. K., & Matthiessen, C. M. I. M. (1999). *Construing experience through meaning: A language-based approach to cognition.* London: Cassell.

Halliday, M. A. K., & Matthiessen, C. M. I. M. (2004). *An introduction to functional grammar* (3rd ed.). London: Arnold.

Harackiewizc, J.M., Barron, K.E. & Elliot, A.J. (1998). Rethinking achievement goals: When are they adaptive for college students and why? *Educational Psychologist, 33*, 1–21.

Harackiewicz, J., Barron, K., Pintrich, P., Elliot, A., & Thrash, T. (2002a). Revision of achievement goal theory: Necessary and illuminating. *Journal of Education Psychology, 94*, 638–645.

Harackiewicz, J., Barron, K., Tauer, J., & Elliot, A. (2002b). Predicting success in college: A longitudinal study of achievement goals and ability measures as predictors of interest and performance from freshman through graduation. *Journal of Educational Psychology, 94*, 562–575.

Harklau, L. (2000). From the "god kids" to the "worst": Representations of English language learners across educational settings. *TESOL Quarterly, 34*, 35–67.

Harklau, L. (2002). The role of writing in classroom second language acquisition. *Journal of Second Language Writing, 11*, 329–350.

Harklau, L., Losey, K., & Siegal, M. (Eds.). (1999). *Generation 1.5 meets college composition.* Mahwah, NJ: Erlbaum.

Harman, G. (1976). Practical reasoning. *Review of Metaphysics, 76*, 431–463.

Haswell, R. (2005). NCTE/CCC's recent war on scholarship. *Written Communication, 22*, 198–223.

Hayakawa, S.I. (1972). *Language and thought in action.* New York: Harcourt Brace Jovanovich.

Hayes, J.R. (1996). A new framework for understanding cognition and affect in writing. In C. M. Levy & S. Ransdell (Eds.) *The science of writing: Theories, methods, individual differences, and applications* (pp. 1–27). Mahwah, NJ: Erlbaum.

He, T. (2005). Effects of mastery and performance goals on the composition strategy use of adult ESL writers. *Canadian Modern Language Review, 61*, 407–431.

Heath, S. B. (1983). *Ways with words: Language, life, and work in communities and classrooms.* New York: Cambridge University Press.

Heller, M. (2002). *Éléments d'une sociolinguistique critique* [Elements of a critical sociolinguistics]. Paris: Didier.

Helms-Park, R., & Stapleton, P. (2003). Questioning the importance of individualized voice in undergraduate L2 argumentative writing: An empirical study with pedagogical implications. *Journal of Second Language Writing, 12*, 245–265.

Herriman, M., & Burnaby, B. (Eds.). (1996). *Language policies in English-dominant countries.* Clevedon, UK: Multilingual Matters.

Herrington, A. (1985). Writing in academic settings: A study of the contexts for writing in two chemical engineering courses. *Research in the Teaching of English, 19*, 331–359.

Herrington, A. (1992). Composing one's self in a discipline: Students' and teachers' negotiations. In M. Secor & D. Charney (Eds.), *Constructing rhetorical education* (pp. 91–115). Carbondale, IL: Southern Illinois University Press.

Hickey, D. T. (1997). Motivation and contemporary socio-constructivist instructional perspectives. *Educational Psychologist, 32,* 175–193.

Hidi, S., & Harackiewicz, J. M. (2000). Motivating the academically unmotivated: A critical issue for the 21st century. *Review of Educational Research, 70,* 151–179.

Hilgers, T., Hussey, E., & Stitt-Bergh, M. (1999). "As you're writing, you have these epiphanies." What college students say about writing and learning in their majors. *Written Communication, 16,* 317–353.

Hinkel, E. (2002). *Second language writers' text: Linguistic and rhetorical features.* Mahwah, NJ: Erlbaum.

Hoffman, A. (1998). An exploratory study of goal setting and the nature of articulated goals in second language writing development. *New Zealand Studies in Applied Linguistics, 4,* 33–48.

Holec, H. (1981) *Autonomy and foreign language learning,* Strasbourg: Council of Europe.

Hornberger, N. (1989). Continua of biliteracy. *Review of Educational Research, 59,* 271–296.

Hornberger, N. (Ed.) (2003) *Continua of biliteracy: An ecological framework for educational policy, research, and practice in multilingual settings.* Clevedon, UK: Multilingual Matters.

Horowitz, D. (1986). What professors actually require: Academic tasks for the ESL classroom. *TESOL Quarterly 20,* 445–462.

Huang, G. W. (2000). A functional analysis of verbal group complexes in English. *Modern Foreign Languages, 3,* 221–236.

Huddleston, R. D., Pullum, G. K., & Bauer, L. (2002). *The Cambridge grammar of the English language.* Cambridge: Cambridge University Press.

Hull, G., & Rose, M. (1990). This wooden shack place: The logic of an unconventional reading. *College Composition and Communication, 41,* 287–298.

Hyon, S. (1996). Genre in three traditions: Implications for ESL. *TESOL Quarterly, 30,* 693–722.

Intaraprawat, P., & Steffenson, M. (1995). The use of metadiscourse in good and poor ESL essays. *Journal of Second Language Writing, 4,* 253–272.

Ivanič, R. (1998). *Writing and identity: The discoursal construction of identity in academic writing.* Amsterdam: John Benjamins.

Ivanič, R., & Camps, D. (2001). I am how I sound: Voice as self-representation in L2 writing. *Journal of Second Language Writing, 10,* 3–33.

Jacobs, S. (1982). *Composing and coherence: The writing of eleven pre-medical students.* Washington, DC: Center for Applied Linguistics.

James, M. (2003). *An investigation of transfer of learning from a university content-based ESL course to other university courses.* Unpublished Ph.D. thesis, Department of Curriculum, Teaching and Learning, University of Toronto.

Jarvis, S., Grant, L., Bikowski, D., & Ferris, D. (2003). Exploring multiple profiles of highly rated learner compositions. *Journal of Second Language Writing, 12,* 377–403.

Johns, A. (1985). Summary protocols of "underprepared" and "adept" university students: Replications and distortions of the original. *Language Learning, 35,* 495–517.

Johns, A. (1992). Toward developing a cultural repertoire: A case study of a Lao college freshman. In D. Murray (Ed.), *Diversity as resource: Redefining cultural literacy* (pp. 183–198). Alexandria, VA: TESOL.

Johns, A. (1997). *Text, role, and context.* New York: Cambridge University Press.

Johns, A. (2003). Genre and ESL/EFL composition instruction. In B. Kroll (Ed.), *Exploring the dynamics of second language writing* (pp. 195–217). New York: Cambridge University Press.

John-Steiner, V., & Meehan, T. (2001). Creativity and collaboration in knowledge construction. In C. D. Lee & P. Smagorinsky (Eds.), *Vygotskian perspectives on literacy research: Constructing meaning through collaborative inquiry* (pp. 31–48). Cambridge: Cambridge University Press.

Jones, C., Turner, J., & Street, B. (Eds.) (1999). *Students writing in the university: Cultural and epistemological issues.* Amsterdam: John Benjamins.

Kaldor, S., Herriman, M. & Rochecouste, J. (1998). *Framing student literacy: Cross-cultural aspects of communication skills in Australian university settings. Tertiary student writing.* Perth: University of Western Australia.

King, K., & Hornberger, N. (2005). Literacies in families and communities. In N. Bascia, A. Cumming, A. Datnow, K. Leithwood & D. Livingstone (Eds.) *International handbook of educational policy, Vol. 2* (pp. 715–734). Dordrecht, Netherlands: Springer.

Kirkpatrick, A. (1993). Information sequencing in modern standard Chinese. *Australian Review of Applied Linguistics, 16,* 27–60.

Kuh, B. (1993). In their own words: What students learn outside the classroom. *American Educational Research Journal, 30,* 277–304.

Knobe, J. (2003). Intentional action in folk psychology: An experimental investigation. *Philosophical Psychology, 16,* 309–324.

Kögler, H.H. (1996). *The power of dialogue: Critical hermeneutics after Gadamer and Foucault.* (Trans. Hendrickson, P.) Cambridge, MA: MIT Press. (Original work published 1992).

Kohlberg, L. (1969). Stage and sequence: The cognitive-developmental approach to socialization. In D.A. Goslin (Ed.) *The handbook of socialization theory and research* (pp. 347–480). Chicago: Rand McNally.

Kohlberg, L., & Mayer, R. (1972). Development as the aim of education. *Harvard Educational Review, 42,* 465–492.

Lam, W. (2000). L2 literacy and the design of the self: A case study of a teenager writing on the Internet. *TESOL Quarterly, 34,* 457–482.

Lankshear, C., Gee, J.P., Knobel, M., & Seale, C. (1997). *Changing literacies.* Buckingham, UK: Open University Press.

Langer, J., & Applebee, A. (1987). *How writing shapes thinking.* Urbana, IL: National Council of Teachers of English.

Lantolf, J. (2000). Second language learning as a mediated process. *Language Teaching, 33,* 79–96.

Lawrence, J., & Volet, S. (1991). The significance and function of students' goals. In L. Oppenhemier & J. Valsiner (Eds.), *The origins of actions* (pp. 133–157). New York: Springer-Verlag.

Lea, M. (1999). Academic literacies and learning in higher education: Constructing knowledge through texts and experience. In C. Jones, J. Turner & B. Street (Eds.), *Students writing in the university: Cultural and epistemological issues* (pp. 103–124). Amsterdam: John Benjamins.

Leki, I. (1995). Coping strategies of ESL students in writing tasks across the curriculum. *TESOL Quarterly, 29,* 235–260.

Leki, I. (1999). "Pretty much I screwed up": Ill served needs of a permanent resident. In

L. Harklau, K. Losey & M. Siegal (Eds.), *Generation 1.5 meets college composition* (pp. 17–43). Mahwah, NJ: L. Erlbaum.

Leki, I. (2000). Writing, literacy, and applied linguistics. *Annual Review of Applied Linguistics, 20*, 99–115.

Leki, I. (2001a). Hearing voices: L2 students' experiences in L2 writing courses. In T. Silva & P. Matsuda (Eds.), *On second language writing* (pp. 17–28). Mahwah, NJ: Erlbaum.

Leki, I. (Ed.). (2001b). *Academic writing programs*. Alexandria, VA: TESOL.

Leki, I. (2003). A challenge to second language writing professionals: Is writing overrated? In B. Kroll (Ed.), *Exploring the dynamics of second language writing* (pp. 315–331). Cambridge: Cambridge University Press.

Leki, I., & Carson, J. (1997). «Completely different worlds»: EAP and the writing experiences of ESL students in university courses. *TESOL Quarterly, 31*, 39–69.

Leki, I., Cumming, A., & Silva, T. (2006). Second-language composition teaching and learning. In P. Smagorinsky (Ed.), *Research on composition: Multiple perspectives on two decades of change* (pp. 141–169). New York: Teachers College Press, Columbia University.

Leont'ev, A. (1972, trans. 1979). The problem of activity in psychology. In J. Wertsch (Ed.), *The concept of activity in Soviet psychology* (pp. 37–71). Armonk, NY: Sharpe.

Leont'ev, A. (1978). *Activity, consciousness and personality*. Englewood Cliffs, NJ: Prentice Hall.

Levinson, S. (1983). *Pragmatics*. Cambridge: Cambridge University Press.

Li, X. (1996). *"Good writing" in cross-cultural context*. Albany, NY: State University of New York Press.

Little, D. (2005). The Common European Framework and the European Language Portfolio: Involving learners and their judgements in the assessment process. *Language Testing, 22*, 321–336.

Little, T., Schnabel, K., & Baumert, J. (Eds.) (2000). *Modeling longitudinal and multilevel data*. Mahwah, NJ: Erlbaum.

Lightbown, P., & Spada, N. (1999). *How languages are learned* (Rev. ed.). Oxford: Oxford University Press.

Locke, E. A. (1996). Motivation through conscious goal setting. *Applied and Preventive Psychology, 5*, 117–124.

Locke, E. A., & Latham, G. P. (1990). *A theory of goal setting and task performance*. Englewood Cliffs, NJ: Prentice Hall.

Lofland, J., & Lofland, L. H. (1995). *Analyzing social settings: A guide to qualitative observation and analysis* (3rd ed.). Belmont, CA: Wadsworth.

Losey, K. (1997). *Listen to the silences: Mexican American interaction in the composition classroom and the community*. Norwood, NJ: Ablex.

Luke, A. (2005). Evidence-based state literacy policy: A critical alternative. In N. Bascia, A. Cumming, A. Datnow, K. Leithwood & D. Livingstone (Eds.) *International handbook of educational policy, Vol. 2* (pp. 661–675). Dordrecht, Netherlands: Springer.

Maguire, M. H. (1994). Cultural stances informing storytelling among bilingual children in Québec. *Comparative Education Review, 38*, 115–123.

Malle, B. F., Moses, L. J., & Baldwin, D. A. (2001). *Intentions and intentionality: Foundations of social cognition*. Cambridge, MA: MIT Press.

Manning, P. K. (1982). Analytic induction. In R. Smith & P. K. Manning (Eds.), *Handbook of social science methods* (Vol. 2, pp. 273–302). New York: Harper.

Martin, J. R. (1992). *English text: System and structure*. Philadelphia: Benjamins.

Matsuda, P. (2003). Second language writing in the twentieth century: A situated historical perspective. In B. Kroll (Ed.), *Exploring the dynamics of second language writing* (pp. 15–34). Cambridge: Cambridge University Press.

McCain, H. J. (1998). *The works of agency: On human action, will, and freedom*. Ithaca: Cornell University Press.

McCarthy, L. (1987). A stranger in a strange land: A college student writing across the curriculum. *Research in the Teaching of English, 21*, 233–265.

McKay, S. L., & Wong, S. C. (1996). Multiple discourses, multiple identities: Investment and agency in second-language learning among Chinese adolescent immigrant students. *Harvard Educational Review, 66*, 577–608.

Mele, A. R. (1997). Introduction. In A. R. Mele (Ed.), *The philosophy of action* (pp. 1–26). Oxford: Oxford University Press.

Mele, A. R. (2001). Acting intentionally: Probing folk notions. In B. F. Malle, L. J. Moses & D. A. Baldwin (Eds.), *Intentions and intentionality* (pp. 27–48). Cambridge, MA: MIT Press.

Mele, A. R. (2003). Intentional action: Controversies, data, and core hypotheses. *Philosophical Psychology, 16*, 325–340.

Mellow, D., Reeder, K., & Forster, E. (1996). Using time-series research designs to investigate the effects of instruction on SLA. *Studies in Second Language Acquisition, 18*, 325–350.

Mey, J. L. (2001). *Pragmatics: An introduction* (2nd ed.). Malden, MA: Blackwell.

Midgley, C., (Ed.) (2002). *Goals, goal structures, and patterns of adaptive learning*. Mahwah, NJ: Erlbaum.

Miles, M. B., & Huberman, A. M. (1994). *Qualitative data analysis* (2nd ed.). Thousand Oaks, CA: Sage.

Mitchell, R., & Myles, F. (2004). *Second language learning theories* (2nd ed.). London: Hodder Arnold.

Moll, L. (1989). Teaching second language students: A Vygotskian perspective. In D. Johnson & S. Roen (Eds.), *Richness in writing* (pp. 55–69). New York: Longman.

Nassaji, H., & Cumming, A. (2000). What's in a ZPD? A case study of a young ESL student and teacher interacting through dialogue journals. *Language Teaching Research, 4*, 95–121.

Newman, M. (2001). The academic achievement game. *Written Communication, 18*, 470–505.

Ng, E., & Bereiter, C. (1991). Three levels of goal orientation in learning. *Journal of the Learning Sciences, 1*, 243–271.

Nishisato, S. (1994). *Elements of dual scaling: An introduction to practical data analysis*. Hillsdale, NJ: Erlbaum.

Nishisato, S, & Nishisato, I. (1983) *DUAL 3: Statistical software series*. Toronto: MicroStats.

Nishisato, S., & Nishisato, I. (1994). *Dual scaling in a nutshell*. Toronto: MicroStats.

Norton, B. (1997). Language, identity, and the ownership of English. *TESOL Quarterly, 31*, 409–429.

Norton, B. (2000). *Identity and language learning: Gender, ethnicity and educational change*. Harlow, UK: Longman.

Norton Peirce, B. (1995). Social identity, investment, and language learning. *TESOL Quarterly, 29*, 9–31.

Ochs, E. (1993). Constructing social identity: A language socialization perspective. *Research on Language and Social Interaction, 26*, 287–306.

Ochsner, R., & Fowler, J. (2004). Playing devil's advocate: Evaluating the literature of the WAC/WID movement. *Review of Educational Research, 74*, 117–141.

Olson, D. (1994). *The world on paper*. Cambridge, UK: Cambridge University Press.

Oxford, R. (1990). *Language learning strategies: What every teacher should know*. Boston: Heinle & Heinle.

Paris, S. G., & Turner, J. C. (1994). Situated motivation. In P. R. Pintrich, D. Brown & C. Weinstein (Eds.), *Student motivation, cognition, and learning: Essays in honor of Wilbert J. McKeachie* (pp. 213–237). Hillsdale, NJ: Erlbaum.

Paris, S., Byrnes, J., & Paris, H. (2001). Constructing theories, identities, and actions of self-regulated learners. In B. Zimmerman & D. Schunk (Eds.), *Self-regulated learning and academic achievement: Theoretical perspectives*, 2nd ed. (pp. 253–287). Mahwah, NJ: Erlbaum.

Parks, S. (2000). Professional writing and the role of incidental collaboration: Evidence from a medical setting. *Journal of Second Language Writing, 9*, 101–122.

Parks, S., & Maguire, M. (1999). Coping with on-the-job writing in ESL: A constructivist-semiotic perspective. *Language Learning, 49*, 143–175.

Perret-Clermont, A. (1993). What is it that develops? *Cognition and Instruction, 11*, 197–205.

Pintrich, P. (2000a). Multiple goals, multiple pathways: The role of goal orientation in learning and achievement. *Journal of Educational Psychology, 92*, 544–555.

Pintrich, P.R. (2000b). The role of goal orientation in self-regulated learning. In M. Boekaerts, P. R. Pintrich & M. Zeidner (Eds.), *Handbook of self-regulation* (pp. 451–502). San Diego, CA: Academic Press.

Plimpton, G. (Ed.) (1963). *Writers at work : The Paris Review interviews*, vols. 1 to 4. New York: Penguin.

Polio, C. (2003). Research on second language writing: An overview of what we investigate and how. In B. Kroll (Ed.), *Exploring the dynamics of second language writing* (pp. 35–69). New York: Cambridge University Press.

Prior, P. (1998). *Writing/disciplinarity: A sociohistoric account of literate activity in the academy.* Mahwah, NJ: Erlbaum.

Ramanathan, V., & Atkinson, D. (1999). Ethnographic approaches and methods in L2 writing research: A critical guide and review. *Applied Linguistics, 20*, 44–70.

Raymond, P., & Parks, S. (2002). Transitions: Orienting to reading and writing assignments in EAP and MBA contexts. *Canadian Modern Language Review 59*, 152–180.

Reid, J. (2001), Advanced EAP writing and curriculum design: What do we need to know? In T. Silva & P.K. Matsuda (Eds.) *On second language writing* (pp. 143–160). Mahwah, NJ: Erlbaum.

Riazi, A. (1997). Acquiring disciplinary literacy: A social-cognitive analysis of text production and learning among Iranian graduate students of education. *Journal of Second Language Writing, 6*, 105–137.

Richards, L., & Richards, T. (2002). *NVivo* (Version 2.0). Thousand Oaks, CA: Sage.

Rosenfeld, M., Leung, S., & Oltman, P. (2001). *The reading, writing, speaking, and listening tasks important for academic success at the undergraduate and graduate levels.* TOEFL Monograph 21. Princeton, NJ: Educational Testing Service.

Ross, S. (1998). Self-assessment in second language testing: A meta-analysis and analysis of experiential factors. *Language Testing, 15*, 1–20.

Rubin, H.J., & Rubin, I. (1995). *Qualitative interviewing: The art of hearing.* Thousand Oaks, CA: Sage.

Rueda, R., & Moll, L. (1994). A sociocultural perspective on motivation. In H. O'Neil & M. Drillings (Eds.), *Motivation : Theory and research* (pp. 117–137). Hillsdale, NJ: Erlbaum.

Russell, D. (1995). Activity theory and its implications for writing instruction. In J. Petraglia (Ed.). *Reconceiving writing, rethinking writing instruction.* Hillsdale, NJ: Erlbaum.

Russell, D. (1997a). Rethinking genre in school and society. *Written Communication, 14*, 504–554.

Russell, D. (1997b). Writing and genre in higher education and workplaces: A review of studies that use cultural-historical theory. *Mind, Culture and Activity, 4,* 224–237.

Ryan, R. M., & Deci, E. L. (2000). Intrinsic and extrinsic motivations: Classic definitions and new directions. *Contemporary Educational Psychology, 25,* 54–67.

Sasaki, M. (2002). Building an empirically-based model of EFL learners' writing processes. In G. Rijlaarsdam (Series Ed.) & S. Ransdell & M. Barbier (Volume Eds.), *Studies in writing, vol. 11: New directions for research in L2 writing* (pp. 49–80). Dordrecht, Netherlands: Kluwer.

Sasaki, M. (2004). A multiple-data analysis of the 3.5 year development of EFL student writers. *Language Learning, 54,* 525–582.

Schunk, D. & Zimmerman, B. (Eds.) (1994). *Self-regulation of learning and performance: Issues and educational applications.* Hillsdale, NJ, Lawrence Erlbaum.

Scollon, R., & Scollon, S. B. K. (2001). *Intercultural communication: A discourse approach* (2nd ed.). Malden, MA: Blackwell.

Searle, J. (1969). *Speech acts.* Cambridge: Cambridge University Press.

Searle, J.R. (1983). *Intentionality: An essay in the philosophy of mind.* Cambridge. UK: Cambridge University Press.

Sfard, A., & Prusak, A. (2005). Telling identities: In search of an analytic tool for investigating learning as a culturally shaped activity. *Educational Researcher, 34,* 14–22.

Shi, L. (2004). Textual borrowing in second-language writing. *Written Communication, 21,* 171–200.

Sinclair, J., & Coulthard, M. (1992). Towards an analysis of discourse. In *Advances in spoken discourse analysis* (pp. 1–34). London: Routledge.

Silva, T. (1992). L1 vs. L2 writing: ESL graduate students' perceptions. *TESL Canada Journal, 10,* 27–47.

Silva, T. (1993). Toward an understanding of the distinct nature of L2 writing: The ESL research and its implications. *TESOL Quarterly, 27,* 657–677.

Silva, T. (2005). On the philosophical bases of inquiry in second language writing: Metaphysics, inquiry paradigms, and the intellectual zeitgeist. In P. Matsuda & T. Silva (Eds.), *Second language writing research: Perspectives on the process of knowledge construction* (pp. 3–15). Mahwah, NJ: Erlbaum.

Silva, T., & Brice, C. (2004). Research in teaching writing. *Annual Review of Applied Linguistics, 24,* 70–106.

Silverman, D. (2001). *Interpreting qualitative data: Methods for analysing talk, text and interaction* (2nd ed.). London: Sage.

Skehan, P. (1998). *A cognitive approach to language learning.* Oxford: Oxford University Press.

Smagorinsky, P. (Ed.) (1994). *Speaking about writing: Reflections on research methodology.* Thousand Oaks, CA: Sage.

Spack, R. (1997). The acquisition of academic literacy in a second language: A longitudinal case study. *Written Communication, 14,* 3–62.

Spada, N. (1997). Form-focused instruction and second language acquisition: A review of classroom and laboratory research. *Language Teaching, 30,* 73–85.

Spolsky, B. (1989). *Conditions for second language learning.* Oxford: Oxford University Press.

Spradley, J.P. (1979). *The ethnographic interview.* New York: Holt, Rinehart and Winston.

Sternglass, M. (1997). *Time to know them: A longitudinal study of writing and learning at the college level.* Mahwah, NJ: Erlbaum.

Stoddard, S. E. (1991). *Text and texture: Patterns of cohesion.* Norwood, N.J.: Ablex.

Stoller, F. (2004). Content-based instruction: Perspectives on curriculum planning. *Annual Review of Applied Linguistics, 24*, 261–283.

Strauss, A. L. (1987). *Qualitative analysis for social scientists.* Cambridge: Cambridge University Press.

Swales, J. (1990). *Genre analysis: English in academic and research settings.* Cambridge: Cambridge University Press.

Tait, J. (1999, March). *Multiple perspectives on academic writing needs.* Paper presented at the 33rd Annual TESOL Convention, New York. ERIC ED432157.

Ten Have, P. (1999). *Doing conversation analysis: A practical guide.* Thousand Oaks, CA: Sage.

Triebel, A. (2005). Literacy in developed and developing countries. In N. Bascia, A. Cumming, A. Datnow, K. Leithwood & D. Livingstone (Eds.) *International handbook of educational policy, Vol. 2* (pp. 793–812). Dordrecht, Netherlands: Springer.

Truscott, J. (1996). The case against grammar correction in L2 writing classes. *Language Learning, 46*, 327–369.

Tucker, G. R. (2000). Concluding thoughts: Applied linguistics at the juncture of millennia. *Annual Review of Applied Linguistics, 20*, 241–249.

Vygotsky, L. (1978). *Mind in society: The development of higher psychological processes.* Cambridge, MA: Harvard University Press.

Walvoord, B., & McCarthy, L. (1990). *Thinking and writing in college: A naturalistic study of students in four disciplines.* Urbana, IL: National Council of Teachers of English.

Wang, J. & Guthrie, J. (2004). Modeling the effects of intrinsic motivation, extrinsic motivation, amount of reading, and past reading achievement on text comprehension between U.S. and Chinese students. *Reading Research Quarterly, 39*, 162–186.

Weimelt, J. (2001). Toward an activity-based conception of writing and school writing contexts. *Written Communication, 18*, 107–109.

Wenger, E. (1998). *Communities of practice: Learning, meaning, and identity.* New York: Cambridge University Press.

Wells, G.. (1999). *Dialogic inquiry: Towards a sociocultural practice and theory of education.* Cambridge: Cambridge University Press.

Wenden, A. (1991) *Learner strategies for learner autonomy.* London: Prentice Hall International.

Wertsch, J. (1998). *Mind as action.* Oxford: Oxford University Press.

Whalen, K., & Menard, N. (1995). L1 and L2 writers' strategic and linguistic knowledge: A model of multiple-level discourse processing. *Language Learning, 45* (3), 381–418.

Widdowson, H. (1983). *Learning purpose and language use.* Oxford: Oxford University Press.

Widdowson, H. G. (2004). *Text, context, and pretext.* Malden, MA: Blackwell.

Wilder, L. (2002). "Get comfortable with uncertainty": A study of the conventional values of literary analysis in an undergraduate literature course. *Written Communication, 19*, 175–221.

Winsor, D. (1999). Genre and activity systems. *Written Communication, 16*, 200-224.

Witte, S., & Haas, C. (2005). Research in activity: An analysis of speed bumps as mediational means. *Written Communication, 22*, 127–165.

Wolcott, W. (1994). A longitudinal study of six developmental students' performance in reading and writing. *Journal of Basic Writing, 13*, 14–40.

Woods, D. (1996). *Teacher cognition in language teaching.* Cambridge, UK: Cambridge University Press.

Yang, B. (2004). Towards a criteria of non-finite clause identification: A systemic functional approach. *Language Sciences, 26*, 233–249.

Yang, L. (2006). *Writing group-project assignments in Commerce courses: Case studies of Chinese-background ESL students at two Canadian universities.* Unpublished Ph.D. thesis, Ontario Institute for Studies in Education, University of Toronto.

Yang, L., Baba, K., & Cumming, A. (2004). Activity systems for ESL writing improvement: Case studies of three Chinese and three Japanese adult learners of English. In D. Albrechtsen, K. Haastrup & B. Henriksen (Eds.), *Writing and vocabulary in foreign language acquisition,* Special Issue of *Angles on the English-Speaking World, 4,* 13–33. Copenhagen: Museum Tusculanum Press, University of Copenhagen.

Yin, R. (1994). *Case study research: Design and methods.* Thousand Oaks, CA: Sage.

Young, L. (1994). *Crosstalk and culture in Sino-American communication.* Cambridge, UK: Cambridge University Press.

Zamel, V. (1995). Strangers in academia: The experiences of faculty and ESL students across the curriculum. *College Composition and Communication, 46,* 506–521.

Zhu, W. (2004). Faculty views on the importance of writing, the nature of academic writing, and teaching and responding to writing in the disciplines. *Journal of Second Language Writing, 13,* 29–48.

Zimmerman, B. (2001). Theories of self-regulated learning and academic achievement: An overview and analysis. In B. Zimmerman & D. Schunk (Eds.), *Self-regulated learning and academic achievement: Theoretical perspectives,* 2nd edition (pp. 1–37). Mahwah, NJ: Erlbaum.

Appendix A
Profiles of 45 students and
5 ESL instructors (Phase 1)

Student Pseudonym	Gender	Age	Country of Origin	First or Dominant Language(s)	Prior Education and Work Experience	Months in Canada	ESL Instructor Pseudonym
Alfred	M	18–23	Israel	Arabic & Hebrew	High school	16	Faith
Boom Hee	F	18–23	Korea	Korean	High school	12	Lulu
Carla	F	24–30	Chile	Spanish	B.A. (business)	4	Faith
Chulsu	M	24–30	Korea	Korean	B.A. (law/business)	3	Leeanne
Claudia	F	24–30	Mexico	Spanish	B.A. (business administration)	2	Linda
Darina	F	31–36	Ukraine	Russian & Ukrainian	M.D. (medicine), physician for 4 years	4	Leeanne
Gabsu	M	31–36	Korea	Korean	B.A. (economics), TV producer for 5 years	1	Faith
Gade	F	18–23	Thailand	Thai	B.Sc. (chemical engineering)	8	Linda
Hana	F	18–23	Japan	Japanese	High school	6	Lulu
Hoa	F	18–23	Vietnam	Vietnamese	University for 0.5 year	8	Leeanne
Hong	F	31–36	China	Chinese	B.A. (advertising)	24	Maria
Jina	F	18–23	Korea	Korean	University student (business administration)	4	Leeanne
Jing	F	18–23	China	Chinese	University for 1 year	4	Lulu
Jooj	F	18–23	Iran	Farsi	High school	6	Faith
Jun	M	18–23	China	Chinese	High school	7	Lulu
Jwahar	F	18–23	Saudi Arabia	Arabic	High school	6	Leeanne
Kazuko	F	24–30	Japan	Japanese	University student for 2 years	16	Lulu
Kim	M	24–30	Korea	Korean	B.A. (graphic design), software programmer	2	Maria
Ladda	F	24–30	Thailand	Thai	B.A. (Japanese), translator for 4 years	1	Maria
Lan	F	18–23	Vietnam	Vietnamese	High school	2	Linda
Lee	F	18–23	China	Chinese	High school	5	Maria
Long	M	18–23	China	Chinese	High school	5	Maria
Lu	F	18–23	China	Chinese	High school	5	Maria
Madlane	F	18–23	Israel	Arabic	B.Sc. (civil engineering)	5	Leeanne
Magie	F	18–23	Iran	Farsi	College for 2 years	7	Faith
Mahshid	F	18–23	Iran	Farsi	B.Sc.	21	Leeanne
Marianne	F	18–23	Morocco	French	High school	1	Maria
Mark	M	18–23	China	Chinese	High school	12	Linda

Student Pseudonym	Gender	Age	Country of Origin	First or Dominant Language(s)	Prior Education and Work Experience	Months in Canada	ESL Instructor Pseudonym
Martha	F	24–30	Mexico	Spanish	B.A. (accounting), accountant for 1 year	1	Linda
Mehdi	M	18–23	Morocco	Arabic & French	College certificate, clerk for 6 months	34	Faith
Pam	F	24–30	Thailand	Thai	M.A. (economics), lending officer for 2 years	1	Leeanne
Paola	F	24–30	Ecuador	Spanish	B.A. (business), actuarial assistant for 2 years	4	Faith
Qing	M	18–23	China	Chinese	High school	12	Maria
Rihoko	F	18–23	Japan	Japanese	High school	18	Leeanne
Sara	F	18–23	Iran	Farsi	High school	5	Linda
Sharon	F	18–23	Israel (born in Russia)	Hebrew	High school	2	Lulu
Sumi	F	24–30	Korea	Korean	B.A. (architectural engineering)	1	Linda
Tommy	M	24–30	Mexico	Spanish	B.A. (architecture)	6	Faith
Wenzhen	F	18–23	China	Chinese	High school	9	Linda
Wu-long	M	24–30	China	Chinese	College certificate (business), financial advisor for 6 years	5	Maria
Xin	F	18–23	China	Chinese	High school	9	Lulu
Yan	F	18–23	China	Chinese	High school	1	Lulu
Yi	F	18–23	China	Chinese	High school (in Canada)	36	Maria
Yingxue	F	18–23	China	Chinese	High school	9	Lulu
Young Hee	F	18–23	Korea	Korean	B.A. (nutrition)	5	Maria

Notes:

Age, prior education, work experience, and months of residence in Canada are reported here from the first interview. Work experience is indicated only for students who had such experience (i.e., most did not). The student participants took the advanced-level English courses for academic preparation from the five instructors (Faith, Lulu, Leeanne, Linda, and Maria) between September 2001 and April 2002.

Appendix B
Profiles of 15 students, their courses, academic programs, and 9 of their university instructors (Phase 2)

Student Pseudonym[1]	L1	Program[2]	Course Pseudonym[2]	Instructor Pseudonym
Lee	Chinese	OAC (grade 13)	International Business (for ESL students)	Mary
Hong	Chinese	Landscape design	Landscape Design	Aliz
Jun	Chinese	Commerce	Oriental Arts	Richard
Long	Chinese	Electronic Engineering	Writing for Engineering (interview 3)	Sally
			Professional Writing for Engineering (interview 4)	N/A
Qing	Chinese	Mineral Engineering	Professional Writing for Engineering	Bruce
Mark	Chinese	Economics	Foundations of Economic Theory	Willy
Wenzhen	Chinese	Commerce	Arts of Discourse: Ancient and Modern	Gloria
Xin	Chinese	Computer Science	Oriental Arts	Richard
Yi	Chinese	Economics	Cultural History of Asia	N/A
Yingxue	Chinese	Commerce	Behavior in Institutions and Businesses	Hatton
Kazuko	Japanese	Political Science	National and International Issues in Democratic Societies	N/A
Rihoko	Japanese	Architecture	Fundamental Issues in Architecture (interview3)	N/A
			Current Issues in Architecture (interview 4)	N/A

Student Pseudonym[1]	L1	Program[2]	Course Pseudonym[2]	Instructor Pseudonym
Darina	Russian	Computer Science	Fundamentals of Computer Science (interview 3)	N/A
		Statistics	Basics of Statistical Modelling (interview 4)	N/A
Jina	Korean	Economics	Foundations of Economic Theory (interview 3)	N/A
			Writing for ESL students (non-credit) (interview 4)	N/A
Sarah	Iranian	Commerce	Canadian Society and Communication	Julianne

Notes:

1. All students, except for Lee and Hong, were in undergraduate (Bachelor's) programs at one of two nearby universities in southern Ontario. Lee enrolled in a pre-university academic program, the final year of secondary school (grade 13), OAC (Ontario Academic Credit) courses. Hong was in a master's degree. Darina changed academic programs. She enrolled in an undergraduate program in computer science for one semester (at the time of interview 3) then transferred to an undergraduate program in statistics (at the time of interview 4). During interview 4, she stated that she was applying for a master's program in physiotherapy at a different university, which she hoped to start in the following academic year (2003/2004).

2. The program listed refers to the first-year program which the 15 students started after leaving the ESL program (i.e., Phase 2 of the project). The courses listed were those that the students selected for interviews. If students switched from one academic program (at the time of Interview 3) to another program (at the time of Interview 4), then both programs are cited.

Appendix C
Protocols for interviews
and stimulated recalls

Interview schedule for students

1. What kinds of writing in English do you expect to do in your future studies at university?

2. What goals do you have for improving your writing for your future studies at university?

3. What kinds of writing in English do you expect to do in your future career or occupation?

4. What goals do you have for improving your writing for your future career or occupation? Is there anything specific that you are now trying to learn or improve in your writing in English? (General) b) How are you doing this? Why? c) Please give examples.

5. Are there specific types of writing that you are trying to improve (e.g., letters, essays, stories, etc.)? b) How are you doing this? Why? c) Please give examples.

6. What is your usual method of writing in English? What do you do first, second, and so on? What steps do you follow? (Composing processes) b) Are you trying to improve these? How? Why? c) Please give examples.

7. What is your usual method of checking or rewriting your compositions? What steps do you follow? (Editing, revising) Are you trying to improve this? How? Why? Please give examples.

8. Who do you write for, when you write in English? (e.g., teachers, other students, friends, family, self) (Audience) b) Are you trying to improve this? How? Why? c) Please give examples.

9. Where do you get your information for writing (e.g., your own ideas, expe-

riences, other people, books, etc.) (Information sources) Are you trying to improve this? How? Why? Please give examples.

10. Are there any special types of writing that you want to do (e.g., description, exposition, narrative, etc.)? (Genres) Or to improve your writing of? How? Why? Please give examples.

11. Are there any special topics that you want to write about? (Topics) b) Or to improve your writing of? How? Why? c) Please give examples.

12. Are you trying to improve your grammar in your writing? (Grammar) What grammar would you like to improve? How are you doing this? Please give examples.

13. Are you trying to improve your vocabulary in your writing? (Vocabulary) What would you like to improve? How are you doing this? Please give examples.

14. How do your teachers help you to write? What methods do they use? (e.g., by giving assignments, commenting on or grading your writing, etc.) (Explicit instruction) b) What would you like to improve about this? How? Please give examples.

15. Could you tell me how other people help you to write? (e.g., classmates, friends, family) (Social interactions) b) Would you like to do this better? How? c) Please give examples.

16. What tools do you use to help you write? (e.g., materials, such as dictionaries, books, computer software; or mental strategies, such as outlines, heuristics) (Tool use) b)

17. Are you trying to improve or change the way you use these? How? Why? c) Please give examples.

18. Does reading influence how you write? (Reading) How? Why? Please give examples.

19. How do you feel when you write in English? (Affect) b) Are you trying to change this? How? Why? c) Please give examples.

20. Do you have a specific identity or "voice" when you write in English? Does it reflect who you are? (your personal or ethnic identity) Is it different from your identity when you write in another language? (Identity) b) Are you trying to change this? How? c) Please give examples.

Stimulated recall protocol for students

1. What was your purpose for this piece of writing (student's goals)? What were you trying to achieve?

2. Why did you choose this composition?

3. Was this an assignment, or did a teacher ask you to write it? If so, what was the purpose the teacher had? (Teacher's goals)

4. Did you achieve these goals? How? Or why not?

5. What would you like to have done better?

6. Please describe the composition in detail, going through each unit (e.g., sentences, paragraphs, sections, depending on the length of the text). What was the purpose of each unit? How well did you achieve the purpose? What did you find was a problem? What were you trying to improve?

7. Has a teacher responded to this piece of writing? What did you think of that? How did you feel? Did you do anything particular as a result of the teacher's response?

Interview schedule for instructors

1. Could you describe the syllabus for the course you are now teaching?

2. Could you provide us with a copy of the course outline?

3. Specifically, do you have goals for the students to improve their writing in English in this course?

4. What writing do students do in this course? Are there particular requirements or formats?

5. Describe how you assess writing in this course.

6. How do these goals relate to the students' studies at university? Please give
   examples.

7. How do these goals relate to the students' future careers or occupations?
   Please give examples.

8. What kinds of writing do you expect these students will do in their future
   studies at university? Please give examples.

9. What kinds of writing in English do you expect these students will do in
   their future careers or occupations? Please give examples.

10. In general, what are the students in this course learning to improve in
    their writing in English? (general) How are they doing this? Please give
    examples.

11. Are there specific types of writing that they are trying to improve, e.g.,
    reports, journals, essays? (text types) How are they doing this? Please give
    examples.

12. What are the students' usual methods of writing in English? What do they
    do first, second, and so on? What steps do they follow? (composing pro-
    cesses) Are you trying to get them to improve these? How? Why? Please
    give examples.

13. When the students check or rewrite their assignments, what do they usually
    try to do?

14. What steps do they follow? (editing, revising) Are you trying to get them
    to improve this? How? Why? Please give examples.

15. Who do the students write for in English? (e.g., teachers, other students,
    friends, family, self) (audience) Are you trying to change this? How? Why?
    Please give examples.

16. Where do the students get their information for writing (e.g., their own ideas, experiences, other people, books, internet, etc.) (information sources) Are you trying to do to improve this? How? Why? Please give examples.

17. Are there specific genres or rhetorical structures that you want your students to follow and practice (e.g., description, exposition, narrative, etc.)? (genres) Are you trying to change this? How? Why? Please give examples.

18. Are there any special topics that you want the students to write about? (topics) Or to improve their writing of? How? Please give examples.

19. Are you trying to get the students to improve their grammar in their writing? (grammar) What grammar? How? Why? Please give examples.

20. Are you trying to get the students to improve their vocabulary in their writing? (vocabulary) What would you like them to improve? How? Please give examples.

21. How do you help the students write? What methods do you use? (e.g., assignments, commenting on or grading papers, etc.) (explicit instruction) Would you like to improve this? How? Please give examples.

22. Do other people help the students to write? (e.g., classmates, friends, family) (social interactions) Do you encourage this? Should they do more of it, or do it better? How? Why? Please give examples.

23. What tools do the students use to help them write? (e.g., materials such as dictionaries, notes, books, computer software; mental strategies such as heuristics, outlines) (tool use) Are you trying to improve or change the way they use these? How? Why? Please give examples.

24. How does reading influence these students' writing? (reading) Would you like the students to improve this? Do you make explicit connections between reading and writing in your course? How? Why? Please give examples.

25. How do you think these students feel when they write in English? (affect) Are you trying to change this? How? Why? Please give examples.

26. Do these students have specific identities or are their individual "voices" evident when they write in English? Do you think that is different from their identities when they write in another language? (identity) Are you trying to change this? How? Why? Please give examples.

Stimulated recall protocol for instructors

1. I would like you to review some pieces of writing that were written by students in your course. These are photocopies with the students' names deleted or changed. For each piece of writing, could I ask the following questions:

2. What was your purpose for this piece of writing (instructors' goals)? If it was an assignment in your course, please explain the goals you had for it.

3. What do you think this particular student was trying to achieve in this piece of writing? (student's goals)

4. Did you think the person achieved both these sets of (instructors' and students') goals? How? Or why not?

5. What do you think the student could have done better? Please show some examples in the piece of writing. Please go through the piece of writing in detail, showing examples for each of the 4 points above.

Subject index

Contributors

Kyoko Baba is a Ph.D. candidate in Second Language Education at the Ontario Institute for Studies in Education of the University of Toronto. Her research interests are in the learning and assessment of vocabulary and academic writing in a second language.

Khaled Barkaoui is a Ph.D. candidate in Second Language Education at the Ontario Institute for Studies in Education of the University of Toronto. His research interests are in the assessment of second-language writing.

Michael Busch is a Ph.D. candidate in Second Language Education at the Ontario Institute for Studies in Education of the University of Toronto. He previously taught at Chiba University and worked as a reporter for the Daily Yomiuri in Japan.

Alister Cumming is professor and head of the Modern Language Centre at the Ontario Institute for Studies in Education of the University of Toronto. He teaches courses and conducts research on second-language writing, assessment, and educational policies.

Jill Cummings is a Ph.D. candidate in Second Language Education at the Ontario Institute for Studies in Education of the University of Toronto. She teaches in the TESL Certificate Program at the University of Toronto and is currently conducting research on literacy programs for adult immigrants in Ontario.

Keanre Eouanzoui is assistant professor of biostatistics in the Department of Public Health and Preventive Medicine at St. George's University, Grenada. Previously he was assistant professor of educational research, measurement and evaluation in the Department of Teacher Education at Niagara University, following his Ph.D. in Measurement and Evaluation at the Ontario Institute for Studies in Education of the University of Toronto.

Usman Erdosy presently directs the Canadian Academic English Language (CAEL) Assessment program at Carleton University, Ottawa. He recently completed his Ph.D. in Second Language Education at the Ontario Institute for Studies in Education of the University of Toronto

Jia Fei is lecturer of Chinese language in the Department of Linguistics, Simon Fraser University. She recently completed her Master's of Education in Second Language Education at the Ontario Institute for Studies in Education of the University of Toronto.

Guillaume Gentil is assistant professor in the Department of Applied Language Studies and Linguistics at Carleton University, Ottawa. Prior to assuming this position he completed a post-doctoral fellowship at the Modern Language Centre, Ontario Institute for Studies in Education of the University of Toronto, following his Ph.D. at McGill University.

William Grabe is professor in the Department of English at Northern Arizona University. He has published widely on second-language writing and reading, edited the *Annual Review of Applied Linguistics*, and served as president of the American Association of Applied Linguistics.

Tae-Young Kim is a Ph.D. candidate in Second Language Education at the Ontario Institute for Studies in Education of the University of Toronto. His research interests are in motivation for learning languages and socio-cultural theory.

Luxin Yang is assistant professor in the National Research Centre for Foreign Language Education of Beijing Foreign Studies University. She recently completed her Ph.D. in Second Language Education at the Ontario Institute for Studies in Education of the University of Toronto.

Ally Zhou is currently a postdoctoral fellow with the International Institute of Qualitative Methodology at the University of Alberta. She recently completed her Ph.D. in Second Language Education at the Ontario Institute for Studies in Education of the University of Toronto.

In the series *Language Learning & Language Teaching* the following titles have been published thus far or are scheduled for publication:

Like New (but Inscrip.)

£20